The Picture Exchange Communication System Training Manual

Lori Frost, M.S., CCC-SLP
and
Andy Bondy, Ph.D.

With illustrations by Rayna Bondy

PYRAMID
EDUCATIONAL
PRODUCTS, INC.

5C Garfield Way
Newark, DE 19713
www.pyramidproducts.com

Pyramid Educational Products, Inc.
5C Garfield Way
Newark, DE 19713
Phone: (302) 894-9155

www.pyramidproducts.com

Published in 2002 in the United States by Pyramid Educational Products, Inc., 5C Garfield Way, Newark, DE 19713

ISBN 1-928598-05-6

Table of Contents

Acknowledgements

We are forever grateful to the many children who have taught us so much—we will continue to learn.

Our own children are the greatest for sharing our time with other children and families, and for letting us "practice" on them all the many times we were problem-solving.

We are indebted to Anne, Chris, Denyse, Diane, Donna, JoAnne, Kate, Mindy, Sarah, Scott, Sue, Susan, Theresa, Tony, and Zena who challenge us to think, share their wonderful ideas with us, and devote so much time to helping children and their teams.

We offer a huge "thanks" to Nathan, Debbie, Robin, and all of the office staff for supporting us every minute of every day and for helping us find time to write.

Special thanks to Jordan for teaching us about long sentence strips and to Josh for teaching us about patience!

Tell me and I will forget
Show me and I will remember
Involve me and I will understand forever

Confucius

Preface

If you are reading this book, you probably have had the frustration of living or working with a child or adult who cannot communicate effectively with speech. You know that these children and adults have wants and needs that they either cannot express or that they express in socially unacceptable ways. Most likely, you have seen children and adults hurting themselves or others, or damaging or destroying the environment around them related to their communication difficulties. You have seen or experienced the devastating impact the individual's inability to communicate has had on his or her family.

This book presents an updated description of The Picture Exchange Communication System. We begin with a discussion of the "big picture," or our view on the importance of laying the foundation for communication training by systematically structuring the learning environment (be it in the home, community or school). This approach, **The Pyramid Approach to Education**, embraces the principals of broad-spectrum applied behavior analysis and emphasizes the development of functional communication skills, independent of communication modality. In creating the foundation for teaching, the Pyramid Approach focuses on functional activities and communication, powerful reinforcers, and behavior intervention plans. The specifics or the "how" of teaching are described through structural elements: specific lesson types, prompting strategies, error correction strategies and plans for generalization. The Pyramid Approach is one of the few approaches that encourages creativity and innovation on the teacher's part through data-based decision making. Throughout our description of the implementation of PECS, we will be referring to the elements of the Pyramid.

Once we describe "setting the stage" for teaching, we describe the six training phases that make up the PECS training protocol. We describe additional, critical communication skills and where and when, within the PECS protocol, each of these skills is taught. We illustrate how to create a visual reinforcement system that interfaces with the overall communication training program.

The final chapter of this book presents a description of PECS and its relationship to B.F. Skinner's 1957 book, *Verbal Behavior*. Skinner's account presents a functional rather than a structural analysis of communication. We will describe each of the phases of PECS in terms of the verbal operants defined by Skinner. We also will describe how our teaching strategies are related to moving from verbal operant to verbal operant as learners move through the phases of PECS.

Throughout this book, we have made a conscious choice to avoid the use of confusing pronouns. We have fond memories of the bewildering "pronoun battles" we've had with several students over the years—we're sure you've had similar when you've tried to explain to a student with echolalia how to use first and third pronouns correctly. It typically goes something like this:

> "If you want to tell me that you want a drink, then say, 'I want a drink,' but if you want to ask me if I want a drink, then you say, 'Do you want a drink?' If you want to tell me that Shawn or Manda want drinks, then you tell me that he or she or they want drinks, but if you are telling them that you want a drink, then you say to them, 'I want a drink.' Do you understand?"

We refer to trainers, educators, teachers, etc, as "she," and to students as "he." We chose to do this solely for ease of description and understanding and because of the demographics of both populations. Also, throughout this book, we refer to anyone who has an instructive interaction with a student as a 'teacher,' 'trainer,' or 'instructor.' We are not referring to a specific profession. We firmly believe that PECS and communication training is a team endeavor and that each member of the team must know how to implement PECS; therefore, we do not differentiate among team members in our labels.

How to Use this Manual

The manual begins with a discussion on the elements that must be in place when creating an effective educational environment. We follow with a description on our definition of functional communication and the history of functional communication training. Next is a description of how to assess your student's current communication skills using The Initial Functional Communication Checklist.

The training protocol begins by describing how to "get ready" for PECS. What you will discover is that there are very few prerequisites for beginning PECS. There are, however, some steps that the *trainer* must go through before beginning the protocol.

We all benefit from visual aids, so we use several throughout this book.

Each training phase is divided into several sections that are your road map for teaching your child to use PECS. Each section has a unique "visual aid" associated with it so that you can find it easily when you need to refer back to it.

> **Terminal Objective:** *This is the expected outcome for a particular phase or what your student should do upon finishing this Phase. The objective is written behaviorally so that observable, measurable behaviors that your student should learn are described.*

Rationale: We want you to know *why* we are teaching a particular skill at a particular time. Our protocol parallels typical language development in the sequence of skills taught. During each phase, the child will learn a skill that will support the skills learned in the next Phases.

As you will read in the chapter on The Pyramid Approach to Education, proper use of reinforcement strategies is essential for effective teaching and efficient learning. This visual aid is a signal or reminder of what the new skill is for you to appropriately reinforce.

The Structured Training Environment

Each phase begins with structured lessons. The trainers come to this type of training with all of their "tools" prepared and with a specific focus in mind for the lesson.

Setting

The setting describes the "who," what," and "where" of the lesson. "Who" specifies how many trainers will be involved in the lesson. "What" specifies the materials that will need to be on hand for a successful lesson. "Where" describes where the trainers and child should be in relation to each other.

notes

1. **This road sign will alert you to some general reminders to keep in mind as you begin lessons within this phase.**
2. **Many of the reminders will be repeated from Phase to Phase because heeding the caution is crucial for correct implementation of PECS.**

Teaching Strategy

Each new skill we teach is associated with a specific teaching strategy. These strategies are described in general in the chapter on The Pyramid Approach to Education and are elaborated upon within this box throughout the description of the training phases.

Error Correction

Even though we carefully plan each lesson and try to anticipate each road block, students will sometimes make mistakes. We need to have a plan in place for how to deal with those mistakes when they occur. The two main error correction strategies we will use in PECS will be The 4-Step Error Correction Procedure and Backstepping. These will be described.

TAKE NOTICE !

This road sign alerts you to specific warnings to pay attention to your own behavior. We point out information that might seem obvious when read but is easily overlooked in the midst of a lesson while you are attending to so many variables. These warnings are helpful to review if you determine that your training is not going as expected.

The Relaxed Training Environment

Setting This section describes training that is conducted "away from the table." We address generalization from the beginning of training, so this section will give you ideas on how to plan for and expect communication across the day.

Assessing the Trainers

Student learning is dependent on the skills of the teacher, therefore, trainers must periodically assess their own or a peer's skills at implementing PECS. Accompanying each phase will be a listing of critical trainer skills. A complete chart can be found in Appendix E.

Cross-Reference with Additional Skills

PECS is part of a complete communication training program. We describe many communication skills that are not part of the formal protocol that we teach while implementing PECS. This section reminds the reader what additional skills the trainer should be teaching to complement the skills currently being addressed within PECS.

Phase I		
	Phase II	
		Phase III
		Phase IV
		Phase V
		Phase VI
		Attributes
	"Do you want?"	
	Request "help"	"I want help" / "I want help with…"
	Request "break"	
	Respond to "wait"	
	Picture Direction Following	
		Schedule Following
	Let's Make a Deal	
	Visual Reinforcement Systems	

??..Frequently asked questions..??

Over the years, we have received correspondence from many people regarding PECS. We have visited many programs and homes where PECS was being implemented. Questions are a logical by-product of a trainer's assessment of a lesson. We have compiled a list of questions that people ask frequently and answer them at the end of each Phase description.

Bright Ideas

This section will include ideas for making your implementation of PECS easier. Tips on preparing, organizing, and storing pictures are included. Suggestions for fine-tuning your training sessions are described.

Monitoring Progress

How do you know if your student is learning your lesson? How do you know if he is making progress or losing ground? The only way to know either is to systematically evaluate the student's performance based on pre-determined criteria. This means collecting data! The terminal objective at the beginning of each Phase lists the specific behavior the child is to engage in and data sheets are presented at the end of each Phase that will help you assess your student's progress. Blank copies of each data form can be found in Appendix G.

We include many charts, data sheets, checklists, etc. throughout the manual. Within the manual these are provided as samples. Reproducible, blank forms are included in the Appendices.

Skill	Example	Appropriate?
1. Request reinforcers		
edibles		
toys		
activities		
2. Request help/assistance		
3. Request break		
4. Reject		
5. Affirm/Accept		
6. Respond to "Wait"		
7. Respond to directions		

Date	Trial	Put picture on strip	Put "I want" on strip	Exchange	Point to pictures	Correspondence Checks
	1					
	2					

Visual Directions	Step	Teacher	Student	
orient to name being signaled		Entice with both items		
"Come here				
"Stop			Gives incorrect picture	
"Sit down		Give corresponding item		
"Give it to me				
"Go get..." (familiar item			Reacts negatively	
"Go to..." (familiar location	MODEL or SHOW	Show/tap/holds up target picture		
"Put it back/down				
"Let's go/ Come with me	PROMPT	Hold open hand near target picture, physically prompt		
Oral Directions				
orient to name being called			Gives target picture	
"Come here				
"Stop		Praise (does not give item)		
"Sit down	SWITCH	"Do this," pause		
"Give it to me				
"Go get..." (familiar item			Performs switch	
"Go to..." (familiar location	REPEAT	Entice with both items		
"Put it back/down				
"Let's go/ Come with me			Gives correct picture	
8. Transition b/w activities		Praise and give item		
9. Follow visual schedule				

1

The Pyramid Approach
to Education*

*Adapted from *The Pyramid Approach to Education in Autism* by Andy Bondy, Ph.D. and Beth Sulzer-Azaroff, Ph.D. (2001) by Pyramid Educational Products, Inc.

The Pyramid Approach to Education

Teaching is a very complex process. It would be wonderful if it were simple and straightforward. Teachers easily would learn a linear model, such as a set of steps on a staircase. However, we know that life is more convoluted and interactive than any linear model could guide us through. A more realistic model for describing the elements necessary to create effective educational environments is portrayed by the Pyramid Approach to Education (see Bondy, 1996, and Bondy and Sulzer-Azaroff, 2001). A pyramid is three-dimensional, and has a wide and firm foundation that must be built before the full body of the pyramid can be constructed. What are the critical elements of this approach?

Consider your first experiences working with children (or adults) with autism or other complex disabilities. You most likely recall a child who engaged in a variety of actions that you were not thrilled to see such as hitting, kicking, running around, rearranging furniture and other parts of your classroom or home,

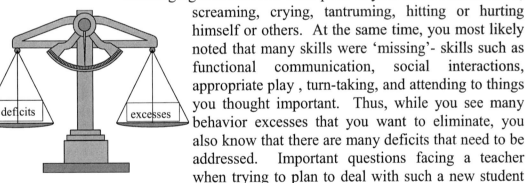

screaming, crying, tantruming, hitting or hurting himself or others. At the same time, you most likely noted that many skills were 'missing'- skills such as functional communication, social interactions, appropriate play , turn-taking, and attending to things you thought important. Thus, while you see many behavior excesses that you want to eliminate, you also know that there are many deficits that need to be addressed. Important questions facing a teacher when trying to plan to deal with such a new student include, "Where do I begin? Should I try to get rid of some behaviors or shall I try to teach new ones?"

One traditional approach is to try to get rid of inappropriate or interfering behaviors in hopes of "getting the child ready to learn." However, the implication here is that unless a child is calmly sitting in a chair, with hands in lap, looking at the teacher for several seconds before the instruction is given, no learning is possible. From a behavioral perspective, this is an unusual stance to take as it implies no learning is possible until some almost magical point in time is achieved. We know that children can learn in any situation- though not always the lessons we want to teach. It is true that our jobs as teachers are 'easier' if the child is attentively sitting in a chair, but making a teacher's job easier is not our goal. Our goal in planning to teach our students is determining what we need to do to make lessons more effective. Some children may engage in actions that interfere with attending to the teacher. However, in many cases poorly designed lessons could lead to inappropriate behaviors. Our preference is to design lessons in such a way that the student learns without necessarily resorting to behaviors that are ineffective or inappropriate. Furthermore, as will be made more clear in a moment, before we try to eliminate a behavior (or reduce its frequency or intensity) we must first determine why the behavior is occurring and then replace that particular behavior with one that meets the same goals for the child and yet is more socially acceptable.

The two terms "Applied Behavior Analysis" (ABA) and "Discrete Trial Instruction" (DTI) are not inter-changeable. DTI is one strategy within ABA.

The foundation of the Pyramid Approach rests upon the field of Applied Behavior Analysis- the field devoted to the science of learning. The basic premise of Applied Behavior Analysis (ABA) and The Pyramid Approach to Education is that behavior is lawfully related to environmental factors (including those within the individual). If we can understand the process of learning then we will be better prepared to effective teach new skills.

The Base Elements of the Pyramid

All buildings require a firm foundation and the Pyramid Approach is no different. The base of the Pyramid involves four elements. These elements deal with the broad issues of *"WHAT"* to teach and *"WHY"* students learn. Of course, our concern about Contextually Inappropriate Behaviors is one of the base elements but it is not were we begin our focus.

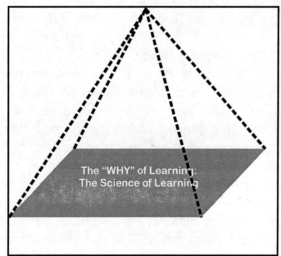

The "WHY" of Learning: The Science of Learning

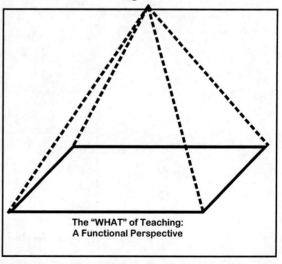

The "WHAT" of Teaching: A Functional Perspective

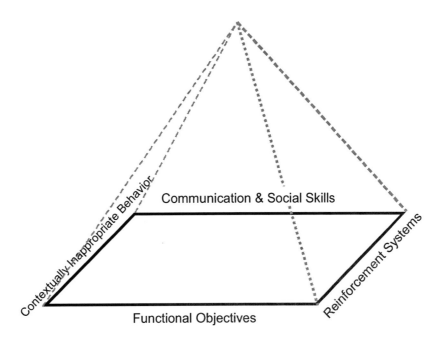

Communication & Social Skills

Contextually Inappropriate Behavior

Reinforcement Systems

Functional Objectives

Functional Objectives

The first element addressed deals with what we should teach children, or *Functional Objectives*. Our goal in teaching children with autism and other severe disabilities should be the same as our goal for educating all students- to teach them skills so that when they leave school, they obtain a good job and go live somewhere other than with their parents! We emphasize the importance of remembering that we teach skills such as reading or math not to end up saying, "He can read at a 3rd grade level" but because improved reading or math skills lead to obtaining a better job or living more independently.

> Functional Objectives involve skills that are necessary for the development of independence.

Related to this issue of functional objectives is our concern about using functional materials. For example, assume that your current developmental profile on your newest 5-year-old student indicates that she does not know her colors. Upon reading the IEP objective, "Mary will learn her colors," most teachers will attempt to create a color lesson for Mary. A common lesson would be to place a red block and a blue block in front of Mary and then say, "touch red" (or some similar variation on this lesson type). As a teacher, we are concerned that this type of lesson is not very thrilling to teach, nor is it very intriguing for students (especially those with autism who may not yet participate in lessons simply to please their teacher). However, in addition to concerns about how motivating this lesson may be is a concern about linking this lesson to other important related skills— how will this skill be used in daily life. We doubt that in Mary's daily life will she be asked or told to touch red or blue blocks!

For example, after lunch, you have Mary brush her teeth. To accomplish this task, she must go into the bathroom and find her toothbrush from among the 8 brushes of her classmates. Most likely, she will need to 'know the color' of her toothbrush. Will months of sitting at a table doing the 'point to red' block lesson automatically transfer to or generalize to the toothbrushes in the bathroom? Unfortunately, practical experience has shown that this transfer does not readily occur. For many children, teachers find themselves teaching the color lesson again in the bathroom with the toothbrushes. We know that teaching Mary to brush her teeth is an important and functional skill. We cannot say the same for touching colored blocks. However, is there any evidence that teaching a student 'colors' with blocks is more effective than using toothbrushes? The simple answer is, "no!" The question is, why do so many of us start the lesson with blocks? Regrettably, the most likely answer is that it is easier to use the blocks than the toothbrushes. We believe that spending time gathering functional materials (in this case, many items involving color that are important to Mary) will more than pay off in the reduction in time for the student to truly acquire the skill being taught.

Powerful Reinforcement Systems

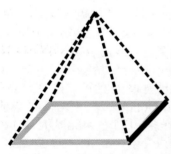

The second core element of the base of the Pyramid involves the use of *Powerful Reinforcement Systems*. One of the issues addressed in this area involves the recognition that students define what is rewarding to them, not teachers. Related to this emphasis is our awareness that we may not like all the reinforcers that are effective for a student! However, while we should work toward developing new sources of motivation for a student (similar to when you or I took an art-appreciation class) such changes will take some time. Until those new reinforcers are effective, we must use what is immediately available (unless, of course, it involves things that are dangerous to the student or others).

We emphasize using reinforcers for completing actions that are as 'natural' to the situation as possible. For example, a natural consequence for putting on sneakers is getting to run around outside. To start a lesson involving learning to lace up sneakers, we use a "reinforcer first" strategy. That is, *first* we

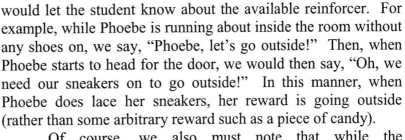

would let the student know about the available reinforcer. For example, while Phoebe is running about inside the room without any shoes on, we say, "Phoebe, let's go outside!" Then, when Phoebe starts to head for the door, we would then say, "Oh, we need our sneakers on to go outside!" In this manner, when Phoebe does lace her sneakers, her reward is going outside (rather than some arbitrary reward such as a piece of candy).

All lessons begin by identifying and signaling the potential reinforcer.

Of course, we also must note that while the consequences for completing a task should be as natural as possible, many activities will require rewards while the skill is being accomplished. In our example, while Phoebe is lacing her sneakers- a complex sequence of actions- we may provide small rewards such as praise or even provide some tokens to help her understand how long this task will last. Such small rewards are identified as within-task reinforcers.

Another central issue regarding the use of reinforcement concerns the timing of providing the reward. We all know that rewards should come quickly after our target skill. However, we want to operationalize 'quickly' by noting that reinforcers that are delayed by more than ½ a second reduce the power of the reinforcer! Whenever a new skill is to be learned, including the steps within PECS, teachers must determine ways to provide positive feedback within ½ second of that new skill!

1/2 sec

Related to the speed of providing reinforcers are factors associated with the differential use of reinforcement. That is, we can reward one behavior but not another or we may reinforce one behavior more than another. In the latter case, each response is followed by reinforcement but one response will be favored because it is connected to more reinforcement. In this way, we can remain positive while teaching, "This response is better than that one!"

"Let's Make a Deal"

Essential to the Pyramid Approach is how we interact with our students. We believe that we should engage in "Let's Make a Deal" with our students. Why make deals with students? Well, teachers expect their students to learn. Learning involves changing behaviors- that is, after a lesson, students should do something that they couldn't do before the lesson (i.e., say something, use a new picture, button a coat, recite the Gettysburg Address, etc.). Thus, teachers want students to do something (learn) for them! The relationship between teacher and student is thus similar to the relationship between a boss and a worker- the boss expects the worker to do something (the job) for the boss! When we work with students, we are "the boss." However, as teachers in a school, we all work for someone- our own bosses. As workers, we have

teacher/student = boss/worker

What do I do?
What will I get?
When am I paid?
What are my perks?
Can I have "time off?"

certain expectations about our relationship with our boss that we believe are equally important to establish in our relationship with our student. If I don't know what I'm going to get paid for a job, I won't start the job. With students, we adopt a similar simple rule- no reinforcer, no lesson!

For example, before we start a job, we want to know what we will get paid, when we get paid, how many vacation days we'll get, and other important factors. Furthermore, even though we have excellent verbal skills (and I'll assume so does your boss!), we want a written contract specifying our deal with the boss- that is, we insist on having a visual representation of the deal. We believe that issues that are important or valued by us should be in place for our students. That is, they too deserve to know what their potential reinforcer is before the lesson starts (i.e., reinforcer first!), when they will receive their reinforcer, and how they will get a break during a lesson. They also should have a visual representation of their deal with us! While this may sound like a mighty large order, by the end of this manual, you will see how simply we can accomplish this goal.

Communication and Social Skills

The next element of the Pyramid involves functional **Communication and Social Skills**. Communication involves certain types of interactions between people. We define *functional communication* as:

> *behavior (defined in form by the community) directed to another person who in turn provides related direct or social rewards.*

In this definition we describe the interaction between a 'speaker' and a 'listener' -regardless of whether speech is used. If there is no 'listener' then the action- even if it does involve vocal noises- may not be communicative.

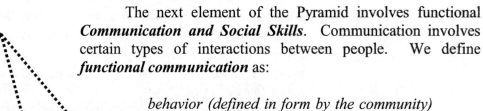

All of the communication issues briefly noted here will be elaborated upon in great detail in the next chapter.

We recognize that there are two broad reasons or functions for communicating with someone. In some circumstances, we make a request or demand something. I may ask for some juice or for you to go

Much of this section is based on the work of B. F. Skinner, in *Verbal Behavior* (1957).

Initiation vs. Responding vs. Imitation

away. The outcome or consequence for this type of communication involves direct reinforcement. On the other hand, at times, upon seeing something interesting, a child may name the object or event not as a request for the item but to engage someone in a simple conversation (such as when Mom says, "Yes, it is a pretty rose!"). Here, the outcome is social in nature. When we are working with young children with autism, we notice that they tend not to be highly motivated by social rewards. Therefore, the type of communication lesson we choose should be related to the types of reinforcers that will be effective for a student.

In addition to noting the type of consequence for communicating, it also is important to note the conditions or circumstances under which communication takes place. At times, upon seeing someone with a cookie, a boy may spontaneously say, "cookie!" At other times, the child may say, "cookie" only when someone says, "What do you want?" or "What do you see?" Finally, a child may say, "cookie" only when someone models the word and prompts the child to imitate. In each of these three situations, the child says the word "cookie." While the form is the same, each response is really a different behavior. That is, initiating is not the same as responding to a prompt or imitating. These three types of behavior initially are acquired independently (for all children, not just children with disabilities). That is, early in language development, if one type of behavior is learned (i.e., imitating a spoken word) the other types of use- initiation or responding to prompts- may not automatically appear (i.e., generalization across these response classes may not occur). Over time and experience, we see generalization readily occur but until that happens, we must plan to teach each skill individually.

Communication is bi-directional. While we may focus a great deal of attention on improving children's ability to use communication, we also want children to understand our communication to them. Here again, the transfer from using communication to understanding others' communication is not automatic early in language development. A child may understand a word but not be able to use it, and a child may also learn to say a word without seeming to understand it when spoken by others.

In our society, speech is the most common mode of communication and obviously the most preferred. However, even those of us who speak use other forms to enhance the effectiveness of what we're saying- we alter our facial expressions, our body movements, our intonation and inflections. Gestures can be formalized into sign language. Furthermore, we use print media to read and write and understand a host of visual signs and cues in the environment (traffic lights, painted lines on the road, arrows, etc.). Is the use of these other modalities dependent upon prior speech development? Certainly not, as we all know that some people learn to sign or even read and write without ever developing speech. Thus, when we note that someone cannot communicate, there are several options to choose from regarding the modality to be taught.

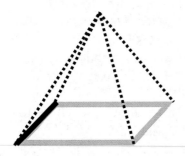

Preventing and Reducing Contextually Inappropriate Behaviors

The final element of base of the Pyramid concerns *Preventing and Reducing Contextually Inappropriate Behaviors*. In this area, we make an important distinction between the form the behavior takes vs. *why* the behavior occurs— the function. Furthermore, the development of effective interventions depends upon a clear understanding of the function of the behavior in question. Three broad types of functions are identified:

1. Behaviors that **gain access** to some type of reinforcement (including attention, materials, sensory stimulation or activities)
2. Behaviors that **escape from or avoid** certain outcomes (including social, activity, or material consequences)
3. Behaviors that are **elicited** by certain events, including the removal or sharp reduction of expected rewards, presence of pain or similar events, or the introduction of powerful rewards

Effective intervention involves identifying the function of the CIB and then assuring that a **f**unctionally **e**quivalent **a**lternative **b**ehavior (FEAB) will be supported. That is, if a child is hitting her head to gain attention, then the child must be taught to calmly request attention. If a child is hitting her head to avoid doing a task, then the child may need to learn to request help or to request a break. If the child is hitting her head

> **FEAB-** Functionally Equivalent Alternative Behavior

because someone has just told her that it's raining so she can't go outside just now, then she needs to learn how to wait. Note that the replacement must serve the same function as the CIB.

Many effective prevention strategies have been developed involving altering conditions that tend to precede a CIB. Successful interventions also involve planned direct reactions when the CIB does occur and implementing strategies to reward the absence of the CIB or the presence of the alternatives noted above.

The Top Elements of the Pyramid

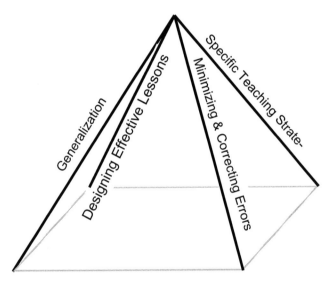

The upper portion of this model deals with issues of *how* to teach effective lessons. Before we begin teaching the lesson, we develop a plan for generalization of the new skill. We design effective lessons using a teaching strategy that is specific to the type of skill being taught. Before beginning to teach, we anticipate what type of errors the student might make and develop a plan for responding to those errors.

Generalization

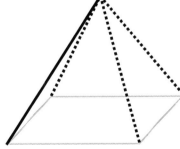

When planning to teach a new skill, we must know how that skill will help the student gain more independence, either immediately or in the future. In other words, we must know "where we're going" with this skill. Is this skill one that will be used as a "stepping stone" for the next skill we teach? Is this skill one that we are teaching after simplifying a broader skill? One unique aspect of the Pyramid model is our emphasis on addressing generalization from the very start of a lesson. That is, rather than working toward skill mastery and then planning for generalization, we think it is important to know where a lesson is going even before beginning.

"Just Noticeable Difference"

Many strategies have been designed to promote generalization from early in a lesson. Most of these strategies involve making gradual, small changes that accumulate over time to result in substantial behavior improvements. The key is to make changes that are large enough for the teacher to know a change has been made but small enough that the student doesn't seem to notice the difference. Making such changes within a teaching session is central to the overall model.

These changes are twofold: First, we can make changes in "stimulus" factors. Stimulus factors include issues related to the "other" people involved in the skill– e.g., Can the student engage in the behavior without close supervision and can he engage in the behavior when in a crowded situation? Stimulus factors involve the places where the behavior will occur– fix a sandwich in a variety of kitchens. Can the student engage in the behavior at various times of day (e.g., can he ask for a drink whenever he is thirsty or only at snack?). Stimulus factors involve the types of materials used in conjunction with the new skill. For example, can the student identify or find the red cup, *and* the red toothbrush, *and* the red coat, *and* the red chair? We look at a variety of environmental factors—can the student greet others when they walk into the room *and* when he walks into a room?

Second, we look for changes in student response factors such as number, rate, duration, complexity, accuracy, durability, and fluency of responses. For example, you have taught your student to help in the school office by sorting teachers' mail into their boxes. You must look at response factors, though, before you consider the skill to be "mastered." Can he sort one envelope or can he sort a whole stack of envelopes? Can he sort quickly and do so for an extended period of time? Can he sort the mail for all of the teachers whose names begin with 's?" Is he accurate when he sorts the materials? Although he can sort the mail for 20 minutes at a time, can he do so 5 days in a row?

Stimulus Factors	Response Factors

1. People
  a. Supervisory distance
  b. Number of others in the area
2. Places
3. Times of Day
4. Types of materials
5. Environmental changes
  a. Entering a room vs. someone else entering a room
  b. Initiation vs. responding
	1. Number of responses
	2. Rate of responses
	3. Duration of behavior
	4. Complexity of response
	5. Accuracy of response
	6. Durability of response
	7. Fluency of response

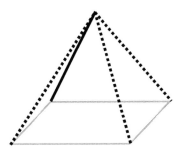

Designing Effective Lessons

When planning to teach a skill, we next consider factors associated with *Designing Effective Lessons*. Specific skills are taught best within specific types of lessons. When deciding on a lesson type, we look at whether the lesson will involve:

1. Relatively direct instructions and simple responses that are teacher-initiated. If so then we use a **discrete trial** format.

   Examples:
   "What's your name?"
   "Draw a line from A to B."
   "Get me the square cracker."

2. Skills that require a series of distinct smaller responses put together in a particular order and that generally are teacher initiated. If so, then we use a **sequential** format.

   Examples:
   washing hands
   completing an art project
   putting away silverware

3. Child-initiated actions that are in response to naturally occurring cues from the physical (things) or social (people) environment. In this case, we use a student-initiated lesson format (including incidental lessons),

   Examples:
   Asking for a drink when thirsty
   Greeting a friend upon seeing her
   Commenting on a loud, sudden sound

Because students ultimately must learn each type of lesson, teachers should develop effective teaching strategies to fit each lesson type. These factors will need to be integrated with other elements of the Pyramid Approach, such as issues associated with emphasizing functional objectives. For example, some lessons may lend themselves to rapid repetition while, for other lessons, immediate repetition would not be natural. If a student is learning to put soap in the dishwasher, it would not make sense to have him repeat this action many times in rapid succession, so we would want to disperse opportunities across the day or across several days. Or if a student is learning to put on a shirt, we would want him to do it at appropriate times. Perhaps before going to gym we would have him change a shirt. It would not make sense for us to have him put on a shirt, take it off, put it on, take it off... because this is not a sequence he's likely to encounter in the "real world."

On the other hand, if a student is doing addition problems, it would make sense to have him do several in a row rather than one per day. Or, if a student is emptying the dishwasher we would want him to sort several utensils into the utensil drawer, not just one each time he unloads the dishwasher.

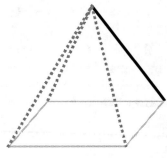

Specific Teaching Strategies

As we make our detailed lesson plans, we must consider *Specific Teaching Strategies*. Most lessons involve a teacher initially helping a student perform a skill. The type of help we provide involves various *prompts*, including verbal, gestural, modeling, and physical prompts. The key to a successful lesson is that it results in a student being able to perform the skill independently of our assistance- therefore, our goal is to eliminate the prompts used to help the student. Once we've eliminated the prompts, the skill then occurs in response to natural cues in the environment, whether physical, social, or internal. These cues are identified as discriminative stimuli because they now have *stimulus control* over the new skill. For example, if we are working with a student who can imitate words, we may hold up an apple and model the word. When the child says, 'apple' he is imitating our actions. Later, when we can only hold up the apple and the child says, 'apple' the stimulus control has shifted from our modeled word to the physical apple.

We differentiate *prompts* from *cues*. The student engages in a behavior in response to a *prompt* that we must eliminate. He engages in a behavior in response to cues that we will not eliminate. For example, in a high school, students arriving at school know to report to their first class in response to a bell ringing. Some students also need us to verbally remind them ("Go to class!"). Our verbal reminder is the prompt that we hope to fade over time while the cue is a signal that we do not intend to fade. Within this differentiation, imagine viewing a stop-sign as a prompt vs. a cue. Do we ever intend to fade the stop sign—do we really expect *all* drivers to learn over time at which corners they must stop? Certainly not! Thus, the stop sign is viewed as a cue, not a prompt. Now, if you are a parent with a teen-aged child learning to drive, you might have to *prompt* your child to stop at a stop sign ("There's a stop sign—stop!!"). We would not let our child drive alone, however, until he learned to respond to the cue (the stop sign) and did not need our additional prompt.

There are a variety of prompting strategies designed to eliminate the prompt while leaving the performance under the control of natural conditions (cues). These strategies include fading, prompt hierarchies (whether most-to-least or least-to-most, delayed prompting (both constant and progressive), and using chaining strategies (both forward and backward chaining).

Shaping is an important teaching technique. In its pure form, it does not involve the use of prompts. Instead, shaping involves the gradual change in the criteria we set for reinforcement. We feel that shaping is a underutilized teaching tool in large part because it does not involve the types of active prompting that so many of us are comfortable using within a lesson.

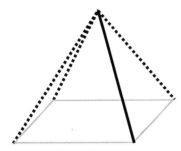

Minimizing and Correcting Errors

The most effective lessons are those that involve few mistakes by the student. Of course, it is virtually impossible to prevent all error. Therefore, the next element involves *Minimizing and Correcting Errors*. Lessons that involve a series of small, gradual changes tend to minimize errors and thus maximize a student's receipt of reinforcement. When errors do occur, we must be aware of the type of lesson we are teaching before deciding what type of correction strategy we want. A correction strategy aims to teach the skill immediately rather than simply fixing the problem caused by the error. For example, if a student fails to tie his shoe properly, I may tie it for him- thus fixing the problem- but the student will have not learned anything new (other than I am likely to solve his problems!).

4-Step Error Correction Procedure. When lessons involve discrete trial formats, we respond with a **4-step** error correction process. First, we will need to model, demonstrate or otherwise indicate the correct response. Then, we need to help the student engage in the correct action. However, at this point we may not want to provide a big type of reward least the student become dependent upon the prompt just provided. Instead, we suggest switching to another task, one that is simple, quick, and mastered by the student. (If there are few such available actions, a delay of some sort may be equally effective.) Then we would repeat the initial part of the lesson and provide a strong reinforcer for a successful response.

For example, during morning circle in a preschool class, the teacher asks, "What day is it?" Mike incorrectly answers, "Tuesday." The teacher says, 'No, it's Wednesday." Mike repeats, "Wednesday." The teacher responds, "Yes!" In this scenario, Mike said the correct word, but he said it by imitating the teacher rather than answering the question. If the teacher were to stop at this point, all Mike would have learned is to repeat the teacher's answers. Minimally, the teacher needs to ask the question again. When she does so and Mike answers, "Wednesday," we are a bit more confident that Mike is learning the lesson. But, many children, with and without disabilities, adopt a "whatever was right last time" strategy. In order to undermine the potential for Mike to use this strategy, the teacher should ask Mike something completely unrelated, but that he can answer, and then re-ask the original question. This time, when Mike answers, "Wednesday," he is doing it solely in response to the question rather than in response to a teacher model or his own last response.

```
┌─────────────────────┐
│       4-Step        │
│                     │
│  1. Model/Show      │
│  2. Prompt          │
│  3. Switch          │
│  4. Repeat          │
└─────────────────────┘
```

Step	Teacher	Student
	"What day is it?"	"Tuesday"
MODEL	"No, it's Wednesday"	"Wednesday"
PROMPT	"What day is it?"	"Wednesday"
SWITCH	"That's right! What's your name?""	"Mike"
REPEAT	"What day is it?"	"Wednesday"

Backstep

Go back to last correct step, prompt through e r r o r s t e p , differentially reinforce

Backstep Error Correction Procedure. Errors that occur within a sequential lesson require different correction strategies. In such situations, it is important to note that we often find the error long after it was made. That is, the error is likely to have occurred some time earlier in the sequence than when we discovered it. In this case, we must help the student go back into the sequence just prior to when the error occurred. Following this type of **Backstep**, we would prompt the correct action in its proper place in the sequence. If we prompt the student from the point where we found the error- the student is in my classroom but he left the water running in the bathroom so I tell him to go turn it off- then I am likely to see that error preserved and repeated on the next opportunity. Once we prompt the student within the Backstep sequence, we then differentially reinforce the completion of the sequence but giving a reward that is effective, but not as powerful as one we would use for independent completion of the sequence.

Anticipate

With a known error pattern, anticipate it, and prompt to prevent it's occurrence

Anticipatory Prompting. In some cases, it may not be possible to immediately go back into the sequence. For example, if we are attempting to teach someone to ride on a public bus and she forgets to pay the bus driver, we will not be able to stop the bus, get off it, and try again. Instead, we must **anticipate** the error on the next natural opportunity and provide a prompt that prevents its repetition (and then fade that prompt over time).

Collecting and Analyzing Data

Data

Collect and analyze date to determine if the lesson is working.

Central to a behavioral or education model is making decisions based upon evaluating what we've done. A core question every teacher must ask about every lesson is, "Is this a good lesson? Shall I keep doing what I've been doing?" Answering this question involves collecting information about the teacher's actions as well as the student's performance. Useful information also may be derived from other sources, including other staff, parents, and peers of the student. To be useful, the data must be gathered and summarized in a manner that permits periodic analysis.

Data collection and analysis can be effortful and time consuming. Thus, the process requires various types of reinforcement. Perhaps the most important rewarding consequence of collecting and analyzing data is having the data help refine a lesson. If the data are not used in a meaningful manner, we tend not to continue collecting it as a way of avoiding wasting our time. While percent-correct may fit some lessons, progress in other lessons may better involve rate, duration, intensity, accuracy, prompt-level, etc. How much data is required, how often should it be reviewed, and what type of potential changes should be made related to our findings, all should be decided upon by the student's full team (rather than individual members of the team).

The type of data collected should reflect the broad range of factors that may be important within different lessons. In some situations, the frequency and rate of an action are most important. In other cases, the duration, intensity, complexity, or accuracy may be focal point of a lesson. Finally, we may observe behavior as it occurs or we may evaluate the product of the lesson (i.e., a clean room, a neatly printed letter, a sentence strip with 3 icons in the correct order within PECS, etc.).

Linking the Elements of the Pyramid

The Pyramid Approach involves a complex model of factors required to make lessons as effective as possible in various environments. The order in which the model has been presented here also is the order in which we support teachers in making changes to implement the full model. That is, it is important to first assure that powerful reinforcement systems are in place before attempting to refine subtle aspect of prompting or error correction. Teaching critical functional communication skills is crucial even before the development of significant behavior management plans for a student. In classrooms and other teaching environments that use The Pyramid Approach to Education, many of the critical aspects noted are prominently posted so that all members of the team are equally aware of the critical information regarding a student.

The elements of lessons involving PECS are very much like any other lesson. First, a reinforcer associated with the skill to be learned must be identified and it's availability made clear to the student. We must determine the type of lesson that leads into a review of potential prompting or shaping strategies. We must anticipate the type of error that can accompany this type of lesson and plan for the corresponding error correction strategy. We must assure that we provide timely reinforcement in amounts that lead to skill growth and long-term independence. We must collect adequate data to justify our current strategies or to help suggest alternative teaching strategies. If inappropriate behaviors occur, we must have a system in place to help determine the function of the behavior, how to respond to the behavior, how to help prevent the behavior, and how to promote functionally equivalent alternative behaviors.

All of these steps require strong and continuous staff and parent training and support. Without adequately trained teachers, we cannot expect students to progress. The Pyramid Approach offers teachers and parents a problem-solving orientation by which they can design and analyze effective lessons, including those for our most complex students.

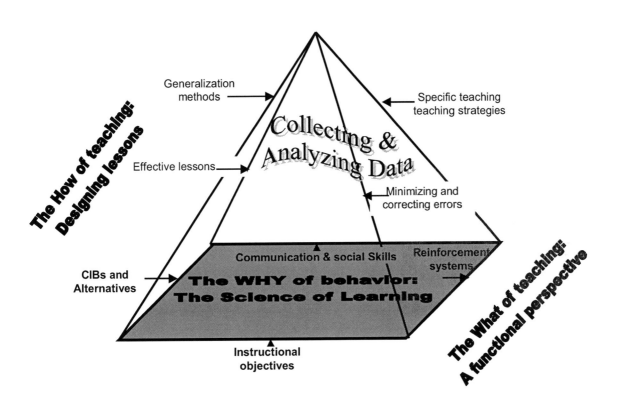

2

Functional Communication

Functional Communication

What is communication?

A small boy tries to reach a plate of cookies, but accidentally knocks it off the kitchen counter. The little boy, about 15-months old and developing quite typically, stops, gasps, and looks at his mother. As she turns to him, he looks back at the spilled cookies and then back to her. He will continue looking back and forth between his mother and the cookies until she, too, sees the cookies and reacts. He has not yet developed any whole words to say but his mother certainly understands that he wants her to react. **Did he communicate?**

> Communication does not always involve speaking.

To help clarify what is unique about communication, let's first look at a situation in which there is no communication. A young boy walks into the family room and goes straight to the television. He does not see his father sitting nearby. The boy pulls a video off the shelf, inserts it into the video player, turns the television on, and begins watching the video. Is this an example of communication? We argue that it is not. Remember, the boy did not know his father was there. The boy simply acted upon something in the real world (the video, the television, the VCR, etc.) and following those actions came a rewarding experience (watching the video). The boy's actions were directed toward various objects in his surroundings. These actions would not have changed if his father were not in the room- that is, his actions were not dependent upon his father.

Actions that are directed to the environment and that lead to rewarding outcomes are not communicative! Some people feel uncomfortable with this conclusion. After all, as the father watches his son, he may think that his son wants to watch a video or that he likes the particular video. That is, by watching his son's actions, the father can interpret what those actions may mean. But our ability to interpret an action does not make that action communicative. Our capacity to interpret someone else's behavior does not change the nature of that behavior. Communication requires something more than simple action upon something in the environment.

Consider a different scenario. A young girl walks into the family room and sees her mother sitting there. The girl approaches her mother and says, "I want my video!" Her mother gets up, walks to the television, inserts a video into the video player, and turns it on to play. The daughter sits down and begins watching the video. First, notice that from the girl's perspective, she obtains the same thing that the boy did-watching a video. However, this scenario does involve communication because the girl acted toward her mother rather than toward some concrete part of the environment (the video player). So, communication requires at least two people and the action of one person **must be** directed toward the other person. The second person, in turn, provides an appropriate response to the first person. In this case, the girl directed her behavior to her mother. And her mother provided the girl with access to the video. What is the role of the person to whom the communication is directed- that is, the person 'listening?' In our example, the mother's role was to provide for her daughter what her daughter wanted- the video. The mother's reaction helps expand our definition of communication:

> **Communication involves behavior (defined in form by the community) directed to another person who in turn provides related direct or social rewards.**

Why do we communicate?

In planning to teach communication, we first must assess all the conditions that might affect a child's communication. For example, sometimes children are very "chatty" and seem to want to just interact with someone with their communication. At other times, the child needs or wants something specific and knows the easiest way to get it is to ask Mom or Dad for it. Some children are great at beginning communicative interactions and some children tend to wait until someone else begins the interaction. Therefore, we need to look at **why** children communicate, and under what circumstances, or **when**, children communicate.

In the above example, the little girl wanted the video and went to her mother to get it. Because the outcome was what the girl asked for (the girl specified the desired outcome), we will call this type of communication a *request*. The *direct* outcome for the girl was something material or concrete that she wanted.

Is there another type of reward for communication? Think about a very young boy sitting in his high chair in the living room. As he looks out the bay window, he suddenly says

This discussion of communication is based on *Verbal Behavior* (1957) by B. F. Skinner

to his mother, "Truck! Truck! Truck!" What does he want? Is it likely that he wants his mother to go outside and get him the truck? No, there is clearly something else he wants. As we continue to observe, his mother replies, "Yes, dear, that's a truck!" Clearly, the boy wants his mother's attention and for her to acknowledge what he is seeing. He wants something social from his mother- her attention, her praise, her apparent enjoyment of her conversation with him. He does not get anything material from his communication, such as the video the young girl requested. Instead, he *commented* to his mother who provided him with a social reaction.

Behavior	Outcome	Type of Skill
"video"	Video (tangible)	Request
"truck"	Attention/ acknowledgement from Mom (social)	Comment

Thus, we can divide the main purposes (or functions) of communication between requests and comments. When we want to teach a lesson involving communication, our first job will be to consider what purpose will the communicative act serve for the child? Furthermore, what we know about the child may influence our lesson goals. For example, we know that social rewards for very young children with autism and related disabilities tend not to be very effective. Therefore, it may be difficult to start communication lessons with very young children with autism by targeting communication skills that primarily serve a commenting function (comments). It is likely to be more useful to the child to begin teaching how to **request** the most important reinforcers.

When do we communicate?

Other factors strongly influence how we will teach communication skills. Just as we look the consequences of communication, we also must look at conditions that exist prior to the behavior. How, then, do various circumstances influence the way we look at certain communication skills?

Beth is standing in her classroom waiting for her students to return from recess. She is eating from a bowl of popcorn. Sarah walks into the room, sees Beth and the popcorn and immediately says, "Popcorn!" Beth gives her some popcorn. Soon, Shawn walks into the room. He walks over to the bowl of popcorn and starts to reach for some- Beth doesn't allow him to grab the popcorn and patiently waits for him to communicate. He remains silent until she asks, "What do you want?" He immediately says, "Popcorn!" She gives him some popcorn. Nathan walks into the room and goes over to the bowl of popcorn. He tries to reach for some. When Beth asks him what he wants, he remains silent. She finally says, "Say 'popcorn.'" He immediately says, "Popcorn!" and she gives him some to eat.

Notice some similarities across children. Each one said "popcorn" and each one got some popcorn to eat. But we recognize that each child actually did something slightly different than the other children. Sarah **initiated**- that is, she saw something she wanted, she saw someone to communicate with, and she spontaneously said something. Shawn said "popcorn" only in **response** to the cue or prompt Beth provided ("What do you want?"). And Nathan only spoke the word when Beth provided a specific type of prompt- that is, she modeled the word "popcorn" which he then **imitated**. Thus, although each child said "popcorn," one child initiated, one child responded to a prompt, and one child imitated a model- three distinct behaviors.

Condition	Behavior	Outcome	Type of Skill
Desire for video	"video"	Video (tangible)	Spontaneous Request
Direct question "What do you want?"	"video"	Video (tangible)	Prompted Request
Model of the request	"video"	Video (tangible)	Imitated Request
Hears the truck	"truck"	Attention/ acknowledgement from Mom (social)	Spontaneous comment
Hears truck and question "What do you hear?"	"truck"	Attention/ acknowledgement from Mom (social)	Prompted comment
Hears truck and model	"truck"	Attention/ acknowledgement from Mom (social)	Imitated comment

Prompted ≠ Spontaneous ≠ Imitated

In terms of teaching, it would be wonderful if each of these types of behaviors automatically generalized from one to the other. Unfortunately, our understanding of typical language development and the general principles of learning leads us to know that such is not the case. Each of these types of communication skills develops independently in typically developing children. At some point in their development, children eventually do learn to generalize new vocabulary across each type of communication skill. However, when we begin to teach children with communication deficits, we will have to arrange to teach each of the communication skills independently and plan for generalization to be promoted. That is, just because a child can imitate a spoken word or respond correctly to a prompt does not guarantee that the child will be able to use that same word spontaneously (either as a request or as a comment).

Three distinct communication skills and lessons:

1. Spontaneous communication
2. Responsive communication
3. Imitation

Communication is bi-directional

So far, we have discussed teaching children to communicate with us. However, it is also important to teach children to understand when we communicate with them! So, in addition to learning to use communication, children must also learn to understand communication directed to them. Some directions immediately benefit the child, as when we say, "Your cookie is on the table; take the big ball and go play." Directions that are functional involve natural consequences associated with the direction. For example, if we say, "Go to the door" or "Go to the refrigerator" then natural consequences associated with each direction should follow. Going to a door should lead to going out the door (for a functional purpose), while going to the refrigerator should lead to opening it and obtaining something good to eat or drink.

Sometimes we give directions because they help **us** in some way. A parent may be thirsty and says to his daughter, "Please bring me a soda." Dad can only get his drink if his daughter understands what he said. But what does his daughter get out of the interaction? Hopefully, her father will politely thank her for getting his drink. Remember that not all children with disabilities find polite praise highly motivating. For these children, teaching them to follow functionally relevant directions is likely to be more successful than teaching them to follow directions that primarily benefit the instructor. Also consider the complexity of the direction itself. Teachers often ask simple questions (i.e., "What's your name? Where is your pencil?"), and give simple instructions ("Go to gym! Line up! Take out your crayons!"). Sometimes these directions are given simply, and sometimes they are embedded in more complex sentences ("It's snowing today, so you will need to get your hats before we go outside"). More complex directions might involve several elements that the child must attend to ("Get your gym clothes and shoes before you line up at the door.").

Again, it would be great if these two skills (using versus understanding communication) developed hand-in-hand and automatically. Careful observation makes it clear that there is

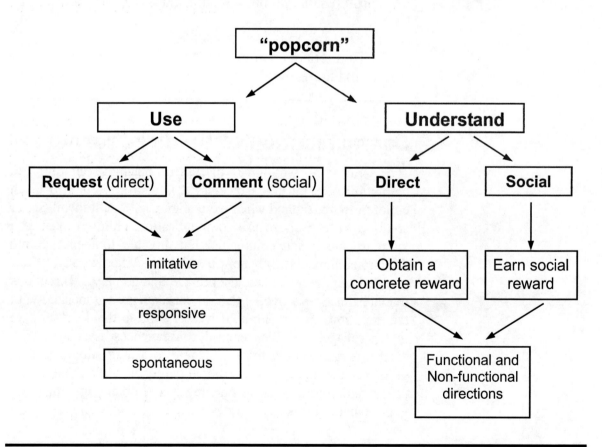

no automatic generalization from using to understanding, or vice versa. We all have known children who can understand a spoken word but not be able to use that same word. That is, John may be able to respond correctly when told to get a spoon, but when he needs a spoon to eat his ice cream, he may not be able to say the word. On the other hand, people who study language development have found that there is a point in early language acquisition in very young children when they can use a particular word but do not respond correctly when that same word is used within an instruction. Therefore, speaking a word and understanding that word spoken by someone else are independently learned. As language development proceeds, children eventually do learn to generalize across these two types of skills.

As we review what we need to teach a child regarding just a single 'word' such as 'popcorn' we notice several factors. We will have to teach children to say popcorn when they want popcorn as well as teach them just to tell us that they see some popcorn. They will need to say popcorn spontaneously AND in response to questions or modeling. Finally, they will need to understand what we mean when we say the word "popcorn," even when the spoken word is accompanied by very little "additional information." Imagine, all these lessons will be needed just for the single word!

Is talking always communicative?

Are there times when we speak but do not communicate? Remember, communicative acts must be directed toward another person. Do you ever hear your child or student singing songs or reciting dialogue from a video when he or she was alone? Do you ever sing in the shower or while driving alone? Do you remember singing songs to yourself as a child –even songs that were in a foreign language? Such talking and singing would not meet our definition of communication because the speaker or singer is not directing his or her words or song to a "listener" or communicative partner. In fact, many of us quit singing when we are joined by another person! As we become more sophisticated speakers, we eventually learn to be our own listeners.

Some children with autism and related developmental disabilities repeat words, phrases, jingles from TV or the radio, or entire dialogues from videotapes without understanding what they are saying. They are not constructing the sentences from words they know how to use but, rather, are repeating the sounds for reasons not related to communication. One reason we may reach this conclusion is that the child may be as likely to say the words or phrases with someone listening as when he or she is alone. That is, his or her words are not targeted to another person. Therefore, when we assess a child's ability to communicate we must go beyond a description of simply noting what words the child can say.

Communicative modality

Have you ever had laryngitis? If you lost your voice completely, speech was virtually impossible. Were you still able to communicate, though? Most likely you used other *modalities* of communication. For example, you might use gestures to get people to understand what you want or what you want them to do with some object nearby. If you knew sign language, you could communicate with full complexity with someone else who understood sign language. With the right tools, you could use writing and reading skills to communicate with others (who also could read and write). If you were a competent artist, you could draw pictures of objects and actions. And if you couldn't draw, you could have access to pictures and visual symbols others have created for you to manipulate.

Each of these examples points out a different type of communication modality- using our hands and other parts of our body, using print or pictures, etc. Each type of communication- including speech- has its advantages and disadvantages. Competent communication is possible through several different types of modalities. Even when we can speak, we often combine several modalities when communicating. Some of us use expansive hand and arm movements to emphasize certain points.

Communicative Modalities:
- Speech
- Gestures
- Sign language
- Pictures
- Writing

Just as we all use a variety of modalities to communicate, we also give directions to children using a variety of modalities. Teachers frequently use written or picture communication to reinforce their spoken lessons. Sometimes teachers use questions or directions with gestures or other *visual cues*. For example, a teacher might hold up a worksheet and point to the top of it as she says, "Write your name at the top." Other times, these directions or questions will be given in isolation.

When we assess a child's communicative skills, we may find that although the child can imitate certain sounds, the child cannot initiate *spoken* requests. Our primary goal is to teach the child to functionally communicate. A secondary goal is to teach the child to speak. That is, we must recognize that communication is the more crucial goal than is speaking. Of course, if we can accomplish both, all the better.

> **Communication is our primary goal**

If communication is our primary goal and our child or student is having difficulty learning to speak, we must consider teaching a modality different from speech. Does this mean that we are giving up on speech? Absolutely not! Our goal is to teach the child to communicate in some manner (or modality) while continuing to address development of speech. Will these alternative modalities "inhibit" speech development? We know from many years of research that the answer is "NO!!" Use of alternative and augmentative communication systems will not inhibit or prevent the development of speech. In fact, many researchers report that these systems actually enhance speech development (Silverman, 1995; Glennen, 1997).

> Augmentative and alternative communication systems will not inhibit speech development.

Throughout PECS implementation we continue to address speech development through a variety of strategies, the details of which are outside the scope of this book. We teach vocal and speech imitation and differentially reinforce interactions in which speech is used. We do so through functional activities rather than in a drill format. Initially, these "speech" lessons are separate from our PECS and communication lessons. In the later Phases of PECS, we will address speech within the communication lesson. We will never, however, require or insist on speech! Our goal is to teach functional communication and we will not withhold reinforcement (social or direct) if our students do not speak.

Critical communication skills

- Rafael goes to his mother and pulls her to the shelves in the play room. He then tries to "toss" his mother's arm up to one of the top shelves. Rafael's mother begins guessing which toy her son wants. When she isn't correct right away, Rafael begins to bite his arm and slap his face.

- Anna's teacher shows her a job to do. Anna drops to the floor and begins hitting her head on the tiles.
- Dominic is gathering his book bag and coat at the end of the day. His teacher comes over to him and says, "Your mom is going to be late today, so you can play longer." Dominic then punches his head.

Each of these children is obviously upset with his or her situation. Rafael wants a specific toy, but cannot calmly communicate this desire. Anna wants *not* to do something but cannot calmly communicate her needs. And Dominic appears to not understand that if he waits for awhile he will be able to get what he wants. Each student must learn certain critical functional communication skills in order to be able to participate independently in daily activities. What are those critical skills?

9 Critical Communication Skills

One set of critical skills deals with expressive or productive communication- that is, skills the child uses to effectively communicate with others. The other set deals with how children respond to the communication of others.

Why are these skills listed as critical? They are critical because, if the student cannot calmly and effectively engage in each skill, then the student will most likely try other means to obtain the same outcome. As noted for Rafael, when he wanted something important (such as a specific train), once his approach to his mother failed, he became upset because he could not get his train.

Productive Skills	Receptive Skills
1. Asking for reinforcers	6. Responding to "Wait."
2. Asking for help	7. Responding to transitional cues
3. Asking for a break	
4. Indicating "no" to "Do you want _____?"	8. Following functioning directions
5. Indicating "yes" to "Do you want_____?"	9. Following a schedule

Asking for a desired item

Asking for a desired item is perhaps the most fundamental communication skill for all learners to develop. Requesting allows us to access items and activities that are essential for day-to-day living or that allow us to enjoy ourselves or our interactions with others.

| Asking for assistance |

Asking for help is universally important because everyone at some time will be in a situation where the solution to a problem must come from someone else. A child may not be able to reach a toy put on a high shelf, a girl may not be able to open a clear container with her favorite snack inside, a boy may not be able to push his straw into the juice box, a girl may not be able to push open a heavy door, etc. In each situation, we may realize what's going on when we see the child crying or acting out.

| Asking for a break |

We all have been in situations where the demand is too high or fatigue has set in due to the length of the task at hand. In these cases, we will ask for a break- some time to recuperate. We are not quitting because we understand that after our break we will go back to work. When we consider a comprehensive contract with our boss, we will be certain to negotiate about our vacation days (breaks) because we know we'll need them sometime during the year. We adults periodically need to avoid or escape from certain events and can do so in a number of socially acceptable ways. Students also need a calm way to ask for a break, so we must teach them to do so. As with learning to ask for help, the key will be for the child to be able to ask for a break before starting to tantrum.

| Rejecting |

Rejecting offers from other people allows us to participate in interactions during which our communicative partner is determining what, specifically, we might want. Billy hates pickles- their very smell makes him gag. Walter walks over to Billy and offers him a pickle. How will Billy react? In large part, it depends upon Billy's communication skills. He may be able to communicate, "No thanks!" However, if he is not able to do so in such a calm manner, he still will convey his disgust- most likely in a dramatic manner that Walter will not appreciate!

| Affirming |

If Walter holds out something that Billy likes, even if Billy cannot calmly communicate "yes" the alternative will be safe for Walter- that is, Billy simply will take the item. But sometimes Billy might be offered an item that the communicative partner is not holding. Calmly taking it will not be an option, so Billy will need to indicate, "Yes, that's what I want."

Notice the functional difference between answering "yes" or "no" to an offer ("Do you want this?") as opposed to the question, "Is this an X?" When we say "yes" to "Do you want a cookie?" we expect to get a cookie (similar to the function of a request). When we say "yes" in answer to "Is this a cookie?" we do not get the cookie- instead, the teacher says, "You're right! It is a cookie!" (similar to the function of a comment). So, we need two different lessons, the first of which is a critically functional skill.

Responding to "Wait"

Dominic was the student who punched his own head when he misunderstood the instruction, "Wait." Who else needs to learn this lesson? Everyone! Even adults could do a little better in the patience department (as our mothers constantly remind us!). What are we trying to communicate to someone when we say, "Wait?" The message is actually complex- "I know what you want and you are going to get it but not right now." The listener must understand that he is not being denied access to the item, that he going to get the item eventually. This is a complex message!

Responding to functional directions

Responding to directions is viewed as critical because of the potential risks associated with failing to understand the message. For example, if a parent tells a child, "Move! There's a car coming!" failure to respond to that direction could be perilous. Therefore, children must learn to follow certain directions that involve functional outcomes. When teachers begin this lesson, the consequences for the direction should be naturally associated with the direction. For example, when we say, "Get your shoes" or "Find your cup" then natural consequences associated with each object should follow. Retrieving shoes should lead to going out the door and finding a cup should lead to someone filling it with something good.

Sometimes we give directions because they help us in some way. A parent may be thirsty and say to his daughter, "Please bring me a drink." Dad can only get his drink if his daughter understands what he said. But what does his daughter get out of the interaction? Hopefully, her father will politely thank her for getting his drink. However, we should recall that not all children with disabilities find polite praise highly motivating. For these children, teaching them to follow functionally relevant directions (directions that are important from the child's perspective) is likely to be more successful initially than teaching them to follow directions that primarily benefit the instructor.

Just as productive or expressive communication can occur with several different types of modalities, so too can directions/questions. We certainly want children to learn to understand what we are saying, however, to be a productive member of our society, we all must learn to respond to many different types of visual cues or directions. For example, anyone who drives must learn to respond to different traffic signs, lights, and solid versus dashed lines painted on the road. We must respond to these visual cues independently of spoken cues. To drive effectively, we must respond to a stop sign without a policeman standing at the intersection saying, "Stop!" Consider how we put together furniture from stores such as Ikea®- they provide all instructions with drawing due to their international clientele. Therefore, we must plan to teach students, whether they communicate with speech, sign, or pictures, to respond to both visual and auditory instructions.

Responding to transitional cues

Have you ever had a student you found crying or screaming as you took him off the school bus? You firmly take the student to the class and after 20 minutes or so, he calms down as he plays with a toy. Then, you approach him and say, "It's time for gym!" The child immediately cries and screams. You firmly take him to gym where he continues to cry for another 15 minutes before settling down to play with a ball. Then, you walk over and say, "It's time to go back to class!" He immediately cries and screams! This cycle is repeated throughout the day, following each transition. What's happening here?

If you open your own day-calendar system, most likely what you have written are the events and activities that you need to complete. Thus, when we communicate with our students, we typically direct them to their activities. Using visual cues may help clarify which activity we mean, but sometimes merely adding visual support will not suffice. Are the students focused on activities, as are adults? More likely the students are thinking about the things they like- that is, their reinforcers. When a child playing with blocks is told to go to gym, the child hears that he must stop playing with the blocks. Once he settles into the routine at gym and is playing with a ball, the direction to go back to class really signals to the child to stop playing with the ball. When reinforcers are suddenly removed from anyone, we can expect a negative reaction. Is there a way to communicate more effectively with the child about the transitions? While the child is playing with blocks in the classroom, the teacher can

approach with a ball that is only used in the gym. In this manner, the teacher is communicating about the next reinforcer rather than the next activity. When the child is playing with a ball in gym and the teacher wants him to return to the classroom for snack time, it would be best to approach the student in gym communicating (with auditory or visual cues) about the snack. In each situation, the student must change activities as a way to obtain the next reinforcer. This strategy shifts the emphasis from what the student must give up to what the student can obtain. So, when dealing with transitions, focus on communicating about the student's primary concerns- reinforcers!

Following a schedule

Most adults keep track of all the important things they need to do across today, this week, or this month by using some type of written calendar system. Children also like to know what is expected of them and when activities will occur. Therefore, we should teach them how to use systems that contain information about their future schedule of activities. A system to provide such information should be as visual for the children as it is for us. We do not simply try to memorize what we need to do. Rather, we write things down to provide a visual source of information. For our students, we also must provide a visual system although using pictures and objects will be necessary for those who cannot understand text.

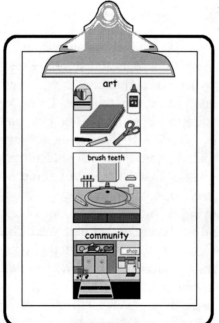

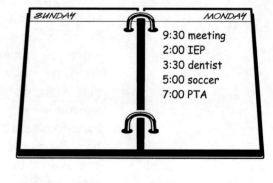

Are visual communication strategies an unnecessary crutch upon which the child might become dependent? Consider how many visual "aids" or visual communication systems are present in our everyday lives. Every time you get in a car, you trust your life to visual aids! We try to observe all road signs and we certainly hope the drivers around us are doing so, too! Many of us keep a personal calendar or organizer handy. Many of us leave notes to ourselves or others. Other visual communications could include:

- Recipes
- "To do" lists
- Overhead aisle markers in grocery stores
- Visual directions for assembling furniture or toys
- Menus (especially those with pictures!)
- Roadside billboards
- "Emergency procedure" card on airplanes
- "Men" or "Women" icons on bathroom doors

A survey of a typical kindergarten classroom yields a vast array of visual signals/cues to which children must respond. These include a variety of directions:

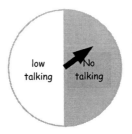

1. What type of talking is allowed during a specific activity

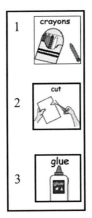

2. The sequence for an art activity

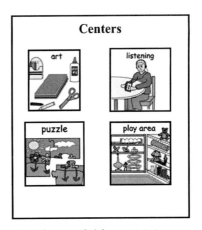

3. The available activities during "center time."

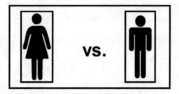

4. Girls vs. boys

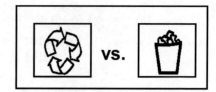

5. Recycle or trash

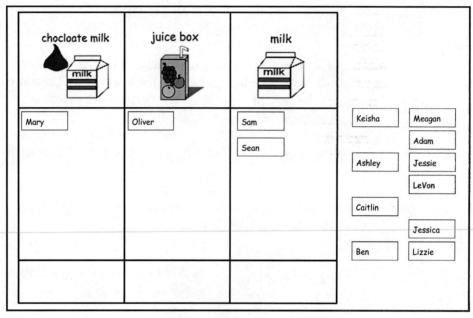

6. Choose a drink for today's snack

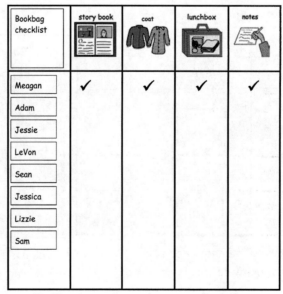

7. Items to remember to take home

Critical Communication Skills Checklist

Before beginning communication training, it is helpful to know how a child currently communicates. Does he/she request specific items or activities? What does he do when you tell him to "wait?" **The Critical Communication Skills Checklist** is used to assess the child's current functional communication skills. The purpose of the checklist is to determine what critical communication skills your child uses or does not use, how he engages in each skill, and whether the manner in which your child engages in each skill is appropriate. Once this judgment has been made, the user can then develop a communication training plan by prioritizing each target skill.

Example #1

In the following example, a five-year-old child lets her mother know that she wants something to eat by pushing or pulling her mother into the kitchen and then pushing her mother's hand/arm toward the cupboard containing the desired food. This action might be a tactic a much younger child uses before he or she develops words, but for a five year old child, a more specific means of requesting particular foods is desirable. Therefore, we would judge this current behavior as inappropriate. Because the child frequently uses this communicative skill throughout a day, we would prioritize this item as a "1" or as a top priority for training.

Skill	Example	Appropriate?
Request - edible	drags Mom to kitchen and pushes her arm to item	no

Example #2

In the next example, a ten-year-old boy goes to the kitchen and finds his food on his own. If something is out of reach, he drags a chair from the table across the room so that he can climb up onto the chair in order to reach items in high cabinets. If he is unable to open a cupboard or drawer, he will find another food that he can access on his own.

Skill	Example	Appropriate?
Request - edible	accesses food on his own	no

In this example, the boy does not communicate with others about his desire for things to eat. (Remember that communication requires a listener!) While it is great that the boy independently can satisfy some of his needs, it will not always be possible or realistic for him to do so. Therefore, we would judge the absence of this skill as inappropriate and consider teaching the child to do so a top priority.

Example #3

In example #3, an eight-year-old boy, tantrums when confronted with activities he does not like or finds difficult. The tantrums can be very severe and may escalate to aggression or self injurious behavior.

Skill	Example	Appropriate?
Protest/Reject - activity	tantrums	no

Although temper tantrums might be a typical sequence children pass through, even in very young children, we try to teach them to say "no" rather than tantrum. Therefore, we would judge this behavior as inappropriate at signaling "no." As this boy progresses through his school program, and as his family continues to teach new skills at home, he is likely to encounter non-preferred activities throughout each day. It would be much simpler for him and his family and teaching staff if he were able to calmly indicate "no." Because of the intensity of this boy's reaction, and because of the potential for this behavior to occur at high rates, we would consider teaching this skill a top priority.

Example #4

In example #4, a ten-year-old girl does not respond when told, "Come here." This often results in threats to her safety, especially during community-based training.

Skill	Example	Appropriate?
Respond to directions "Come here"	Does not do	no

The potential for harm when not responding to this direction is of grave concern. Therefore, teaching the girl to respond appropriately would also be a top priority.

Summarizing the checklist

Once you have completed the checklist, summarize which skills you have designated as "not appropriate." These skills will be the first to be addressed within communication training. For some of these skills, such as requesting, PECS will be used with the children with no functional speech. The children will be taught to use gestures with other skills (shaking/nodding his or her head for affirming and rejecting). These skills can be translated very easily into objectives for Individualized Education Plans (IEPs), Individualized Family Service Plans (ISPs), etc.

When summarizing the checklist, you might notice that your child does engage in some appropriate communication skills, but only in response to a specific cue or prompt (e.g., the student can ask for a desired item, but only when asked, "What do you want?"). Fundamental to PECS across all communicative behaviors is that the student learns from the very beginning of training to *initiate* communicative exchanges. This lesson is accomplished through the use of specific teaching strategies designed to limit, control, and eliminate the amount and type of prompts that are used. Strict adherence to the teaching principles outlined in the initial two phases of training is vital if the desired outcome is a child who **spontaneously initiates communicative interactions.**

See Appendix A for sample IEP/IFSP objectives for PECS implementation.

See Appendix B for a blank "Critical Communication Skills Checklist."

CRITICAL COMMUNICATION SKILLS CHECKLIST

Name: **Bryan**   Age: **5**   Date: **7/27**

Skill	Example	Appro-priate?
1. Request reinforcers		
edibles	takes/leads adult to desired item	no
toys	gets toys on his own-not interested in toys out of reach	no
activities		
2. Request help/assistance	cries	no
3. Request break	tantrums to escape an activity	no
4. Reject	screams, cries, hits	no
5. Affirm/Accept	takes offered items	yes
6. Respond to "Wait"	tantrums	no
7. Respond to directions		
VISUAL DIRECTIONS		
Orient to name being signaled	not attempted	
"Come here"	only if speaker shows desired item and gestures	yes
"Stop"	does not respond	no
"Sit down"	only if offered desired item	yes
"Give it to me"	does not respond	no
"Go get..." (familiar item)	does not respond	no
"Go to..." (familiar location)	if shown car keys will go to door	yes
"Put it back/down"	does not respond	no
"Let's go/ Come with me."	does not respond	no
ORAL DIRECTIONS		
Orient to name being called	does not respond	no
"Come here"	only if speaker shows desired item	no
"Stop"	does not respond	no
"Sit down"	does not respond without gesture and showing desired item	no
"Give it to me"	does not respond	no
"Go get..." (familiar item)	does not respond	no
"Go to..." (familiar location)	does not respond without visual cue	no
"Put it back/down"	does not respond	no
"Let's go/ Come with me."	does not respond	no
8. Transition b/w activities	tantrums	no
9. Follow visual schedule	does not do	no

A Brief Review of the History of Communication Training

Historically, therapists working with children with autism have utilized a broad array of training protocols, strategies, and curricula to teach communication skills. We divide these approaches into three broad categories:

1. Speech imitation protocols
2. Sign language protocols
3. Picture/symbol based protocols

Speech Imitation:

When children fail to develop speech, then speech production often has become the primary goal of intervention. To this end, professionals have used a variety of speech imitation training protocols. The basic premise of these approaches is that children can be taught to speak by teaching them to imitate the sounds and then words of the trainer. Often times, speech imitation is initially difficult for children. The task is simplified, then, by teaching the child first to imitate specific non-speech actions of the therapist. If, however, a program is to rely on a child imitating the therapist, then the therapist must insure that the child is paying attention to her or him. Therefore, what must first be taught are basic attending skills such as sitting appropriately and looking at the therapist. Once children are sitting calmly, they then learn to imitate various actions of the therapist. Typically developing children learn to imitate others because of the social consequences associated with doing so. Because many of the children with whom we work are not responsive to social reinforcement, we typically use some sort of direct, or tangible, reinforcement to respond to their imitating. Because this approach relies strongly on imitation skills, many children spend many months in this type of training before the first words are spoken, and many children fail to develop speech at all. In using this protocol, trainers often spend weeks and months trying to develop motor and/or vocal imitation skills. While doing this, many student continued to have no appropriate or reliable means of making basic needs and wants known. Consequently, they often expressed these needs in a variety of "inappropriate" ways.

Speech Imitation protocols require many prerequisites before communication training:

- Eye contact
- Gross motor imitation
- Oral/motor imitation
- Speech imitation
- Word imitation

Sign Language:

Therapists recognizing the limitations of speech imitation training programs have looked for alternative communication modalities to teach while speech is developing. One system is manual sign language. Children were taught to imitate signs made by the educator and to use these signs to label or request items. Many of our very young students had fine motor deficits that interfered with the clarity of their sign formations. The number of people who understood their idiosyncratic sign formations was limited to those working directly with or living with the child. Some of our students were successful at learning a few signs, but this communicative modality precluded the children's independent functioning out in the "real" world. If the goal of intervention is use of communication in a variety of settings, then sign language presents limitations merely because of the limited number of communicative partners available to the user.

Picture/Symbol Systems:

Another alternative communication modality we have attempted to teach our students is picture- or symbol-based communication. These systems require a user to point to or touch pictures/symbols in order to encode a specific message. Some programs involve matching-to-sample formats as prerequisite skills to communicative use of the pictures. It isn't until the child is able to match objects to objects, pictures to objects and objects to pictures, etc. that communication is addressed. When we attempted to teach picture-point systems, we found either that the children had many competing hand movements so that messages were difficult to "read" or that they did not initiate communicative exchanges by directly interacting with a "listener." For example, some students could not isolate their index fingers in order to point to a picture. These children often "slapped" the communication book, making contact with several pictures at the same time. It was up to us to "interpret" the message. Other children would point to a picture but look away from the pictures and the trainer. This, too, was difficult to interpret, as we often weren't sure if the child was communicating. In other words, these picture-based systems taught students to act on a picture rather than another person, thus ignoring the "social approach" that is a part of communication.

Speech training, sign language, and picture-point systems are highly dependent on a variety of prerequisite skills, particularly eye contact and imitation. Typically developing children learn each of these skills, in part, because of their associated social consequences. Very young children with autism are not highly responsive to these types of rewards, and, thus, training protocols must include non-social rewards (Bondy, 1988). For example, a child with autism might be given candy for looking into the teacher's eyes. Such attending may take the form of normal eye contact, but because it does not have the same consequences, it does not serve the same function. Furthermore, such training does not teach the child to initiate social contacts, but, rather, focuses upon how he or she should respond to social approaches by teachers and other adults.

The Picture Exchange Communication System (PECS)
was developed in 1985 in response to our difficulty in successfully using a variety of communication training programs with young students with autism. PECS originally was developed for use with preschool-aged children with Autism Spectrum Disorder (ASD), and other social communicative disorders who display no functional or socially acceptable speech. By this, we mean that these children do not speak at all, speak only in a "self-stimulatory" manner, speak only when prompted to do so, or are extremely echolalic. These children's communicative difficulties are socially-related in that the children do not routinely approach others to communicate, actively avoid interaction with others, or only communicate in response to a direct cue to do so. Over the years, we have recognized that many children, in addition to children with ASD, have difficulty learning speech. We now teach PECS to a variety of children and adults with a variety of diagnoses or educational classifications. We have taught PECS to thousands of children from around the world, in family and educational settings. Children using PECS first learn to approach and give a picture of a desired item to a communicative partner in exchange for that item. By doing this, the child initiates a communicative act for a concrete outcome within a social context.

> PECS is used with children and adults with a variety of disabilities.

The PECS training protocol is based on research and practice in the principles of Applied Behavior Analysis. Distinct teaching strategies, reinforcement strategies, error correction strategies and generalization strategies are essential to use to teach each skill. The PECS training protocol also closely parallels typical language development in that it first teaches the child "how" to communicate or what the basic rules of communication are. Then the children learn to communicate specific messages. Children using PECS learn to communicate first with single pictures, but later learn to combine pictures to learn a variety of grammatical structures, semantic relationships, and communicative functions.

3

Getting Ready for PECS

Getting Ready for PECS

Setting the Stage for Communication

Communication is an all-day, every-day activity. Each and every moment of the day, we all have opportunities to communicate as long as we can find someone to listen to us. The ability to spontaneously interact with another individual in order to access a particular outcome is a skill that many of us take for granted in our own lives. But the inability to do so is perhaps the most significant obstacle to independent living for those with disabilities.

Typically developing children begin learning to communicate from birth! For example, infants are born showing a preference for the sound of their mothers' voices. At birth, infants can distinguish between sounds such as *ba* and *pa*. They show a preference for looking at items with varied shapes and sharp contrast between dark and light. The human face has both variations, so infants look at Mom's and Dad's faces right from birth. Infants begin smiling at around 3 weeks! These actions all are directly related to how a child learns the sophisticated skill we call language. Infants listen for and to Mom and Dad. They look at Mom and Dad. They coo and babble to Mom and Dad. Mom and Dad react to these actions in a manner that encourages the baby to continue and to initiate these interactions.

During their first 6 months, infants make lots of sounds—crying, laughing, burping, raspberries, screeches, and cooing (strings of vowel sounds such as "*ooooo*"). When the infants smile, look at their parents, or make sounds, think of Mom's and Dad's reactions! They speak in an excited voice to their baby, smile at him, pick him up, and make noises back to the baby. The infant, in turn, responds positively to this! This cycle leads Mom and Dad to interact more and more with the baby and the baby to learn more and more about interacting. So far, the behaviors the babies are displaying are not *intentionally communicative*. That is, the baby is not engaging in these behaviors in order to deliver some sort of specific message to his parents.

Intentional communication develops during the next couple of months. By six months of age, babies are making

See "Beyond Baby Talk" (2001) by Kenn Apel and Julie J. Masterson sounds that are more and more like the sounds in their native language. By six to nine months of age, babies begin to "communicate" with others in order to request and comment. They do not have words, yet, but communicate with "jargon" and gestures. The baby will look at or reach for something, then look to Mom or Dad, and then back at the item.

Usually around the time the baby is 12 months old, he says his first word. By 18-24 months of age, he is combining these words. By two years, he can say about 50 different words.

In terms of quantity, the amount of time an infant and toddler spends "learning to communicate" is phenomenal! At 11 months of age, he is vocalizing/verbalizations about 132 times per hour. At 19 months of age, this rate more than doubles—to over 304 per hour. He points to and reaches for objects abut 20-30 times per hours. By 12-19 months of age, he engages in an average of 96 interactive episodes per hour— more than half initiated by the child touching, babbling, and offering (Hart and Risley, 1999).

In our discussion about the types of reinforcement associated with communicating, we identified both social and tangible outcomes. Typical language development is the product of both types of outcomes. Children who are typically developing acquire communication skills without specific, systematic language training. They do so through the interactions with their parents and other more mature language models (Halle, 1984). These interactions, alone, however are not sufficient in terms of quantity or quality for children with Autistic Spectrum Disorder.

Children with Autistic Spectrum Disorder are not responsive to social reinforcement, so we wouldn't expect that their language would develop typically. When we live and work with children who are not developing language along the usual timelines, we must develop a plan for actively teaching language. We need to build learning environments in which children are likely to develop functional communication skills. We do this by creating *many* opportunities for communication within physical environments which contain interesting materials and useful activities. Mere exposure to these materials and activities is not sufficient, however, to foster development of communication skills. We also must capitalize on these opportunities by employing specific strategies to teach specific communication skills. As a result of many confounding variables in our classrooms and homes, we often create environments which are not conducive to language development. Halle (1984) described ways in which we often undermine or pre-empt communication, and consequently fail to create or effectively use communicative opportunities.

1. **Environmental Preempting** occurs when everything is easily accessible and available "at no charge." Why would a student need to communicate a need or desire to someone when everything is readily available? For example, at breakfast we make sure that the student has have everything he wants and needs available to him.

2. **Nonverbal Preempting** occurs when we are not familiar with a student's current skills and capabilities, and, consequently, do not expect or teach the next step. For example we might make sure that we remember to give a child juice at breakfast because we don't know whether or not he can ask for it and that we should, therefore, teach it.

3. **Verbal Preempting** occurs when we take the lead and don't allow opportunities to initiate. We actually discourage language initiations with children who have some functional communication. We might say, "Here's your juice," at breakfast time rather than teaching the student to ask for it.

An environment that is conducive to communication development for our students is one in which we

1. **create many opportunities for communicating**
2. **know our student's current skills and can plan to teach the next**
3. **expect communication**

Create many communicative opportunities. When we look at the day we spend with our students, what we see is a series of activities. At home we get dressed, prepare and eat meals, play, run errands, watch videos... At school we have lessons, gym, art, recess, lunch, snack...Within each of these activities we must arrange for communicative opportunities by creating situations in which a student is likely to want something so that we can teach him how to communicate in order to get it. To do this, we

This "desire" or "need" is referred to as the "*establishing operation,*" (Michael, 1983).

- identify what our student is likely to want given the current activity
- arrange for that item to "disappear" long enough to begin to need or want that item.

For items to "disappear" we must organize the physical environment so that items are not easily accessible. For example, we put favorite toys on a shelf so that they are in sight but out of reach. We put our student's preferred snacks and drinks on the top shelf of the refrigerator. We put a favorite food in a container the student cannot open. When we notice that a student is interested in a particular item, we capitalize on this interest by expecting and teaching communication. This strategy, called "Incidental Training," (Hart and Risley, 1982) has been widely used with a variety of students for many years. Or we attract the student or tempt the student in order to build the desire for that item. We then carefully control the student's access to the item so that we are the means for obtaining the item. Wetherby and Prizant (1989) describe several ways to "set the stage" for communication. They refer to these as **"Communicative Temptations."** Some of these include:

1. Eat a desired food in front of the child without offering any.
2. Activate a wind-up toy, let it deactivate, and hand it to the child.

> This also is referred to as "contriving" the establishing operation.

3. Open a container of bubbles, blow some, close the container and give the container to the child. Blow up a balloon and slowly deflate it; then hand it to the child or hold it up to your mouth and wait.
4. Hold a food item or toy that the child dislikes near the child.
5. Place a desired food item or toy in a clear container that the child cannot open while the child is watching and then put the container in front of the child and wait.

In addition to creating communicative opportunities, we also should capitalize on opportunities as they occur across the day. For example, imagine that you are finishing a meal and your student is sitting quietly. You notice that he is looking at a toy across the room. Turn this into an opportunity for requesting by picking up the toy and teaching a request at that moment!

> This also is referred to as "capturing" an establishing operation.

Remember that typically developing children have virtually thousands of communicative opportunities each day. So, once we've created one communicative opportunity and taught communication within it, we must arrange for the next communicative opportunity. This means that we must teach communication all day! We should not merely "plan" for a communication training time and write it into our schedule, so that, for example, we actively teach communication from 10:30

until 11:00 every day. Rather, we must ensure that communicative opportunities are occurring within all activities.

Some activities are more conducive to creating communicative opportunities. The activity must contain materials that the student likes, so that when we arrange for these to disappear, they are motivated to get them back. For example, if a student loves to color with markers, giving him only one marker (and a dried out one!) and a piece of paper is likely to motivate him to ask for another. On the other hand, if at lunch you are trying to get your student to eat a new food, he is not likely to want to ask for it! This does not mean, though, that we should not include this type of activity in our daily schedule.

Know our student's current skills in order to plan for the next.

If we are teaching our student to request, we must know how he currently does so. Completing the "Critical Communication Skills Checklist" provides us with this information. We then must know what skill we actively want to teach. For example, if your student fusses at breakfast when you don't include the expected Poptart with his cereal, you can teach him to exchange a picture for that Poptart. If he can ask for items using a single picture or word, you can teach him to use a phrase.

Expect Communication.

Once we have arranged our environment to elicit communication and know what skill to teach, we must **expect** the student to communicate. In many situations, our lives (and our students') are easier if we just give them the item they need or want. If you have a busy household and a chaotic mealtime, dinner is less hectic if you make sure that the student has everything—his plate, silverware, cup, napkin, food and drink. At school, when it's time for recess, our classes run more smoothly and quietly if we give the students their coats and mittens before going out. Snack time is less complicated if we offer only one item and give it to each student right away. If we are always "doing for" the student, though, then we cannot teach communication.

Assessing Reinforcers

Because communication training within PECS begins with functional acts that bring the student into contact with effective reinforcers (requests), the trainer must first determine, via consistent observation, what a student wants. This step is done by conducting a **"reinforcer assessment."** A reinforcer assessment can be conducted in many ways. We generally use a three-step process to help us determine what a student likes:

1. Interview significant others. Parents and those who have worked with the student are great sources of information on what the student likes. We ask family members, staff, and anyone else who knows the student to complete a Vocabulary Selection Worksheet (See Appendix D) so that we get a general idea of what the student likes

2. Observe the student in an unstructured, "frcc access" situation. A powerful method to assess preferences is to spend time observing what the student plays with or eats when given free access to many items. The items the student chooses most frequently or spends the greatest amount of time with are likely the most reinforcing. Pay attention to how much effort a student puts into getting particular items. The amount of effort he is willing to expend in gaining access to an item is a great indicator of how reinforcing it is.

3. Conduct a formal reinforcer assessment.
Before beginning PECS, we need to determine which items a student likes more than others or which items are the most powerful reinforcers. We prioritize a student's particular preferences by determining a **"reinforcer hierarchy."** For that reason, once we informally have observed the student's likes and dislikes, we conduct a more formal reinforcer assessment. Using the following sequence is helpful in ranking a student's preferences by comparing a student's reactions to various potential reinforcers. The specific reactions we will be observing include:
- what he does when offered an item (reaches for or pushes it away)
- what he does with the item (eats it, plays with it, or politely holds it)
- what he does if we try to take the item away (protests,

has no response)
- how he responds when we offer it again

Establishing Reinforcer Hierarchy

1. Begin by offering the child one of the items you think he likes. Observe his reaction. Does he reach for it and take it? Does he reject it in some fashion?
2. If he takes the item, immediately try to take it back. Observe his reaction. Does he protest or try to get it back? Does he let you take it? Give it back to him and note his subsequent behavior.
3. While the student has the item, watch what he does with it. Does he consume it or play with it (appropriate play is not required!). Does he make sounds of enjoyment or smile? Does he persist in playing with it? Does he hold it "politely," but not play with or eat it?

Item	Rejects	No reaction	Reaches for	Protests when taken away	Shows signs of pleasure	Takes again
pretzel			✓		✓	
Koosh			✓			
applesauce	✓					
potato chips		✓				
spinning top			✓	✓	✓	✓
Whipped cream			✓	✓	✓	✓
markers		✓				
Jack-in-the-Box			✓	✓	✓	✓
Modeling clay	✓					

For example, when presented with a pretzel, Fritz quickly reached for it. Before he could eat it, the trainer tried to take it away, but he quickly turned away and put the pretzel into his mouth to eat it. While he was chewing it, he closed his eyes and hummed, a reaction that others often observed when he was eating something he really liked. Fritz next was shown a koosh ball. He immediately took it and manipulated it for 15 seconds but did not resist when it was taken away and did not show any obvious and overt signs of pleasure. When the evaluator offered it again, he did not reach for it. Next, the evaluator offered a small bowl of applesauce. Fritz screamed, pushed it away, and turned away from it. When potato chips were offered, he looked at them, but did not react either by reaching for them or by rejecting them...

4. Once the assessment is completed, list the items that the student took, reacted negatively to when it was taken away, and consumed or played with when given back.

5. Present the student with a selection (2-4 at a time) of items from this group. Note which item the child reaches for first. Repeat this several times.

6. Remove most preferred item (selected most often) and present remaining items and one new item. Continue offering groups of items and removing the most frequently selected item.

Item	1	2	3	4	5	6	7	8	9	10	
Spinning top	X+	X+	X+	X+						X+	5/5
Pretzel	X	X			X	X		X	X		0/6
Jack-in-the-Box			X	X	X+	X+	X+				3/5
Whipped creme							X	X+	X+	X	2/4

7. Summarize and rank the items by determining which item from a specific grouping was selected most often.
8. Continue presenting groups of items and removing the most preferred until a pool of 3-5 items has been determined to be "most preferred."
9. Present these most reinforcing items and repeat the above procedure until you are able to determine which item is first, second, and third.

When offered three foods, the student consistently took the whipped cream.

When offered three toys, the student consistently took the spinning top.

When offered the whipped cream and the spinning top, the student consistently took the spinning top.

Preferred	Non-Preferred	Neutral
1. Spinning top	applesauce	Potato chips
2. Jack-in-the-Box	Markers	
3. Whipped cream		

"What happens if..."

1. ...I can't find anything reinforcing? Occasionally we meet a student for whom it is very difficult to identify any potent reinforcers. Often during the assessment, the student sits or stands passively and does not reach for anything. If this happens, determine if the student is not reaching because he is not interested in the item or if he is not reaching because he doesn't know how to reach or has been taught not to reach. If he is not reaching because he is not interested in the items, continue looking for potential reinforcers. Explore various types of sensory input such as lights, sounds, vibrating items, etc. Occupational therapists are great sources for these types of items.

2. ...my student is not reaching because he doesn't know how to reach or thinks he shouldn't reach? Perhaps yours is a student who has been taught to not reach or has never learned to reach. In this situation, then, you will have to teach him to reach for and take desired items. We have worked with older students who have been consistently reinforced for "hands down" behavior and, no matter what we present to them they will not reach unless given permission. If this happens, it will be necessary to "un-train" this behavior so that the student once again freely reaches.

3. ...I have a student with visual impairments? We also have worked with students with visual impairments and have discovered that many are individuals who do not actively explore their environment with their hands. If this is what you encounter, it will be necessary to spend some time teaching these individuals how to use their hands to reach for and search for items. Also, note that these individuals do not see you offering an item or putting it on the table in front of them. So, rather than doing this, very noisily present the item. Rattle wrappers, bang toys, turn on radios, etc. Let these individuals smell the item and touch the item. Take his or her hand and put it on the item and then move the item away just slightly.

Preparing Materials

Once you have assessed your student's communication skills, organized your training environment, and established a reinforcer hierarchy, the final step before beginning PECS is to prepare your materials. The first item to prepare is the symbol you will be using to begin training. As you will read in the following chapter, we do not initially address picture discrimination skills—we will not expect the student to be able to tell the difference between pictures when we begin training. Therefore, the symbol you choose to begin with is entirely up to you. We do not teach the student to "understand" the picture prior to training, nor do we conduct any kind of assessment to determine if one symbol type should be preferred over another. We will address both of these issues within the functional context of communication when we begin discrimination training in Phase III, rather than spend valuable time teaching this in a non-functional drill format prior to teaching the student how to communicate.

We use many commercially available black-and-white line drawings, colored line drawings, digital images, photographs, clip art, and product logos. We also like to make our lives and jobs as easy as possible, so we begin training with the symbols that are initially easiest to create or that we already have on hand. Many symbols are available commercially—either in printed format or via computer software.

Picture/Symbol Sources

1. **Pyramid Educational Products, Inc**
   "PECS 151"
   Schedule pictures
   Attribute, songs, body parts
   5 Garfield Way, Suite C
   Newark, DE 19713   .
   www.pyramidproducts.com
   888-732-7462

2. Imaginart
   307 Arizona St.
   Bisbee, AZ 85603
   (800) 828-1376

3. Broderbund Software
   "Click-Art"
   Available wherever graphic software is sold
   T/Maker Company/Broderbund Software
   P.O. Box 6125
   Novato, CA 94948-6125
   415-382-4700

4. Attainment
   Attainment Co.
   P.O. Box 930160
   Verona, WI 53593-0160
   Phone: 608-845-7880;
   800-327-4269
   FAX: 800-942-3865

5. **Mayer Johnson Co.**
   "Boardmaker" computer software
   P.O. Box 1579
   Solana Beach, CA 92075
   (619) 550-0084

6. **www.trainland.tripod.com**
   (downloadable digital images)

7. *Flash!* Digital images software
   Shops.looksmart.com/aba

8. *Picture This* software
   www.silverlining.com

Pictures are the most important "ingredient" for beginning PECS training, but you will also need:

☐ Velcro® hook
☐ Velcro® loop
☐ communication binder
☐ sentence strip
☐ insert pages
☐ oak tag paper
☐ laminating supplies
☐ book strap

To make the pictures durable, we print them on or glue them to thick paper— "cardstock" paper. This paper can be found at most office supply stores—look for paper that says, "Index stock," "Card stock," or "110 pound." If you are printing pictures on this paper, you can load use this paper with most printers either through the paper feed mechanism or by manually loading each piece. Once you have the pictures printed, cover them with a clear, durable material—either contact paper or lamination film. Desk top laminators are a great tool—if you buy one, make sure that it will accommodate laminating pouches that are at least 5ml thick.

We prefer to use Velcro® to put on the communication binder and on the back of the pictures. We use the rough or "hook" Velcro® on the book only because it is easily cleaned with a dry toothbrush. Sources for Velcro® include:

1. **Pyramid Educational Products, Inc**.
   5C Garfield Way
   Newark, DE 19713
   (302) 894-9155

2. **John Bead Corporation**
   19 Bertrand
   Scarborough, Ontario
   CANADA
   (416) 757-3287

3. **Therapro 1-800-257-5376**
   224 Arlington Street
   Framingham, MA 01701

4. **Sammons 1-800-323-5547**
   P.O. Box 386
   Western Springs, IL 60558

5. **Velcro USA, Inc.**
   6201 Randolph St.
   City of Commerce, CA 90040
   (213) 255-8530
   (800) 950-3233
   FAX: (213) 255-8956

6. **Lockfast:**
   10904 Deerfield Rd.
   Cincinnati, OH 45242
   (513) 891-5020

7. **Best Priced Product, Inc.**
   P.O. Box 1174
   White Plains, NY 10602

8. **Fastenation, Inc.**
   87 Somerset St.
   Garfield, NJ 07026
   800 876-9922

Each student must have his own communication binder or book. We use small three-ring binders-we put Velcro® strips on the cover and inside the book and add pages as needed. Because each student will be expected to take his book wherever he goes, we put some sort of carry-strap on the book. In Phase IV of training when we introduce using multiple pictures, you will need to add a "sentence strip" to each student's book—this is a sturdy piece of plastic or cardboard to which the student will affix 2 or more pictures in sentence fashion.

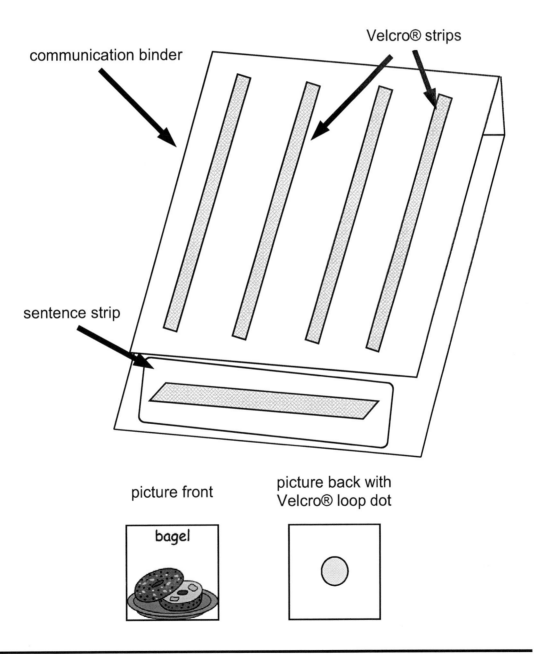

communication binder

Velcro® strips

sentence strip

picture front

bagel

picture back with
Velcro® loop dot

4

Phase I

"How" to Communicate

Phase I -"How" to Communicate

> **Terminal Objective:** *Upon seeing a "highly preferred" item, the student will pick up a picture of the item, reach toward the communicative partner, and release the picture into the trainer's hand.*

Ack!!

Rationale: Typically developing children learn the "nature" of communication as early as 6 months of age when they begin interactive routines with Mom or Dad. These routines do not involve actual words, but, rather involve an *approach* (the infant gets Mom's or Dad's attention), an *action* directed to the audience (the vocalization, babbling, or pointing), and an *outcome* (Mom and Dad laugh, smile, give the baby something, or repeat the vocalizations). Because the outcomes involve items or events the child likes (i.e., these are reinforcers), then he will likely repeat this behavior. The approach is controlled by the potential "listeners." The baby learns that the action he engages in results in a desired outcome only through this audience. The action the baby engages in is controlled by something in the environment (a train whistle) or by some need (hunger).

For example, parents often report that at a very early age, their baby began getting their attention by making a loud noise, crying, or (if mobile) crawling to them. They report that the baby would differentially cry—they recognized that their baby cried in a specific manner when hungry and a different manner when he wanted to play. Many parents also report that, before his first birthday, their child "babbled" with realistic intonation patterns and that he took turns "conversing" with his parents.

In Phase I the student is taught the "nature" of communication—he will learn to approach another person (reach toward), direct an action (give a picture), and receive a desired outcome, i.e., the item requested. Just as typically developing children do not use actual words during this early learning period, PECS students also will not yet choose a specific picture. Instead, he uses the single picture that is provided for him by the teacher. A child does not have to have mastered discrimination between symbols or pictures before learning the basic elements of communication. Just as with typically developing children, learning to use a specific word or symbol will come later. Typically developing children learn both to request and to comment at virtually the same time because tangible and social reinforcement are equally effective for them. Once developed, commenting and requesting are the skills that serve as the foundation for conversation throughout life!

Whereas typical communication development involves outcomes that are either tangible or social, children learning PECS firstwill learn to communicate for tangible outcomes (foods, toys, etc.) because these are the most effective reinforcers. So when we begin the protocol, we teach requesting. We will discuss later how to teach commenting and other types of communication that result in social outcomes.

The Structured Training Environment

Setting The student and two trainers are in a common area, often seated, though not necessarily so. One trainer (the communicative partner) is in front of the student. The other trainer (the physical prompter) is in back of the student. A "highly preferred" item is held by the communicative partner out of reach of the student. The picture of the item is on the table (floor, etc.) between the student and the communicative partner.

notes

1. **Two trainers are required to teach initiation.**
2. **No verbal prompts are used during this phase.**
3. **Present one picture at a time.**
4. **Do not conduct all training in a single session—arrange for at least 30-40 opportunities throughout the day for the student to request.**
5. **Use different types of reinforcers—food, toys, etc.**
6. **Modify the symbol/picture to match motor skills of the student.**

Teaching Strategy

Backward Chaining: This strategy teaches a chain, or sequence, of behaviors by reinforcing mastery of the last step, then the next-to-the last step and so on (Sulzer-Azaroff and Mayer, 1991.) The behavior engaged in closest in time to receiving the reinforcer is the most easily learned step. The trainer prompts the student through the initial steps of the chain, and assistance to complete the chain is faded first at the "back end" of the chain. The student initially masters the final step, then the final two steps, then the final three steps, and so on.

Two-Person Prompting: To facilitate rapid fading of prompts, prompting is provided from outside the social interaction. This strategy requires two trainers. The first trainer, the communicative partner, interacts with the child. The second trainer, the physical prompter, prompts the student from behind (or next to) and does not interact in any social manner with the student such as by providing reinforcement. The physical prompter steadily fades all prompts via backward chaining so that the student performs the desired behavior independently.

Communicative Partner's responsibilities:

- **Entice the student**
- **Reinforce the student's exchange (with the item) within 1/2 second**
- **Pair social praise with the tangible reinforcement**
- **Time the open hand appropriately**

Physical Prompter's responsibilities:

- **Wait for the student's initiation**
- **Physically prompt the student to exchange the picture**
- **Systematically fade prompts**

TARGET SEQUENCE: Pick up ➔ Reach ➔ Release

Teaching Spontaneity.

As we described earlier, a limitation of many traditional training protocols is that the students do not learn spontaneity. This is not a failing of the student or a symptom or characteristic of a particular disability. Rather, it is the logical result of a "teacher-led" training strategy. Spontaneity involves "going first."

To teach spontaneity in Phase I, we must ensure that the student "goes first." Initially, we elicit this behavior by identifying a powerful reinforcer, withholding it for awhile, and then presenting or showing it to the student. The student's most likely response is to try to get the item or to *reach for* it. This reach is the student's "going first" behavior.

It initially is not communicative because the student is directing this behavior to the reinforcer, not the communicative partner. The physical prompter waits for this reach, though, and over successive trials uses physical prompts to shape this behavior into picking up a picture, reaching to the communicative partner, and releasing the picture into the communicative partner's hand. As the communicative partner systematically reinforces this behavior by providing the tangible item, this "reaching" behavior becomes communicative when the student reaches to the communicative partner with a picture.

To begin training, ensure that the item you are using is still reinforcing. Even if you just completed the formal reinforcer assessment, your student's interests might have changed. We use a "First One's Free" strategy to quickly assess the current value of the item. Offer a bit or let him play with the item for a few seconds—if he does so, then assume the item is still reinforcing. The communicative partner "entices" the student by showing him the powerful reinforcer. Both trainers must **wait for the student to reach for the item—this is the student's <u>initiation</u>!!.** <u>As</u> the student reaches for the item, the physical prompter immediately physically assists the student to pick up the picture, reach to the communicative partner, and release the picture into the communicative partner's open hand. The communicative partner opens her hand to receive the

"First One's Free"

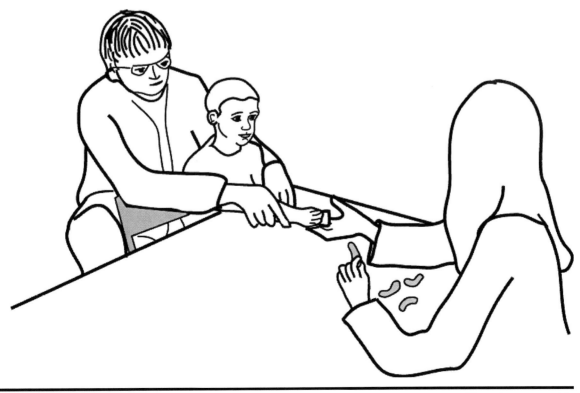

picture ONLY AFTER the student has reached. The moment the student releases the picture into the communicative partner's open hand, she immediately gives the student the reinforcer and praises ("Cheesie!!!").

While the student is eating, drinking, or playing with the item, the two trainers get ready for the next trial—put the picture back in front of the student and get another bit of food or drink ready. If the student is requesting a "non-consumable" item (one that doesn't disappear such as a ball, etc.), calmly take the item from the student. Entice the student again, wait for the initiation (the reach), and repeat the physical guidance again.

> If the student is requesting a toy, allow him to play with it for 15-20 seconds before calmly taking it back and beginning the next trial.

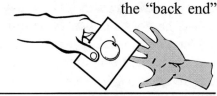

Using backward chaining over successive trials, the physical prompter fades the amount of physical guidance from the "back end" of the prompting sequence (the pick up, reach and release) over a series of trials. In other words, the physical prompter is going to continue to **WAIT** for the student to initiate, and then provide assistance to pick up and reach, but will fade assistance to release the picture. Once the student has released the picture into the trainer's hand, the communicative partner immediately gives the student the requested item and simultaneously praises him.

Once the student independently releases the picture into the communicative partner's hand, the physical prompter begins fading physical assistance to reach toward the trainer's hand. The communicative partner continues to show the student her open hand only when the student reaches for either the item or the picture. Over successive opportunities, the physical prompter continues to help the student pick up the picture, but provides less and less physical prompting to reach until the student independently is reaching with and releasing the picture.

Finally, the physical prompter begins to fade assistance to pick up the picture. Continue this step until the student, upon seeing the desired item, independently picks up the picture, reaches toward the trainer, and releases the picture into the trainer's open hand. The communicative partner continues to immediately give the student the item and provides verbal praise. Remember that your verbal praise should be enthusiastic but not overbearing!

Reinforcement
Reminder

The new behavior being reinforced is releasing the picture into the communicative partner's open hand. The reinforcement must be immediate, so make sure you are prepared by having the appropriate items on hand and immediately accessible. If you delay the reinforcement by more than a half-second, the student will not quickly learn what behavior is being reinforced. During your delay, he might have scratched his nose or wiggled in his seat. If this happens, the student might incorrectly conclude that it is nose scratching and wiggling that is critical in getting access to the desired item, and these actions might occur again.

The effective reinforcement is the item being requested. We pair this reinforcement with social reinforcement, typically in the form of praise, a pat, a tickle, a hair tousling. The form of your praise is dependent upon what the student can understand and tolerate. At a minimum, name the item ("Book!"). You can elaborate on this by saying, "I want book," "You want a book!" or similar phrases. If your student imitates actions, sounds, or words, avoid saying, "You want..." as this is the phrase the student most likely will imitate.

"What happens if..."

1. ...the student does not reach for the reinforcer on the first trial? If the student does not reach for the item, reconfirm that it is a highly desired item. Give the student a "free sample" and observe his reaction. If he plays with it or consumes it, then try using the item again. If he does not play with or consume it, or if he overtly rejects it, find a new item! Many students' preferences change quickly!

2. ...the student "gets tired of" the item after a couple of trials? If the student quits reaching for the item or for the picture of the item, you have two options: You can end the session. Or, you can offer another reinforcer. Remember, continue using one reinforcer and one picture at a time!

3. ...the student has difficulty picking up the picture? Sometimes during Phase I, the student has physical difficulty picking up the picture or holding onto it. If this appears to be the case, consult with an occupational or physical therapist to determine what, if any, modifications can be made to the symbol. For example, if the student has difficult picking up the picture, make it thicker. You can do

this by printing it on thicker paper, mounting it on a block of wood, etc. We save the lids from frozen juice containers or baby food jars and mount pictures on them— they are rigid and virtually indestructible! Another strategy is to put some sort of "handle" on the symbol. Again, mount it on a thick piece of wood and screw a dowel into the wood to act as a handle (similar to puzzles with knobs).

4. ...the student seems to be waiting for some signal that it's okay to pick up the picture? The communicative partner should entice silently and minimize use of "attentional cues", e.g., calling the student's name, noting what is available by saying, "I have pretzels," etc., as students might begin to wait for this announcement. These attentional cues used "ritualistically" can become a prompt for the student to communicate. Do not use direct prompts such as "Give me the picture," or "What do you want?" Be sure that the student is not waiting for the communicative partner to show her open hand. If this happens, it is because the communicative partner has been sloppy about when to open her hand to the student. The open hand is an informational cue to the student—it signals where to put the picture and should not prompt the exchange. Begin to fade the open hand by waiting increasingly longer to show your open hand. The child should pick up the picture and begin reaching to you before you open your hand. Allow the student access to the item and continue to provide simultaneous praise.

5. ...the student gets very upset when I try to take the non-

consumable item from him in order to begin another trial? If you anticipate before beginning training that this might be a problem, begin with a less-desired item. Go back to your reinforcer hierarchy and begin with item #4 or #5. Then while the student is playing with that item, entice with a slightly more reinforcing item. The student's likely response upon seeing something that he wants more than the item he is holding is to drop it and reach for the new item. This is the next initiation! Continue "moving up" the reinforcer hierarchy. Alternatively, offer additional samples of the desired item. What's better than one toy car? Two, or three, or four! Remember, if the student protests when you take the item from him, treat this protest as the next initiation. The physical prompter must quickly prompt the next exchange—before the student reacts so strongly that he loses his attention to the available reinforcer. If the student has a tantrum, etc., end the session rather than trying to get him to request in the midst of a tantrum. When you begin training again, use a less powerful item.

During Phase I of training, the student learns the physical exchange in order to gain access to a variety of items. Therefore, the trainer must switch between reinforcers during training while continuing to present one picture at a time!!! It may not be crucial for you to switch pictures as you switch reinforcers because the student is not yet expected to look at the picture itself or to "know" what the picture means. He really needs only to look closely enough to locate the picture card on the table. However, we have found that some children do begin looking at the picture itself and, if they can discriminate between pictures, become confused when we do not switch pictures. For this reason, if possible, switch pictures as you switch reinforcers.

Occasionally the student is attracted to some aspect of the picture itself—the shape, the sharp corners, a reflection or glare on the lamination, etc. Sometimes the student waves the picture in front of his eyes, plays with the corners, crushes the picture, etc. If this behavior is allowed to occur over a few trials, it can become a ritualistic part of the exchange. If the student picks up the picture and does anything except *reach* to the communicative partner, the physical prompter should interrupt this behavior. If the physical prompter doesn't prevent the behavior or interrupt it immediately, the Backstep procedure (See next box) should be used so that the inappropriate use of the picture is not reinforced. The physical prompter should put the picture back down, and the exchange should begin again. If the student is particularly attracted to some aspect of the picture, make sure that the reinforcer you are offering is more desired than playing with the picture. Alternatively, you can modify the aspect of the picture that attracts the student. Use non-glare contact paper to cover the picture if the student likes the glare. Make the pictures circular if he likes the corners. Mount the pictures on a firm material if he crushes or crumples the pictures (juice lids work well for this!).

Pay careful attention to your student so that you know when he is tiring of a particular item. The success of Phase I is directly related to the student's interest in the items being offered, so switch items as frequently as necessary. End your session before the student is no longer interested in available items (or when you are out of time). **END WITH SUCCESS!**

Error Correction

The two-person prompting strategy essentially is an errorless learning strategy. If the physical prompter systematically fades prompts and the communicative partner entices with items that are reinforcing, errors should not occur. Occasionally, though, the student will not perform on a particular trial as expected. For example, the child might pick up the picture, begin reaching, and then drop the picture before completing the exchange. This error takes place within a sequential lesson, so the appropriate error correction strategy would be the **Backstep:** the physical prompter takes the child back in the sequence to the last step completed correctly and then provides extra assistance to complete the sequence. In this example, the physical prompter would pick up the picture (do not make the student pick it up from the floor!), put it back on the table, and the sequence would begin again with the communicative partner enticing. Once the student picks up the picture, the physical prompter would provide more physical assistance than on the previous trial by physically prompting the child to reach to the communicative partner. Once the student reaches the communicative partner and gives the picture, the communicative partner differentially reinforces the exchange.

The Relaxed Training Environment

Setting

Anywhere the child is likely to find something he wants! This should include all areas of the classroom, in various parts of the house, indoors, outdoors. Two people need to be on hand so that as one person notices that the child is interested in a particular item, she can call for the physical prompter to help.

Phase I of PECS training can be conducted at any time of the day in practically any environment. It should NOT be conducted ONLY during structured training. To assure generalization across a variety of elements, make sure to plan for a variety of trainers to participate. Initially, the communicative partner and the physical prompter can trade places so that the student, from the very beginning, has opportunities to request from two different people. Vary the reinforcers you offer when you entice the student. Conduct training in a variety of environments— different areas of the classroom, different classrooms, different rooms at home, outside, etc.

We conduct a lot of what we call **"Stop/Drop/and Talk"** training. This means that whenever a communicative opportunity arises, grab your physical prompter, stop for a moment, get at your student's level (on the floor, on the jungle gym, etc.) and do a PECS trial! This ensures that generalization is being addressed from the very beginning of training. For example, on the way outside, if you notice your student is looking longingly at a ball on a shelf, conduct one PECS trial right then and there. Grab a picture, call for someone to act as physical prompter, and conduct one PECS trial on the spot.

Stop, Drop, and Talk

Capitalize on each communicative opportunity when it arises.

Examples of Potential Stop, Drop, & Talk opportunities include:

1. In the cafeteria, you notice that your student is interested in his peer's pretzels. "Borrow" one or two from the peer, and use them for a PECS opportunity.
2. At Grandma's house, your daughter notices and tries to

climb into the new hammock swing on the porch. Grab a picture and grab Grandma and teach a PECS trial.

3. At the end of a work session, you give your student some chips as a reward. You know that chips will make him thirsty, so have some water on hand and a picture of the water.

4. Always carry some simple reinforcers and their corresponding pictures with you. Between activities, during "down time," do one or two PECS trials.

When you are in a classroom with students who are new to PECS, and you are thinking about these Stop, Drop, and Talk opportunities, you realize the importance of teaching everyone in the classroom how to implement PECS. If you expect to do one or two PECS trials on a moment's notice, you will need to have other staff on hand who can step in and be a physical prompter or a communicative partner.

Think about your routine or schedule and envision when and where PECS trials could occur. Determine for each student based on a specific activity, what the potential reinforcers are. Your staff/family should be prepared, too, so that anyone, on a moment's notice can assume either trainer's role.

Wear a carpenter's apron or a waist pack when working with students who are at the beginning of PECS training. Because these students use one picture at a time, carrying several pictures around in your pockets helps to have a picture ready for those Stop-Drop-and-Talk opportunities. Also, carry small items in a pocket to entice students with during "down time." When you have a spare moment (and a physical prompter), entice a student with a desired item and conduct a quick exchange.

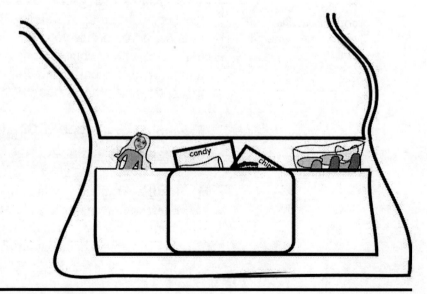

Assessing the Trainers

Before beginning Phase I, the two trainers should participate in role playing with each other so that they are able to refrain from verbal prompting and use appropriate levels of physical assistance. Ideally, this should be done under the supervision of a "seasoned" PECS trainer. Both trainers should be able to do each of the following skills— they should be able to take the part of either trainer. The two trainers can assess each other or a third experienced trainer can assess both new trainers.

The communicative partner must select a powerful reinforcer with which to begin training. The physical prompter waits for the student to initiate and then provides physical guidance to pick up, reach, and release the picture. The communicative partner immediately gives the item to the student and praises. This sequence is repeated over successive opportunities as the physical prompter fades the physical guidance.

PHASE I Communicative Partner
• Arranges training environment effectively –pictures available one at a time, trainers positioned appropriately, control of reinforcers
• No verbal prompting
• Entices appropriately
• Uses open hand prompt effectively- appropriate timing
• Reinforces within ½ second and provides social reinforcement
• No insistence on speech
• Returns picture (while student consumes/plays with R+)
PHASE I Physical Prompter
• Waits for student to initiate (reach for REINFORCER)
• Physically guides to pick up, reach, release
• Fades prompts effectively
• Interrupts/prevents student's interfering behaviors
• No social interaction with student

Cross-Reference with Additional Skills

As soon as you identify powerful reinforcers, you can begin PECS training. For the majority of students, this means the first day we work with them! The social approach/request that we teach in Phase I is the foundation for all of our interactions with the student. The student learns that we are a source of "good things." Once this relationship is established, the next skill we introduce is "Let's Make a Deal." Initially, these deals are short. The student asks you for a drawing toy and you quickly have him do one small task—Pick up a dropped pencil, put the last piece in a puzzle, put one spoon in the drawer.

See Chapter 13 for a detailed description of how to teach each of these skills.

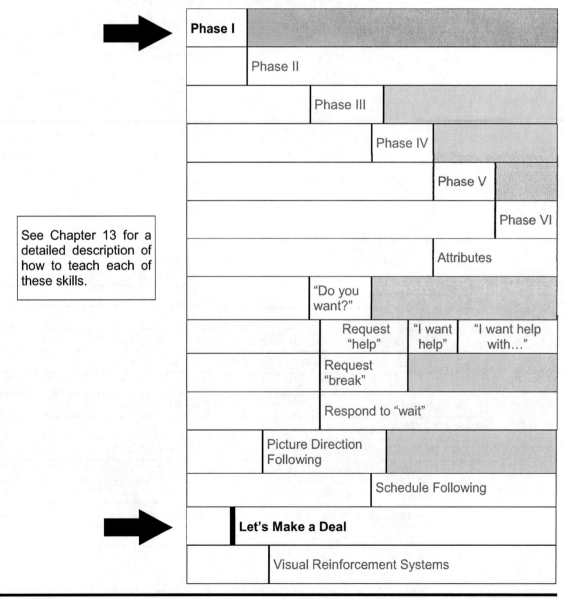

??..Frequently asked questions..??

1 **How long should a training session last?**
Simply put, as long as you have the student's interest.
You can conduct one trial or you can conduct 20 trials as
long as your student continues to **INITIATE**. Once your
student no longer is interested in what you have to offer
(doesn't reach for the item or begin the exchange), you have
two alternatives:

1. Switch reinforcers and continue the session
2. End the session

The second course of action creates a dilemma when one of
the trainers is a speech/language pathologist conducting a
"traditional" speech/language session. "Traditional"
sessions typically last for 20-30 minutes and if cut short,
result in other staff having to adjust their schedules.
Therefore, an appropriate "service delivery" model for
speech/language pathologists conducting PECS training is
an integrated model in which the therapist is available to
conduct one trial whenever the opportunity arises and isn't
committed to interacting with the student for any minimum
amount of time. In a setting where speech/language
services are integrated, the therapist typically is actively
involved in the daily classroom schedule and, consequently,
is interacting with the students throughout regular
classroom activities. Remember to end the session before
the child tires of the offered item.

In settings where integrated services are not feasible,
develop a plan for beginning training in the service setting
and for quickly generalizing to all other settings. If you
begin services in a clinic, have teaching staff and parents
participate in the training so that they can transfer the
training to school and/or home. An ideal strategy for
ensuring that two trainers are available is to use staff or
family members in this setting during initial training.

2 **How many pictures do you introduce during Phase I?**

Because we plan for generalization from the beginning of training, our aim is to teach across a variety of reinforcers, activities, locations, and people. The number of pictures introduced in Phase I is dependent on the number of reinforcers identified during the assessment and the number of trials/sessions, etc. needed for the student to master Phase I. We have seen many children and adults learn the first phase in just a few trials, while one picture was introduced. In this case, we try to introduce additional reinforcers during subsequent lessons—either at the Phase I level or as we begin Phase II.

For students who need more time to master Phase I, the number of pictures is determined by the number of strong preferences and how they relate to the activities occurring when Phase I training is being conducted. If, during your reinforcer assessment, you identified 5 highly preferred items, then these 5 items should all be introduced in Phase I (one at a time with one picture at a time). If, on the other hand you only identified 2 or 3 items the student showed a strong motivation to access, then you would introduce just those items/pictures.

3 **Will using pictures prevent or interfere with the development of speech?**

We have implemented PECS with hundreds of preschool children with autism and related disabilities, and know of no cases of a child losing established speech. Research conducted over the past 30 years (Silverman, 1995, Glennen, 1997) has demonstrated that augmentative and alternative communication strategies (sign language, picture systems) do not inhibit the development of speech. In fact, many researchers have reported a facilitation of speech when AAC strategies are used.

Of course, there is no guarantee that all children who use PECS will develop speech. For children older than 6 or 7, there are fewer known cases of the development of speech. It is important to understand that PECS is used because it provides a child with a rapidly acquired functional communication system. The development of speech is not the primary purpose of using PECS. However, the long term data with over 70 preschoolers who have used PECS for over one year indicates that more than two-thirds of these children have developed independent speech

See Chapter 14 for more information on research related to PECS.

and another 20% use some speech while they use PECS (Bondy and Frost, 1994).

4 **If we are not teaching the child to recognize and use a specific symbol, why use specific pictures rather than a "generic" picture such as an "I want that" picture?**

Many children, especially those with autism and related disorders, seem to be very interested in pictures or other visual materials. They often are referred to as "visually oriented" or "visual learners." These children look at catalogs and magazines, look at signs, and spend a lot of time looking at pictures on objects rather than the object itself. For this reason, we try to use a specific picture. If we change reinforcers within a lesson, we also change the picture. Often when these children first are introduced to PECS, even though we are not formally teaching it, they attend to the pictures themselves. This is okay!! Some children begin PECS already knowing how to discriminate between pictures but not how to use them to communicate, so they still need the lesson taught within Phase I. When we later get to discrimination training, these students don't then require much formal discrimination training.

5 **What happens when the student tries to interact with the physical prompter?**

The physical prompter should provide only the physical assistance necessary to guide the student through the pick up, reach, and release. She should not reinforce the child vocally or non-vocally. She should refrain from touching the student between trials. Most often, when the physical prompter uses appropriate prompting, and if the offered item is extremely desirable, the student will not attend to the physical prompter. If the student does, the physical prompter should not respond to the student—she should look away and turn away, and the communicative partner should regain the student's attention by re-enticing with a desired item.

Bright Ideas
(Phase I)

1. Decide on a symbol system. We use symbols from many different sources. We also use product logos, pictures from catalogs, scanned images, digital photos, and pictures from the boxes toys come in. It's fine to mix picture types—one student's communication book could have several product logos, some digital images, and line drawings. If the student has more than one book (a separate on for home vs. school, make sure that the pictures are the same, though, in each book (the same "apple" picture in each book. We have found it important later in the protocol for the pictures to all be the same size. We generally start with pictures that are about 2 inches by 2 inches—this seems to be a great size for most beginning PECS students.

2. We have found that simple drawings are the easiest to begin with because of their quick availability and because the majority of the students respond well to them. **REMEMBER!** ➤ REMEMBER, THOUGH! The picture system you choose in Phase I is not relevant to a student's success as he is not discriminating between pictures during this phase!

3. Attach Velcro® from the beginning. The pictures are placed on a table at the beginning, so the Velcro® is not necessary. Add it anyway— having the Velcro already attached to the picture raises the edges of the picture from the table surface, making it easier for the student to grasp them and pick them up.

4. Standardize your Velcro®! Decide for all students and staff which side (hook or loop) of the sticky-back Velcro® you will use on the picture backs and which side on the book or page surface. We generally put the hook on the book because the hook is much easier to clean than the loop. When the Velcro gets dirty, just use a dry toothbrush to brush off dirt, crumbs, and unidentifiable substances.

5. The pictures wear out, get lost, disappear, etc. and rather than having to take the time to make a new one, it's easier to reach for one already made. When you decide on which pictures you will need, make two,

three, or more copies of each. Store extras in an alphabetically divided index card box, three-ring binder with Velcroed pages, small drawers that you find in the tool department at department stores, or slide protector pages.

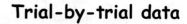

Monitoring Progress

Date	Trial	Pick Up	Reach	Release	Picture	Activity
2/25	1	FP	FP	FP	cookie	1:1 structured
	2	FP	FP	FP	cookie	"
	3	FP	FP	FP	cookie	"
	4	FP	PP	+	cookie	"
	5	FF	+	+	cookie	"
	6	PP	+	+	cookie	"
	7	PP	+	+	pretzel	"
	8	+	+	+	pretzel	"
	9	PP	+	+	pretzel	"
	10	+	+	+	pretzel	"

+ =Independent, FP=Full Physical prompt, PP=Partial Physical prompt

This sample shows a student's initial Phase I lesson. In Phase I monitor the level of assistance the student needs with the <u>pick up,</u> the <u>reach,</u> and the <u>release.</u> Because we use backward chaining and are fading prompts, track whether the student completed each step of the exchange independently (+) or if he needed a Full Physical (FP) prompt or a Partial Physical (PP) prompt. In the above example, note that the student required full physical prompts for all three steps in the exchange sequence but that these prompts were diminished and then eliminated over time from the end of the 3-step sequence. The student tired of cookies after 6 trials, so the trainer switched to pretzels.

Phase I Anecdotal data

Monitoring Progress

Date of Session/ Activity	Approximate # trials	Location and Length of session	List icon(s) used	Initials of Trainers	Status of Physical Assistance
10-21-98 morning	15	Classroom At the table used for snack and group 7 minutes	Apple, Chocolate, Barney (2" X 2" Colored icons)	AH/MG	Partial Physical with the pick-up, indep. with the reach and release
10-21-98 after work session	6	5 minutes	Legos	AH/DB	Indep. Exchange for the last 3
10-22-98 free play in the morning	10	Classroom Free play area	Train, train track, blocks	AH/SP	None needed for last 5 trials

This anecdotal form can be used immediately following a session during which trial-by-trial data were not collected. This example shows three sessions over two days. Training took place in a variety of locations, with a variety of objects/pictures, and with a variety of trainers. The student clearly showed progress in that less physical prompting was needed as training progressed. If the student had not been showing progress, the trainers would have arranged for additional training and would have collected trial-by-trial data.

This form was created by Anne Hoffman, M.Ed., of Pyramid Educational Consultants, Inc.

Anecdotal data

Monitoring Progress

Date of Session/ Activity	Ap-proximate # trials	Location and Length of session	List icon(s) used	Initials of Trainers	Status of Physical Assistance
12/2 Afternoon snack	10	Classroom Snack table 10 minutes	Pretzels Juice bananas	AH/MG	Complete physical as-sistance
12/2 Free play	16	5 minutes	balls	AH/DB	Complete physical as-sistance
12/3 Individual work	12	Classroom Free play area	Pretzels bubbles	AH/SP	Complete physical as-sistance

This example shows three sessions during one afternoon. Training took place in a variety of locations, during a variety of activities, with a variety of objects/pictures, and with a variety of trainers. Across these three sessions, the student made no progress (the physical prompting was not reduced). Consequently, trainers will conduct future sessions using the trial-by-trial data sheet to determine specific areas of weakness.

This form was created by Anne Hoffman, M.Ed., of Pyramid Educational Consultants, Inc.

Picture Exchange Communication System- Long-term Progress©

Name: Data Period:

		DATE	11/2	11/16	12/7	12/21	1/11	1/25	2/15	3/1	3/15	3/29	4/12	4/26	5/3	5/17									

Phase VI
- Spontaneously comments — 58
- Discriminates all Sentence Starters — 56
- 2nd comment question — 54
- Com ? + Request ? + Spont. request — 52
- Discrim. comment vs. request S.S — 50
- First comment question — 48

Phase V
- Answers AND spontan. requests — 46
- Answers independently — 44
- 3-5 second delay — 42
- 0 second delay — 40

Attributes
- Uses multiple attributes — 38
- Uses multiple exemplars — 36
- Discrim 2+ prefer. attribute icons — 34
- Discrim. High vs. low attribute icon — 32
- Constructs 3-icon sentence — 30

Phase IV
- Points to pictures during read-back — 28
- Constructs entire strip — 26
- Adds R+ icon to sentence strip — 24

Phase III
- Looks inside book — 22
- 5 High Preference — 20
- 4 High Preference — 18
- 3 High Preference — 16
- 2 High Preference — 14
- High preference vs Low/non preference — 12

Phase II
- Travel to book — 10
- Travel to Comm Partner — 8
- Remove picture from book — 6

Phase I
- Independent Exchange — 4
- Physically Assisted Exchange — 2

> Once your student begins using PECS, you'll find it useful to track progress over time. This data sheet allows you to track Phase acquisition (shaded bars), number of pictures in the student's repertoire (lines connecting the letter "P"), and if applicable, the number of spoken words acquired (lines connecting the letter "W").
>
> In this example, across 28 weeks, this student mastered Phase IV and had 28 pictures in his repertoire. He said his first word after 8 weeks of PECS use and by the end of the 28 week period had learned to say 18 words.

P = Number of Pictures

W = Number of Spoken Words

Shaded Area = PECS Acquisition

5

Phase II

Distance and Persistence

Phase II –Distance and Persistence

> **Terminal Objective:** *The student goes to his/her communication board, pulls the picture off, goes to the trainer, gets the trainer's attention, and releases the picture into the trainer's hand.*

Rationale: In Phase I we taught students to exchange a picture within very specific parameters. We made sure a picture was in front of them and that a communicative partner was nearby waiting expectantly. Typically developing children learn to persist in their communicative initiations when these parameters change. For example, a young girl might repeat herself, raise her voice, or touch or tug on the communicative partner (imagine what these children do to get your attention when you are on the phone!). They learn that they must get a listener's attention in order to communicate, and they will do this by going to find someone or by calling someone. Children with autism and other disabilities often do not develop this persistence when communication efforts are not immediately successful. These children often <u>attempt a communicative interaction once</u>, and <u>if it is not successful</u>, either quit or <u>revert to previous behaviors</u>. Children using PECS can't raise their voices, and often find it easier to either not re-attempt communication or to use previously learned strategies such as tantrums.

In order to teach our students to be persistent, we must arrange for their communicative initiations to become slightly more difficult over time. So, in Phase II, we teach the students to communicate in "real world" situations. We teach them to "keep trying" when their initial attempts don't work. We do this by systematically eliminating both environmental and "listener" prompts that might be leading the student to initiate communication. Initially, the students are taught to "keep trying" when the communicative partner does not respond immediately to them. First, we teach the students to go to their potential "listener" and to persist in getting this person's attention prior to exchanging the picture. Next we teach the students that the pictures with which they are communicating don't always "magically appear" in front of them when they need them. We teach the student to go get the picture when he has something to "say." The student learns that he doesn't have to be in a specific location, that he doesn't have to be sitting, that he doesn't have to be with a specific person, or in a specific activity, in order to use PECS.

Phase II is the Phase that lasts forever! We teach persistent communication by arranging for multiple opportunities to communicate in a variety of environments, for a variety of items, with a variety of communicative partners, across a variety of obstacles. Each time a student masters a new skill from this point forward in PECS, we will re-visit Phase II issues by ensuring that the student can use the new skill while "traveling" and in all the various circumstances listed below.

Phase II Variables	
"Listener" Factors	Environmental Factors
Distance to communicative partner	Distance to book
Variety of communicative partners	Variety of rooms (environments)
Expectant Look	Variety of reinforcers
Enticement style	Variety of activities (lessons)
Eye contact	Sitting vs. standing vs. "on the move"
Body orientation	Furniture
Taking picture from room to room to find communicative partner	

The **Structured**
Training Environment

Setting
Attach one picture of a highly preferred item via Velcro® to the front of a communication book. Student and trainer are seated at a table/on the floor as in Phase I. Have several items and their corresponding pictures available.

notes

1. **No verbal prompts used during this phase.**
2. **Teach a variety of pictures— presented one at a time.**
3. **Conduct reinforcer assessments frequently.**
4. **Use a variety of communicative partners.**
5. **In addition to structured training trials, create many opportunities for spontaneous requesting during functional activities each day.**
6. **The new skill to reinforce is traveling.**
7. **Create lessons that don't look like lessons.**

Teaching Strategy

Shaping: Shaping involves teaching new behaviors by "upping the ante" from trial to trial. The trainer does this by reinforcing behavior that is slightly better (closer to the "new" target behavior) than the behavior exhibited on the previous trial. The trainer must decide what the terminal behavior will be (crossing the room to reach a communicative partner or crossing the room to retrieve a communication book) and then define how large each step size should be from trial to trial so that expectations for each trial are determined prior to training. In Phase II, we shape the student's skill at "traveling" greater and greater distances to reach the communicative partner or his communication book. The communicative partner does this by moving slightly farther away from the child from trial to trial or by moving the child's pictures slightly further away from him from trial to trial. The key is to make a change that is big enough for you to notice but small enough that the child does not notice.

Step 1. Remove the Picture from the Communication Book.

In order to keep up with each student's pictures, we begin storing them in a communication binder. During training, we arrange for the target picture to be on the front of the binder, and we store the "extras" inside the book.

Allow the student "free access" to one item to "set the stage." After the student has consumed the item or played with it for 10-15 seconds, arrange for the first training trial by putting the single picture on the cover of a communication book and enticing the student. The student is to remove the picture from the communication board, reach to the trainer, and release the picture into the trainer's hand. If needed, the physical prompter can provide physical assistance to guide the student to remove the picture, but only after the student initiates in some fashion (at this stage in training, by reaching for the picture). The physical prompter fades assistance until the student independently removes the picture from the book and exchanges it with the communicative partner.

Step 2. Increase Distance Between Trainer and Student.

The student initiates the exchange- removes the picture and reaches for the adult. As the student is reaching for the trainer, the trainer holds her hand close to her body so that the student has to reach slightly further to exchange the picture. As the exchange is completed (the picture is released into the trainer's hand), verbally praise the student and provide access to the item. On the next trial, move slightly further back from the student so that he has to reach even further. Then, begin backing away from the student so that he has to stand up in order to reach the adult.

Continue training in this manner, gradually increasing the distance between the student and the trainer by inches then feet, then yards, etc. Eventually, the student should be able to cross the room to reach the communicative partner. Maintain the close proximity of the picture to the student.

Because the training strategy is **shaping**, the student should not have difficulty traveling the entire distance. Sometimes, however, we increase our increments too much, and the student hesitates, pauses, or stops before reaching the communicative partner. It is at this point that it is critical to have the second trainer on hand who will physically guide the

Teaching Strategy

Two-Person Prompting: As in Phase I, we will facilitate rapid fading of prompts by using a second trainer to physically prompt the student from outside the social interaction. If necessary, the physical prompter guides the student from behind (or next to) and does not interact in any social manner with the student such as by providing reinforcement. The physical prompter steadily fades all prompts so that the student engages in the desired behavior independently.

student to the communicative partner. On the next trial, the communicative partner be closer to the student. The physical prompter should provide this assistance the moment the student pauses, though.

> ## Error Correction
>
> **Backstep**– Follow the same procedure described in Phase I in which you take the student back in the sequence to the last step he performed correctly. Then provide physical assistance to complete the sequence and differentially reinforce the traveling.

If the prompter waits for the student to move toward the communicative partner and then pause for several seconds, the student will learn that all he has to do is move forward a bit and then wait for the physical prompter to guide him the rest of the way. If the student surprises you, though, and walks toward the communicative partner and pauses, and the physical prompter is not able to prompt immediately, then consider this an error within this sequential task. Respond with the Backstep Error Correction Procedure—the physical prompter takes the student back to the last correct step and provides physical assistance to complete the sequence. In this case, that would mean essentially starting the trial over by putting the picture back on the book. The communicative partner re-entices and the physical prompter makes sure that the student walks the entire distance smoothly. Remember, when you use the Backstep procedure, to reinforce the student by providing access to the reinforcer, but in a smaller quantity (differential reinforcement).

The communicative partner should not provide any prompting!! She should not say, "Come here," etc. or gesture to the student to continue. The communicative partner also should not move closer to the student once he pauses. If the communicative partner does this, then what the child will learn is "walk toward the person holding what I want, pause, and then she'll come to me!!!"

Step 3. Increase Distance Between Student and Communication Book.

Once the student reliably and independently is traveling to the communicative partner when the partner is at least 5-8 feet from the student, begin systematically increasing the distance between the book and the student so that the student must go get the picture and then go to the adult to complete the exchange. Typically, we begin this with the communicative partner nearby and by moving the book slightly (by a few inches at a time) away from the student. The student now has to reach further to get the picture. Over several trials, move the book further and further away from the student so that he has to get up and walk to it.

Finally, move the book to one side or the other so that it is no longer directly in line between the student and the communicative partner. Instead of "encountering" the picture on the way to the communicative partner and the "goodies," the student has to detour just a bit—veer a bit off center in order to get the picture. Continue moving the book further and further away from the student so that, over time, he learns to go and get his communication book or a picture from his book when the book is on the other side of the room. Begin storing the student's book in a specific location so that he can easily find it when he wants to communicate.

At this point in training, it is up to the communicative partner and the physical prompter to work cooperatively so that the correct picture is on the cover of the book depending on the current activity and the student's current preferences. Once the student has given the picture to the communicative partner, either trainer can put the picture back on the book, as long as this does not prompt the student to initiate another request. The student should initiate a request because he sees the communicative partner with a desired item, not because he sees the teacher putting the picture on his book.

As with distance to the communicative partner, sometimes we increase the distance between the student and his picture too much on a particular trial. If the physical prompter can get to the student almost immediately, she physically assists the student to complete the distance. Then, on the next trial, the picture book is placed closer to the student. If the physical prompter cannot get to the student immediately, and the student pauses for several seconds, respond with the Backstep Procedure.

A different type of error occurs when the student sees the communicative partner with something he wants and starts moving directly to the communicative partner, rather than toward the picture. In this scenario, the student makes an error in the sequential task at the very beginning of the sequence, so the Backstep Procedure would involve starting the trial over, providing extra assistance, and then using differential reinforcement.

The student must learn to travel to the communicative partner AND to the book during one communicative exchange.

Once the student can move away from the communicative partner in order to get a picture, reintroduce traveling to the communicative partner so that the objective of the lesson is traveling to the book AND to the communicative partner. Think of a "triangle" when envisioning this, with the student being one corner of the triangle, the book another, and the communicative partner the final.

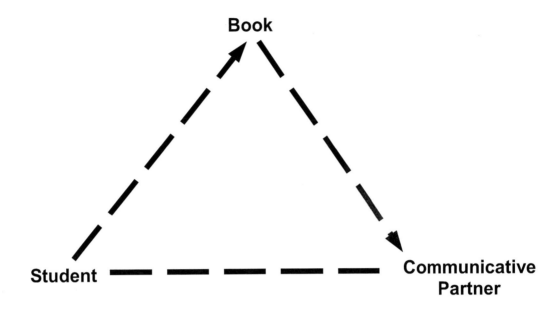

Book

Student

Communicative Partner

Step 4. Assess and Eliminate Additional Prompts.

During Phase II, it is important to eliminate ALL prompts or cues which might remind the student to communicate with the communicative partner.

A. The "Expectant Look"

This is a signal that all educators use. It is a signal that many parents use as they learn not to use verbal prompts with their children. It involves looking at the student with a questioning look: raised eyebrows, hunched shoulders, and raised arms. It is the "body language" often associated with "What do you want?" This is a prompt that we have seen students wait for before communicating, therefore it is one we want to eliminate. Practice with other trainers or in front of a mirror using your "poker face" so that your student doesn't come to depend on those facial signals from you.

B. Aspects of the Physical Environment

We sometimes begin PECS training in a highly structured situation where the student is seated in a chair at a table with the physical prompter behind the student and the communicative partner across the table from the student. As we begin the "distance" training, we usually move the student slightly away from the table so that he can walk to the communicative partner. We frequently see students who are extremely reluctant to give up their chairs! Sometimes they even try to take their chairs with them by scooting it toward the communicative partner while still sitting in it. This especially is common in older students who have been reinforced for "in seat" behavior. The PHYSICAL PROMPTER should help the student out of his chair! We also have seen students who are hesitant about moving away from a table if that was the initial training environment. Make sure that if you begin training seated at a table, you quickly move to the floor, outside, standing by a shelf, etc.

C. High Drama

In Phase I we talked about the importance of "enticing" the student or getting the student to attend to the reinforcer he is learning to request. Because the communicative partner does this silently, she or he often exaggerates her facial expressions or the physical manipulations she engineers with the item itself. We discussed making sure that you have the student's attention by showing him what you have to offer rather than speaking to him. Sometimes the communicative partner does such a wonderful act of enticing that the student begins to wait for the "drama" to begin before requesting. Take care that you don't fall into the habit of waving items flamboyantly. Eventually, the students should learn even to ask for items that are out of sight or items that you can't actually hold in front of them (the playground, tickles, etc.).

D. Body Orientation

Students often become quite adept at looking for and waiting for signals to engage in a specific behavior. We sometimes see students who mistakenly have learned to wait for a communicative partner to be facing them before they will initiate a communicative interaction. While you are moving further and further away from the student while teaching him to "travel," gradually turn away from him so that eventually he becomes persistent at getting your attention even when your back is turned. If necessary, the physical prompter guides the student to tap, touch, turn, etc., the communicative partner to get her to turn around. Initially, the communicative partner might have to face away from the student while making sure that the reinforcer is still in sight. Eventually, combine turning your back with eliminating the dramatic enticement.

E. Eye Contact

Just as students might learn to wait for your enticement, your body orientation, and your drama, they, too, might become dependent on your eye contact. Even before you move away from the student, drop your eyes or look away from the student so that he learns to initiate an exchange without waiting for you to look at him.

F. Variety of Environments/Rooms/Activities

We might begin PECS training in a structured environment—the student and trainers seated at a table where all of the materials are carefully organized. Many times, though,

we begin PECS in whatever location is of interest to the student—we go where the reinforcers are. This could be in the play area, the playground, the kitchen, etc. Regardless of where we begin PECS, we must plan to teach PECS in a variety of environments or rooms and across a variety of activities. At school, if you begin PECS in a classroom, make sure to

quickly create communicative opportunities on the playground, in the cafeteria, in the art room, etc. At home, if you begin in the playroom, remember to create communicative opportunities in the kitchen, the family room, the bedroom, etc. Go outside, in the car, to the park. Also remember the community—go to the mall or to a favorite restaurant.

The **Relaxed** Training Environment

Setting

Anywhere the child is likely to find something he wants! This should include all areas of the classroom, in various parts of the house, indoors, outdoors. Ideally, two people need to be on hand so that as one person notices that the child is interested in a particular item, he or she can call for the physical prompter to help.

In Phase I we recommended reinforcing EACH request that the student makes so that the he is likely to request again. Essentially, we are establishing ourselves as sources of "good things." As the student approaches us and we respond positively to him by effectively reinforcing the approach, we can expect the student to approach us more and more frequently and for reasons in addition to request from us. One analogy we use is making deposits in a coin bank. During Phases I and II, more and more coins are added to the bank each time a child makes a request and that request is quickly honored. If we do not respond or if we delay our response too long, a coin disappears. When you are eliminating the various prompts you have identified in Phase II, be attentive to how many of your student's requests are correct and reinforced (adding a coin) and how many are incorrect and, therefore, not reinforced or reinforced after a delay for error-correction (deducting a coin). Throughout all of our communication training, during all of our interactions with our student, our goal is to maintain a "positive balance" in the coin jar. As long as we do this, we can expect our interactions with the student to be beneficial to both of us.

Because "traveling" is involved in Phase II, this is a great time to do a lot of unstructured training. By this we mean move away from the table and onto the floor or outside. Many lessons should be devoted to creating new "challenges" to your student's spontaneity. Create lessons that will involve being more persistent at finding a communicative partner and at getting the communicative partner's attention even when she is distracted or interacting with someone else. Your student should learn that choosing a communicative partner involves more than approaching the adult who is the closest in distance to the student or most familiar to the student. He even must learn that the communicative partner is not always an adult!

Traveling From Room to Room

Teach the student that the communicative partner is not always in the same room as he is! This is another lesson that will involve shaping. The communicative partner, instead of only moving to the far side of the room, should actually move into the doorway, then to the other side of the doorway. Eventually the communicative partner should move out of the doorway into the next room. Do this gradually, so that the student, across subsequent exchanges, sees you in the doorway, then sees you half-way in the doorway, and then sees only your foot or hand in the doorway.

Staff Party

One of our favorite activities in a school setting is what we call the **"staff party."** This involves the staff suddenly withdrawing attention from the student(s) and instead focusing on the students' favorite items. For example, one staff member can walk into the classroom eating a bowl of popcorn. Another could sit down on the floor and begin playing with a set of toys. Don't overtly attend to the students, but instead, boisterously attend to the food or toys in order to gain the students' attention. We want the students to get a picture and come and ask us for some of what we're enjoying. If they resort to "old patterns" of requesting, pretend that you don't understand them or turn away from them. Have a physical prompter available to guide students to their communication books or to a communicative partner if necessary.

> Conduct these "Staff Parties" throughout the rest of PECS training. Expect the student to request items using PECS at a level he has mastered.

This staff party is an activity that we do often but in unpredictable ways. Vary the items you use at your parties. Vary when and where you have the parties, and invite new people with whom the students can interact. Even within one activity use a variety of items. Don't get stuck on food! PECS is not the "menu" for snack or meal times. Assess each of your activities across the day and determine what is reinforcing to the child within that activity. Then, create PECS opportunities and staff parties within those activities.

Who has the "goods?"

Another important lesson for everyone using PECS is to determine whom to ask for a particular item. By this point in training, the student should be able to exchange pictures with a variety of communicative partners. What should the student do, though, when several people are on-hand as potential communicative partners? If only one person has what the student wants, the most expedient way to get it would be for the student to ask that person. Often what we see, however, is the student going to the nearest person or the most familiar person to exchange the picture rather than going directly to the person with the desired item.

We create lessons to teach this very skill. Arrange for two or more people to be near the student, one holding the item the student wants at that moment. Two scenarios are possible:

1. The student goes directly to the person holding what he wants. If this happens, great!!!

2. The student goes to the person who does not have the "goods" or the *specific* item he wants. The natural response during this scenario would seem to be that this person would direct the student to the person holding the item. If this scenario happens frequently, though, the student is likely to learn the error pattern of approaching the nearest person with the picture

and then waiting for that person to direct him to the correct communicative partner. This lesson is a sequential lesson (go to communication book, remove picture, identify communicative partner, go to that person, exchange picture), so **BACKSTEPPING** should be used to respond to this error. Take the student back to his book, put the picture back on the book, and then guide the student to remove it again and take it to the correct communicative partner. Quickly recreate the situation so that the student can respond more independently.

Eye Contact

Although making eye contact is not a skill the student must have acquired before beginning PECS, we do think it is important for the student to use eye contact in a social manner. We previously described the type of eye contact typically developing children make with parents at an early age as a behavior that is maintained by social reinforcement. We discussed that because of their lack of responsiveness to social reinforcement, eye contact is a skill that children with autism don't usually develop without intervention.

Think for a moment about a typically developing three-year-old's interactions with her mother when Mom is talking on the telephone. It seems always to be the case that the moment the telephone rings, the child develops a tremendous thirst. Because the telephone conversation is an important one, Mom doesn't respond when her daughter initially approaches and starts asking for juice. As Mom continues not to attend to her daughter, the girl becomes more intense in her attempts to get Mom's attention. She uses a louder voice and she begins tugging on Mom. Initially she tugs on Mom's jeans. As she continues to get no response, she tugs higher on Mom's clothes—her sleeve, her shoulder, etc. Finally, in exasperation, she grabs Mom's face and turns it to her, loudly saying, "Mommy!" This girl knows that her communicative interactions will be most effective if she gets Mom to look at her. So, typically developing children learn not only to look at Mom and Dad when they look at them, but to get their parents to look at them during social interactions. Consequently, when we want to teach students about eye contact, we need to consider two skills—*responding* to someone's eye contact and *eliciting* eye contact from others.

Teaching students with autism and related social communication difficulties to elicit eye contact is a natural extension of Phase II training. As the communicative partner moves further and further away from the student, she begins to turn away from the student until her back is turned and she seemingly is paying no attention to the student. The physical prompter physically guides the student to tap the communicative partner (gently!!). The communicative partner very dramatically turns to the student, the student gives her the picture, and the student learns that he must get the communicative partner's attention (eye contact) in order to successfully interact.

> Eye contact must be important from the student's perspective. With PECS, it becomes important to get the communicative partner's eye contact before exchanging a picture.

Using PECS with Peers

We began teaching PECS with adults acting as both the student's communicative partner and physical prompter because adults typically control access to items and activities the student wants. Children become quite persistent at approaching adults with PECS, but don't do so with peers unless we specifically teach that. Children with autism won't learn to interact with peers merely by being with them.

A very successful strategy was developed at the University of Washington at Seattle (Schwartz, Garfinkle, and Baur, 1998). In their integrated preschool program, they systematically taught children to use PECS with their peers by initially arranging for peers to control access to the PECS users' favorite items at snack. The children using PECS were all persistent users with adults, and in this situation, some spontaneously requested from their peers while others needed  guidance to do so. All of the children learned to request from a variety of peers at snack time (including peers using PECS). When Schwartz, et al. probed a daily free time activity, they observed the children also using PECS with peers in that setting, despite no formal training to do so. The researchers did note one crucial aspect of this training was encouraging the peers to share!

When planning activities to encourage your student to interact using PECS with other children, three elements must be in place:
1. Peers and siblings must control the reinforcers. For example, select a "snack captain" who is responsible for distributing the food and drink items at snack.
2. Peers and siblings must know what the pictures mean so that they can respond with the appropriate items.
3. Peers and siblings should be encouraged, supported, and rewarded for sharing.

Throughout the entire PECS training protocol, arrange frequent opportunities for the students to interact with their peers. They should do so using PECS at a level they have mastered in communicating with adults.

Assessing the Trainers

During Phase II, the two trainers again should practice before working directly with students. This phase requires the trainer to identify and eliminate listener and environmental prompts upon which the student might be relying. The trainer **"shapes"** the student's behavior so that on each trial the trainer expects a slightly more difficult response from the student. Initially the trainer will shape the student's ability to travel farther and farther to reach the communicative partner with the picture. The trainers should set a goal for how far they expect the student to "travel" and then shape the student's ability to do so, by reinforcing "successive approximations" toward the end product. This process begins by the communicative partner first moving her hand further from the student until the student learns to **reach** further. Once the student travels to the communicative partner, the trainer arranges for the pictures to be further and further away so that the student learns to go get his picture and then go to the communicative partner.

PHASE II Communicative Partner:
• Plans for each student to have own communication book
• Arranges training environment appropriately—pictures available one at a time, trainers positioned appropriately, items available but inaccessible
• Entices appropriately
• Gradually increases distance between student and communicative partner
• Teaches student to cross room to reach communicative partner
• Gradually increases distance between student and communication book
• Teaches student to cross room to reach communication book
• Reinforces appropriately—new behavior within ½ second
• Turns away from student-eliminates subtle "body language" cues
• Reinforces appropriately– new behavior within ½second
• Teaches student to travel from room to room
• Does not insist on speech

The physical prompter participates in the lesson as minimally as possible. She uses physical guidance if the student needs help reaching or walking further to the communicative partner or communication book. The physical prompter fades the guidance as quickly as possible. If, during a specific trial, the student pauses on his way to the communication book or to the communicative partner, the physical prompter should use the Backstep error correction procedure.

Phase II Physical Prompter:
• Waits for initiation
• Prompts removal of picture from book if necessary
• Physically guides student to trainer if necessary
• Physically guides student to communication book if necessary
• Does not interact socially with the student.
• Uses backstepping if necessary

Cross-Reference with Additional Skills

As the student becomes more persistent in Phase II, set deals that are a bit more complex. Give the student a puzzle and have him complete the last 4 or 5 pieces. He might sort 10 pieces of silverware. As the delay between setting the deal and the "payoff" increases (even by a few seconds), introduce a visual reinforcement system to help the student remember the agreement. Typically, the actual item is placed on or near the job card. As the student becomes more proficient in use of pictures, a picture of the item is on the job card.

Begin single picture direction following—using a visual representation of a direction you give the student. Teach a variety of these directions as they are the foundation for schedule following.

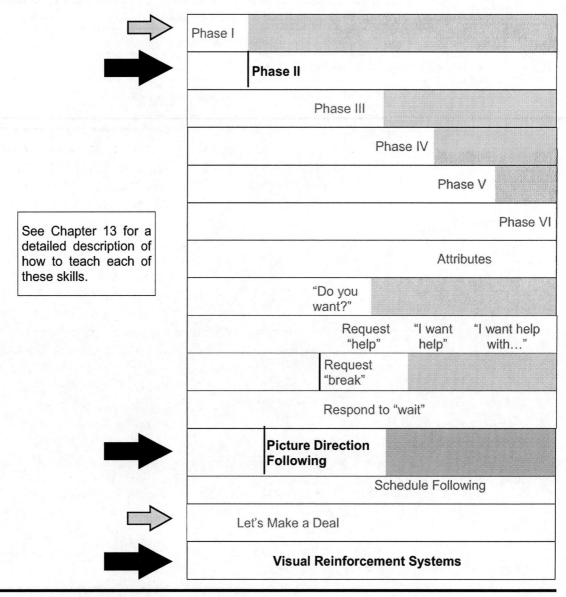

See Chapter 13 for a detailed description of how to teach each of these skills.

Phase I

Phase II

Phase III

Phase IV

Phase V

Phase VI

Attributes

"Do you want?"

Request "help"   "I want help"   "I want help with…"

Request "break"

Respond to "wait"

Picture Direction Following

Schedule Following

Let's Make a Deal

Visual Reinforcement Systems

??..Frequently asked questions..??

1 **What is the role of imitation training, especially vocal imitation?**

Imitation is an extremely important skill. Many children with autism and related disabilities demonstrate very poor imitation. Imitation may involve body actions (i.e., clapping hands), manipulating objects (i.e., bouncing a ball) or vocal acts (i.e., sounds, words, or phrases). If a child does not imitate one of these types of behaviors, it is very important to teach the skill. However, it is not necessary to imitate a word in order to be able to effectively communicate. Many of the children we have worked with have acquired important functional communication skills via PECS while improving their imitation skills, including vocal imitation. For many of these children, when their vocal imitation skills significantly improved, they have been able to imitate the words corresponding to the pictures they are using. However, during the period of time that they acquired vocal imitation, children using PECS still were able to communicate in a functional manner. Therefore, we strongly suggest that while children are taught PECS, parents and staff continue to teach imitation skills. However, it is best to teach one skill per lesson. Thus, during PECS lessons, imitation is not the focus, while during imitation lessons, PECS is not the focus. Many staff and parents work on vocal imitation within activities wherein PECS use is unlikely, as during playtime during which the child already has desired items. Many staff use a morning-circle routine to promote imitation of words, sometimes within a song or other established routine. In short, there is no conflict between PECS and imitation training, nor is it an either/or situation. The best practice involves choosing goals and strategies to match student needs and situational factors.

2 **What happens when the student leaves the classroom? Should he carry his book with him? What about at home?**

He take his communication book with him! In school settings, children often leave the main classroom to go to gym, art, lunch, music, recess, etc. Because communication occurs all day and across all contexts, the students must learn to take their books with them. Again, this training should be done using the 2-person prompting procedure and should be a gradual process as described earlier.

In home settings, it is often inconvenient to be in one room and to have to go to another to get a communication book. We often set up "mini" books in various locations throughout the house. For example, a student about to step into a bath tub for bath time should not have to run downstairs and all the way to the kitchen to get his communication book in order to ask for his tub toys. We sometimes build mini communication books in the kitchen, in the bedroom, in the playroom, etc.

For more information on these "mini books," see Frequently Asked Questions in Phase III.

3 My student is in a wheel chair and can't walk to the communicative partner or to get his book. Does this mean he is not an appropriate candidate for PECS?

Not at all! Your student can maintain spontaneity and persistence by calling a communicative partner to him rather than traveling to the communicative partner. We assume, though, that because you are using PECS with your student, he is able to manipulate the pictures. If he is not able to walk, though, we use some type of recorded message ("Come here, please" or "I have something to say.") or bell that the student activates in order to initiate an interaction. We use a small talking picture frame that is activated by opening the cover an pushing the "play" button. We adapt the frame by putting a bumper of some sort on the play button so that with the lid closed, the student has only to tap the frame in order to activate the message. Use the 2-Person Prompting Procedure to teach the student to activate the switch and then to exchange a picture once the communicative partner has approached. Remember, separate the function of gaining the attention of a communicative partner (Phase I) from the function of selecting a specific message (as in Phase III).

Bright Ideas
(Phase II)

1. Prepare communication boards using small 3-ring binders; small notebooks; small, firm boards, etc. Remember to use the same side of the sticky-back Velcro® (hook **or** loop) on all boards in your classroom, home, workshop, etc. This way, pictures can be recycled from board to board without worrying about mis-matched Velcro®.

2. Because the student is not yet discriminating pictures keep the one picture being used at a particular moment on the outside cover of the communication book, and house the rest of the student's pictures inside the communication book. Thus, the communication book will have Velcro® both on the outside and inside. Attach pages to the inside of the book as additional space becomes necessary.

3. Never take away the student's book or any picture within the book as a way of controlling when he can communicate. We can't take words away from speaking children; we respond to their incessant requests in a variety of ways and will eventually do the same with children using PECS.

4. Because we respond to these students as if they are verbal, the trainer is responsible for returning pictures to the communication book once a student has given the picture. Don't tell the student to "Put your picture back."

5. If more than one student in a classroom or home is using PECS, when you make a picture for one, put his initials on the back of the picture. Then, when you find stray pictures while cleaning up an activity, you know right away whose picture it is.

Monitoring Progress

Date/ Trainer initials	Item(s) requested	Distance to listener	# trials at target distance:	# independent trials at target distance:
2/28 JM	Cheese, raisins, ball	start: 0 1 2 ③ 4 5 6 7 8 9 10 end: 0 1 2 3 4 5 6 7 8 9 10	4	4
		Distance to book	# trials at target distance:	# independent trials at target distance:
		start: 0 1 2 3 4 5 6 7 8 9 10 end: 0 1 2 3 4 5 6 7 8 9 10		

Comments: first travel lesson– didn't work on travel to book

Date/initials	Item(s) requested	Distance to listener	# trials at target distance:	# independent trials at target distance:
2/28 LW	Bigwheel, therapy ball, bubblegum	start: 0 1 2 3 4 5 6 7 8 ⑨ 10 end: 0 ① 2 3 4 5 6 7 8 9 10	5	4
		Distance to book	# trials at target distance:	# independent trials at target distance:
		start: 0 1 2 3 4 5 6 7 8 9 10 end: 0 1 2 3 4 5 6 7 8 9 10	1	1

Comments: Communicative partner turned her back on last two trials. Began travel to book on last trial.

This was the student's first and second lesson involving travel in Phase II. Initially the two trainers targeted traveling to the communicative partner only—the book remained close to the student. On the first trial, the trainer was right in front of the student. On the last trial she had moved to three feet away from the student. The last 4 trials were at the target distance and the student was independent on allof those trials.

During the next lesson on the same day, a different communicative partner was able to move up to 9 feet away from the student. The last 5 trials the partner was 9 feet away from the student. The student crossed the distance independently on 3 of those trials. The trainer also began moving the student's book away during the last trial

This form was created by Victoria Bluett-Murphy of Applied Behavior Consultants, Inc.

Monitoring Progress

Date	Trial	Travel To Trainer	Dis-tance To Trainer	Travel To Board	Dis-tance To Board	Picture	Activity
3/2	1	+	1ft.	NA	NA	ball	free play
	2	+	1ft.	NA	NA	ball	free play
	3	+	1ft.	NA	NA	ball	free play
	4	+	18in	+	6in	ball	free play
	5	+	2ft.	+	6in	bubbles	recess
	6	+	3ft.	-	1 ft.	bubbles	recess
	7	+	3 ft.	+	1ft.	juice	lunch
	8	+	4 ft.	+	1 ft.	juice	lunch
	9	+	5ft.	+	2ft.	pretzel	"staff party"
	10	+	10 ft.	+	2ft.	pretzel	"staff party"

(+) = Independent   (-) = Prompted Note distance in inches, feet, room-to-room, etc.

In this example the student has just begun walking further and further to reach the communicative partner without prompts (physical guidance) from the physical prompter and is going to get the picture when it is not directly in front of him. Initially, the communicative partner moved one foot from the student and kept his book within reach in front of him. Eventually, the communicative partner also began moving the student's book further away from him, so that by the end of this session, he was able to walk two feet to get his book and then 10 feet to get to the communicative partner.

Monitoring Progress

Date	Location/ Length/ Activity	List icons used	Comm. Partner (s)	Status of Physical Assistance	Distance to Comm. Partner	Position of Comm. Partner	Distance from Comm. book
11-2-98	Classroom 15 min. Approx. 25 trials snack	Popcorn, juice, shoelace	AH, MG	A slight physical prompt to stand when seated on floor or in chair	6 feet	standing	A few inches
11-2-98	Classroom 10 min. Free play	Legos, toy cars	MG, DB	none	7 feet	Sitting and standing	2 feet
11-2-98	Playground Less than 1 min 1 trial	Frisbee	MG	none	4 feet	Standing with back turned	2 feet

This data form summarizes three separate training sessions conducted during one day. Training took place with a variety of trainers, for a variety of reinforcers, and within a variety of locations and activities. While the child required assistance to travel to the communicative partner, the book was kept nearby. As the child developed more independence at traveling to the communicative partner, the distance to the book gradually was increased.

This summary demonstrates that the child made progress across training during one day. It provides enough information for the next trainer to assess at what level (distance) to begin training during the next session.

This form was created by Anne Hoffman, M.Ed., of Pyramid Educational Consultants, Inc.

6

Phase III

Picture Discrimination

Phase III -Picture Discrimination

Terminal Objective: *The student requests desired items by going to a communication book, selecting the appropriate picture from an array, going to a communication partner, and giving the picture.*

Rationale: By the time your student is ready for Phase III, he should be a very persistent communicator. He even "nags" you! He has learned the **POWER** of communication. He has learned that communication involves approaching a person and exchanging a message for a reinforcer of some kind. Most importantly, he is acting within a **SOCIAL** context to impact on someone else's behavior. He is now ready to begin formulating specific messages, so it is time to teach him to discriminate between specific symbols. Many traditional picture-based communication programs begin picture discrimination by teaching the student to "match to sample." These lessons involve having the student match objects to objects, objects to picture, pictures to objects, and so on. For many of our students, this lesson is not fun (socially reinforcing), so we must encourage the student to participate in it by offering reinforcers that are effective (tangible). When a student masters these lessons (which can take quite awhile), we then assess whether the student can effectively use the pictures within a communicative context; we are assessing whether what the student learned in the matching to sample lessons generalized to a communicative context. This doesn't always happen!

For this reason, we plan for "picture learning" to occur within the communicative context from the very

> **Remember:**
> Typically developing children learn "how" to communicate before they can speak single words!

 blocks
 play clay
 chips
 banana

beginning. It is not necessary for the student to learn picture matching tasks in a "structured" lesson in which tangible reinforcement must be used to teach a skill that will eventually be used within a social context.

We begin teaching discrimination by presenting the student with a choice of two pictures. Which two pictures we begin with is critical! If we began discrimination training by presenting the student with two pictures of equally desired items, the student could conceivably give us one picture, expecting to get the other item, but still be happy when we give him what the exchanged picture represents. The initial lesson in discrimination training should be one that teaches the student that there are specific consequences for exchanging one picture versus another. This lesson is more salient when the consequences for one versus the other are vastly different. Consequently, when we begin Phase III, we initially use a picture of a desired item and a picture of an item that the student does not want. The student learns that giving a specific picture results in access to a preferred item, while giving a different picture results in access to something he does not want.

highly preferred
versus
non-preferred
We know the "correct" picture and the consequences are more meaningful to the student.

Highly preferred

Distracter

highly preferred
versus
highly preferred
We don't know the "correct" picture and the consequences are relatively the same (n o t i n i t i a l l y meaningful).

Highly preferred

Highly preferred

The **Structured** Training Environment

Setting

The student and teacher are seated at table, facing each other. Have available several pictures of desirable or contextually appropriate items, pictures of "irrelevant" or non-preferred items, and the corresponding items.

notes

1. **No verbal prompts used during this phase.**
2. **Conduct reinforcer assessments frequently.**
3. **Use a variety of trainers.**
4. **In addition to structured training trials, create many opportunities for spontaneous requesting during functional activities each day.**
5. **Vary position of pictures on the communication board until discrimination is mastered.**

Teaching Strategy

Discrete Trial Instruction: This methodology is used when the skill being taught can "stand alone." It is a useful strategy when staff want to have many repetitions of the target behavior. The sequence involves four steps:

(1). The trainer's presentation—the trainer will place two pictures on the communication book and entice the student.
(2). The student's response– the student selects one picture and gives it to the communicative partner.
(3). The consequence—the student gets the requested item.
(4) A short pause before the next presentation– the student consumes or plays with the requested item.

In the case of an error, Step 3 also involves an error correction sequence.

Discrete trial instruction can involve many repetitions within one lesson (massed trials) or can involve trials spread across a broad period of time (dispersed or distributed trials). Discrete trials do NOT need to begin with a verbal stimulus.

Phase IIIA. Discrimination between a highly preferred icon and a distracter icon.

The general sequence during this step is to present the student with two items and their corresponding pictures. One item is something that the student really likes and one is an item that he does not like or that does not "fit" during this activity. For example, if you begin this training during free play, the student likely won't expect an empty box to be part of the routine.

In discrimination training, the new skill being taught is choosing the correct picture, rather than putting the picture into the communicative partner's hand. We observe this new behavior the moment the child touches the correct picture. As Karen Pryor points out in _Don't shoot the dog: the new art of teaching and training_ (1999), we should never try to teach two lessons at once- we should split them into two separate lessons. Putting pictures into someone's hand is a Phase I and II lesson while discrimination training- selecting the correct picture- is a Phase III lesson. We know that the closer in time the reinforcement is delivered to the targeted response, the greater the strengthening effect of the reinforcer. Therefore, we _must_ reinforce the selection of the correct picture as soon as it happens- that is, _**the instant the child touches the correct picture!**_ We do this by providing the child with some vocal feedback ("Yes!" "Uh-huh," "That's right!"). This feedback serves as a **conditional** or **secondary** reinforcer as it reliably precedes the established reinforcer—the requested item.

Do not wait for the student to pick up the picture and put it into your hand- that delays the reward far too long and leads to the student looking for little cues in your expression or body posture as to which response is correct. If the student is slow in reaching and giving selected pictures, then focus on that aspect of the skill without presenting a discrimination, i.e., use only one picture (this is a Phase I skill). Remember, as soon as the student touches the correct picture, vocally respond! When the picture is placed in your hand, then give the student the item he requested.

Sometimes, the student will reach for the incorrect picture (the distracter picture). When this happens, we could say, "No," or "Hmmmm," but we are not sure the student will be able to discriminate this as negative feedback versus the happier tone of voice we used for positive feedback. So, we say nothing when this happens, and wait for the exchange to be completed and then give the student the distracter item.

> Phase III is not a lesson about initiation. Initiation was taught in Phases I and II, so in Phase III, one trainer is sufficient.

> Entice with both items in one hand so that you have a free hand for accepting the picture.

Step 1. To begin, set up a familiar situation during which the student is likely to want a particular item (i.e., something that fits the context or situation). Arrange the communication board with two pictures on it: one of a highly reinforcing or contextually appropriate item and one of a non-preferred, or contextually irrelevant item.

Because the new skill to learn is discrimination, other aspects (mostly Phase II issues) of the lesson can be simplified. Therefore, have both the book and the communicative partner nearby. Entice the student as in previous lessons and wait for him to request. As soon as he reaches for the correct picture, begin praising him. Once he has put the picture into your hand, give him the corresponding item. If the student reaches for the the picture of the "irrelevant" object (i.e., a picture of a "sock" while sitting at the dinner table) the trainer gives no social reaction. Once he gives the picture, give him the "irrelevant" object. Watch the student's reaction. If he has any kind of negative reaction (e.g., cries, throws the item, pushes the item away, etc.), **THIS IS GOOD!!** Now we can teach the student that he must use a specific picture to get the item he wants. Respond to this error using the **4-Step error correction procedure.** A summary of the sequence is:

Step	Teacher	Student
	Entice with both items	
		Gives incorrect picture
	Give corresponding item	
		Reacts negatively
MODEL or SHOW	Show or tap target picture (get S to look at the target picture on the book)	
PROMPT	Hold open hand near target picture, physically, or gesturally prompt	
		Gives target picture
	Praise (do not give item)	
SWITCH	"Do this," pause, etc.	
		Performs switch
REPEAT	Entice with both items	
		Gives correct picture
	Give item and praise	

Correct use of this error correction procedure is very important! It would be very easy for us to simply show the student which picture is correct and then give him that item when he gives us the picture. If we do this, however, we will be reinforcing a prompted response. In essence, all the student has to learn is to wait for you to point to the correct picture and then give you that picture in order to get something good! He is not likely to give you the correct picture independently.

Why do we do the "switch?" Many children- with or without disabilities- adopt a "do whatever was right last time" strategy. After having a response reinforced, they logically conclude that this response must be the way to go! So, on

subsequent opportunities, they will stick with that response ("If it worked once, it should work again!"). We do the switch in order to "change the subject." Within PECS discrimination training, the subject change serves to visually distract the student from the pictures. Switching to a known task is crucial. It is the trainer's opportunity to insert a quick trial into the sequence that is unrelated to choosing a picture. That way, when we get to the "Repeat" portion of the 4-Step sequence, the student can't merely do what was right the last time. If imitating your motor action was the "switch" then on the "repeat," the student must independently choose a picture to give because repeating the imitated motor action won't work.

What you select as your "switch" is important. It should be a known task so that the student's response will be successful. Because he is successful, we have an additional opportunity to provide some positive reinforcement in the midst of the sequence by praising the student for complying with the switch. If we chose a task at which the student is inconsistent, then we will get bogged down in the midst of the error correction sequence in training this unrelated task. If your student does not perform the well-known task, then question general motivation issues related to this lesson: does he or she really want the item you are offering?

Many children who are new to PECS also are new to any type of intervention. Consequently it might be difficult for us to identify a "switch" that he will successfully complete. The switch can be something as simple as gesturing to the student to pick up a pencil you dropped or drawing his attention to an unrelated object. The point is to do something that will visually distract the student for a moment. If you can not identify ANY behavior to which you can switch, then use a **DELAY** as your Step 3 in the sequence. Move the book away or turn the book over for a couple of seconds and then allow the student to turn it back over once you have enticed again.

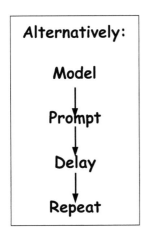

Alternatively:

Model

↓

Prompt

↓

Delay

↓

Repeat

"Switch" ideas:

■ Give the student a single task to complete (clap your hands, touch your hair, stand up, turn around, etc.).

■ Show the student something unrelated to the task (remember, your goal is to visually distract the student).

■ Gesture for the student to pick something up from the floor (something you "accidentally" dropped).

■ Turn PECS book over.

■ Model a motor action for the student to imitate.

The goal in this step of discrimination training is for the student to consistently exchange the picture of the desired item. That picture will change depending on what currently is reinforcing to the student. During a single discrimination lesson, try to vary the item the student is requesting so that he is exposed to a variety of pictures. Use the "first one's free" strategy when you switch reinforcers and when conducting mini-reinforcer assessments.

Vary your switches. Within the 4-Step error correction sequence, step 3 (the switch) shouldn't always be the same action. Use a variety of actions during the "switch" so that the student does not learn the motor component of the switch as a "step" in the exchange. We have seen students for whom this action was not varied. They will give the trainer a picture and as soon as they see the trainer reach for the distracter item, they start clapping their hands or turning around! The new sequence they have learned is 'give a picture, look at the trainer, clap hands, give another picture, get item, .' So in order to avoid this, remember to **"switch your switches."**

In addition to varying the desired item, remember to vary the distracter item, too. If you always use a wooden spoon as the distracter, all the student needs to learn is to avoid that picture! We find it helpful to identify several potential distracters and to keep a variety of these items and their corresponding pictures on hand.

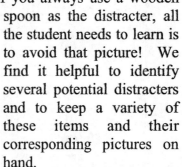

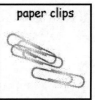

Sometimes students make an additional error during the error correction procedure. You go through the MODEL, the PROMPT, the SWITCH, and the REPEAT, but on the "REPEAT," the student makes another mistake. Cycle through the 4-Step procedure once again. If the student makes another error, cycle through one more time if the student remains motivated to access one of the items. If the student continues to make errors, consider that this lesson is not going to be successful, and plan to end the lesson successfully. The best way to do this is to quickly rearrange the cover of the book to a *level of mastery*. This means going back to one picture of a highly reinforcing item. The student should now be able to make a correct exchange so that you can end the lesson successfully.

Within one trial, repeat the 4-Step Error Correction Procedure two to three times at most!
End successfully by backing up to the level of mastery!

The student is learning to discriminate between pictures—he is not memorizing the position of a particular picture on the book. So, when the student successfully requests an item by giving you the picture of the preferred item, reinforce this behavior appropriately, and then rearrange the pictures on the front of the book before the next trial begins. Make sure that you rearrange the pictures in a variety of ways and that you switch the two pictures within each array. Do not simply move the picture back and forth from left to right. Move them all around the book early in this level of training. Do not rearrange the pictures within an error correction sequence.

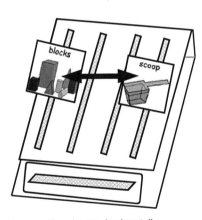

Arrange the pictures horizontally

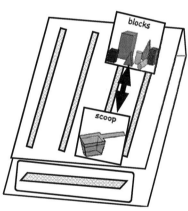

Arrange the pictures vertically

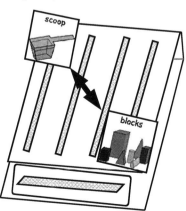

Arrange the pictures diagonally

Arrange them haphazardly!!

Alternate Discrimination Training Strategies

With each strategy, introduce fading as soon as discrimination is evident. The longer the prompt remains, the more difficult it will be to fade!!

Continued errors at Step 1 require special discrimination training strategies. Your task is to determine what visual discriminations the student currently makes and build from that point. Following are several strategies that we have tried when students are having difficulty learning to discriminate between a picture of a reinforcing item and a picture of a distracter. Each strategy involves adding a visual prompt, so remember you will have to eliminate that prompt over time! This list is not exhaustive, but is a compilation of suggested strategies!!!

1 Use a highly preferred reinforcer/picture paired with a blank or faintly copied "distracter" picture. This highlights the visual difference between the pictures. If the child gives the distracter picture, indicate that you are giving him "nothing" (hold out empty hands, etc.) or that you don't understand, and complete the 4-Step error correction sequence. As the child consistently is successful with this variation, begin "drawing" on the blank picture or copying it more darkly so that it begins to look more and more like a picture. Remember, the final step within this variation is for the student to get to the point where he can discriminate between two symbols with the same visual characteristics (line thickness, darkness).

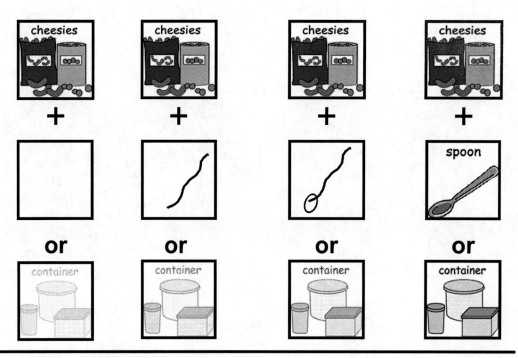

2 Enhance the visual difference between the pictures by using color, photographs, labels or logos from packages, etc. We use wrappers from candy bars, the logo from a package of cookies, or a cut-out picture of the cereal from the cereal box. If you started PECS with black and white line drawings, try colored line drawings. Look at a variety of different symbol sets available commercially. Use a scanner or digital camera to create "realistic" symbols. If your child likes videos or books and has preferences for which one to look at during a particular time, color copy or scan the box to make a symbol. These "custom" symbols should be the same size and shape so that it is the picture to which the student is attending, not the size or shape.

3 Maximize the size of the pictures and maximize the distance between the pictures. If the child is having difficulty discriminating one size picture, use larger pictures. Keep the distance between the pictures as large as possible, even exaggerating the placement by putting one picture on one end of the table (or on one table) and the other picture at the other end (or on another table). Fade this prompt by moving the pictures closer together, making them smaller, and then putting them back on the book.

4 There are a host of procedures that are identified as *errorless learning* procedures. The point of these strategies is to prevent errors from occurring rather than reacting to errors after they occur. The underlying principle for these procedures is very gradually to change some characteristic of the stimulus comparison. For example, if a student has learned to give you a picture when only one picture is available, then the teacher may gradually introduce a second picture into the student's visual field. If the student is accustomed to picking up the picture of "cookie" from near the bottom edge of a table, a picture of something else may be introduced simultaneously near the top left (or right) corner of the table. The student's previous tendency should lead him to select the picture in its familiar location and ignore the new picture in the new location. Over time, the second picture can be brought closer and closer to the other picture. If an incorrect selection occurs, the picture arrangement should return to a safer, more successful distance on ensuing trials.

In a similar fashion, if a student responded by selecting a **LARGE** picture of the desired item versus a *small* picture of the distracter item, then over time the size of the pictures can be gradually made more similar. Or, if the student discriminates between a picture that is colored (within the picture or via a frame) versus a black-and-white picture, then the difference between these styles can be gradually removed, either by adding color to one picture or removing color from the other. Highlighting a feature within one picture may enhance initial discriminations; thereafter, the highlighted feature needs to be gradually removed.

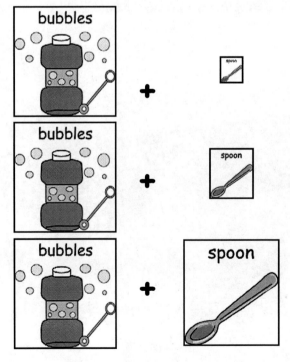

5 Arrange the pictures to spatially correspond to the placement of the actual items. For example, you could place a sock on a table to the child's left and milk on the right. Place the corresponding picture immediately in front of each item. Remember, this visual arrangement is the prompt! Over time, the pictures should gradually be placed further and further away from the items and closer together in order to foster visual discrimination between the pictures as opposed to the location of the items.

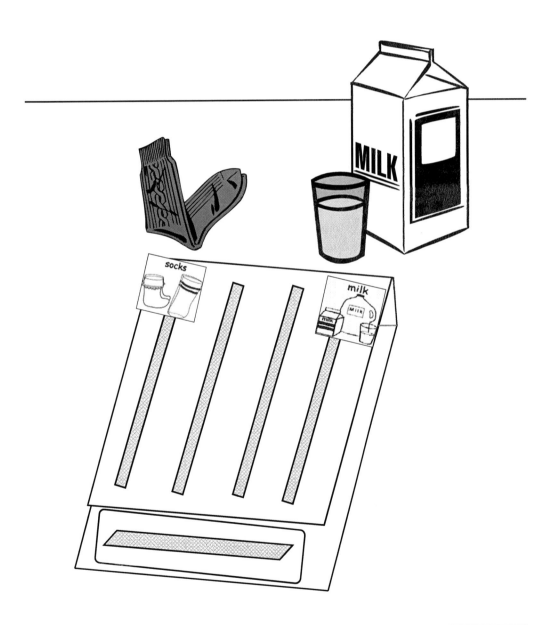

6 Place the pictures on the desired items or on transparent containers filled with the desired items. Over time, alter the container to translucent material so that the child must rely upon the visual cues associated with the picture rather than the specific item. Remember, if you place a picture on the item, as soon as discrimination is clear, gradually move the picture away from the item.

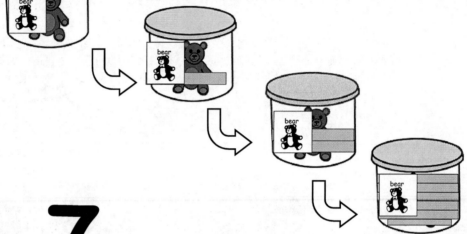

7 Use 3-dimensional representations of the pictures. We actually glue candy, cookies, etc. to the 2-inch cards cut from poster board and cover them with a hard finish. Or, we use miniature representations of the objects. Refrigerator magnets and craft store miniatures are an excellent source. As a child masters discriminating between three dimensional/miniature items, and as he builds vocabulary, keeping up with all of these items becomes quite a chore. Housing them in a communication binder is possible but not practical. Therefore, we suggest converting these three dimensional symbols into line drawings. This can be done by gradually covering the three dimensional symbol with a line drawing and then removing the three dimensional symbol so that we are just left with the line drawing (Frost and Scholefield, 1996).

Each of these strategies relies upon the student having demonstrated clear discrimination skills regarding real objects. For example, PECS should not be started unless the student has demonstrated skills associated with retrieving items directly. The student should be able to pick desired items and move toward them as well. (Note: We may have to use a different definition of "move towards" for non-ambulatory students, but the overall concept remains the same.) Perhaps more revealing for discrimination lessons is determining whether the student can act appropriately in situations wherein objects should be strongly associated with other objects or outcomes. For instance, if a student has finished juice or milk in a cup, the student should move toward a container of juice or milk, or take the cup to the container. If the student does not move toward the container with the empty cup, it is highly unlikely that the student would move toward an adult to give a picture of the juice in order to receive juice.

You may need to teach discrimination skills for objects, such as taking the empty cup to the table with the milk container but bringing the empty plate to the table with cookies on them. (Here, too, you may want to maximize the contextual difference between the choices and, of course, randomly change locations of the containers.) If that discrimination is mastered, then you may want to place the items into boxes (or similar containers) and place a large picture corresponding to the item outside the box. This procedure resembles an object-object association format, yet it is within a functional context with a functional outcome.

Phase IIIB. Discrimination between pictures of two reinforcing items.

Once the student has mastered discrimination between a picture of highly preferred item and the picture of the contextually inappropriate or undesired item, our new goal is to teach discrimination between two reinforcing items. Set up the communication book as in the beginning of Phase III, but put pictures of two reinforcing items on the outside. Because both pictures now represent items that the child likes, we don't know before his first exchange which item he wants. We need to be able to check that the student is using the correct picture to get the specific item he wants. The way we do this is to check to see if what he asks for is what he indeed wants. We do this by conducting **CORRESPONDENCE CHECKS**:

1. Show the student a tray with two highly preferred items on it. Have the communication book nearby with the two corresponding pictures on the front of it.

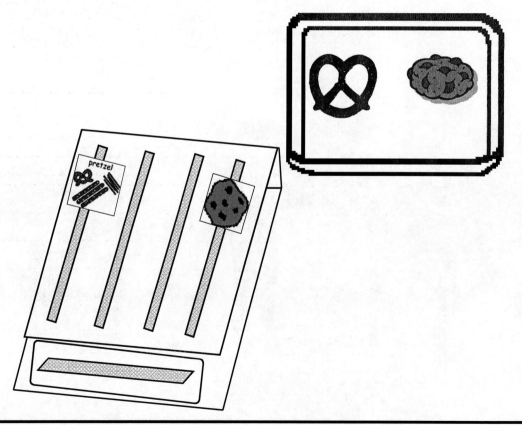

2. Once the student has given a picture, indicate that he is to take the appropriate item — Holding out the tray, say "Good! Go ahead and take it!" or a similar phrase.

3. The new behavior in Phase IIIB is taking the item that corresponds to the picture that the student exchanged. So, begin reinforcing the student (with verbal praise) the moment he reaches for the correct item. As soon as the student reaches for the correct item, praise him and allow him to take it. Taking what he asked for is an indication that the student is using the picture correctly.

4. If the student reaches for the incorrect item, **block** his access to it, and use the 4-step error correction procedure in response to this ERROR. We assume that when told, "take it," the student reaches for the item he really wants. So, model the picture that corresponds to the item the student reached for. We call this, "**Teach the Reach**."

STEP	TEACHER	STUDENT
	Entice with both items	
		Gives a picture
	"Take it," "Go ahead," etc.	
		Reaches for wrong item
	Block access	
MODEL or **SHOW**	Point to, tap correct picture	
PROMPT	Hold open hand near target picture or physically/gesturally prompt	
		Gives target picture
	Praise (do not give item)	
SWITCH	"Do this," or other known task	
		Performs switch
REPEAT	Entice with both items	
		Gives picture
	"Go ahead," etc.	
		Takes correct item
	Allow access and praise	

When you conduct the correspondence check, it is important to just say, "Take it" or a similar phrase during the correspondence check. Do not name the item—do not say, "Take the cookie." If you name the item and the student takes the correct item, you will not know whether he took it because you named it (an example of correct auditory discrimination) or because of the picture (an example of correct visual discrimination). The lesson to be learned at this point is picture discrimination, so not naming the item will ensure that the student is attending to the picture itself. Once the student takes the correct item, then name it.

Remember, if the student makes an error (reaches for the incorrect item), and you do the 4-Step error correction procedure, you must end the error correction with another correspondence check. If you started the trial with a correspondence check, you must end with a correspondence check!

If your student continues to make errors as you begin teaching this level of discrimination, consider whether or not the student is ready for discriminating between pictures of two preferred items. Some children do best when we teach one or more intermediate steps:

distracter vs.
blank vs.
preferred

distracter vs.
distracter vs.
preferred

Preferred
item from one
category vs.
preferred
item from a
DIFFERENT
category

Discrimination between multiple pictures

Add pictures so that the child learns to request from among numerous pictures. Begin by moving to three pictures of preferred items. Now the tray you use to offer the items for enticement and correspondence checks will have three items on it. Because items tend to roll around, we use a muffin tin or egg carton to house the items. Which

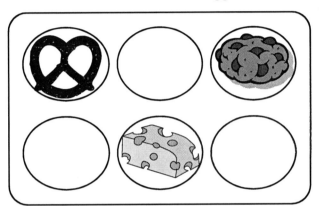

pictures are targeted for training is determined by which items are currently available and reinforcing given the activity.

If the student makes errors during discrimination between three pictures, continue to use the 4-Step error correction procedure. Remember, these error corrections must end in a correspondence check! Some students have difficulty progressing from two to three pictures. Again, an intermediate task is to have pictures of two preferred items and one distracter. If a student can discriminate between these, then move on to discriminating between pictures of three reinforcing items.

Once the student masters discriminating between three pictures, go to four and then to five. Conduct correspondence checks with four and then five items on the tray.

When the student discriminates from among five pictures, he is ready to finish discrimination training. We have not found it necessary to teach the student to discriminate from among six, then seven, etc. With five pictures arranged on the book in an "X" fashion, the student visually has to scan vertically, horizontally, and diagonally. Those are all of the options!!!

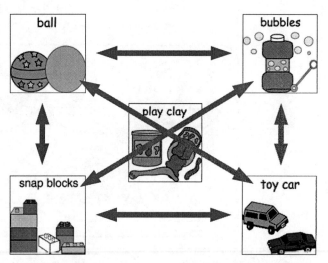

The final step in discrimination training is to teach the student to look inside his book for a specific picture. To do this, clear all pictures from the front cover of the communication binder. Open the binder and place one or two pictures of highly preferred items inside the book. Entice the student with the items, and as he reaches for the picture inside the book, gently close the book. The student should open it to retrieve the correct picture. If he does not, physically prompt him to do so and fade this assistance. If the student has more pictures than will fit inside the book, add pages to the inside of the book. Teach the student to "thumb through" the book by clearing all pictures except one or two on the second page, entice the student, and close the book as he reaches for the picture. Again, provide physical assistance as needed.

Once the student is proficient at opening his communication book and "thumbing" through the pages to find the picture of what he wants, rotating the location of the pictures is no longer necessary. Begin to organize the pictures within the book using a categorization system that will be functional to both you and your student. Many teachers organize the book by specific vocabulary categories such as food, toys, places, etc. Some books are organized according to activities of the day.

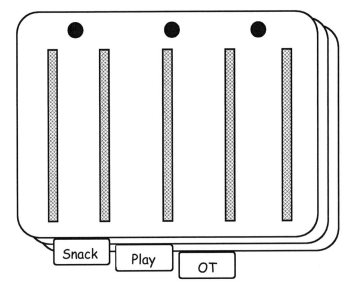

Create some type of visual signal to this organization. Some teachers organize by using a specific color page for a specific set of vocabulary items. Others use pages marked with tabs to delineate the specific category.

Throughout the remainder of PECS training, adding vocabulary typically is not difficult. Most students who have mastered discrimination and have moved on in the training protocol need only to see the picture a few times in order to begin using it meaningfully. When introducing a new picture, arrange a "mini-lesson." Put the new picture on the front of the book with a couple of other pictures, entice with the new item, and conduct a correspondence check to make sure the student correctly uses the new picture. Once you are sure he is doing so, move that picture into the appropriate place within the book.

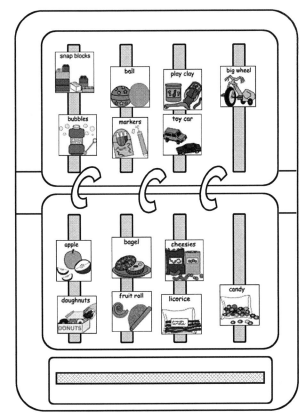

At the completion of Phase III, the student's team should decide on how to organize the book throughout the remainder of PECS. Many teams decide to keep "frequently used vocabulary" on the front cover of the book and to store other vocabulary inside the book according to the agreed upon strategy. Some teams prefer to keep the front of the book empty so that the vocabulary for specific training activities can be housed there as needed. Whatever system you decide to use, make sure to maintain consistency for each student. If the student uses one book at school and a different one at home, both should be organized in the same manner.

The **Relaxed** Training Environment

Setting

The training should continue to be widespread—in a variety of environments, with a variety of communicative partners, for a variety of desired items, and within a variety of activities. Continue the "staff parties," and remember to include different items during these events.

When we began discrimination training and when we did any "troubleshooting," we simplified the rest of the PECS lesson in order to highlight discrimination. Consequently the student has not been doing much "traveling" and might not have been communicating with a variety of trainers. Therefore, we must also create many opportunities throughout the school/home day during which the skills learned in Phase II can be maintained. Continue the STOP/DROP/TALK activities described in Phase I and the "staff parties" described in Phase II. The first time you re-introduce traveling once you have begun discrimination, you might need to simplify the discrimination task temporarily or even eliminate discrimination by presenting only one picture. Eventually the student must learn to travel AND discriminate within a single communicative exchange.

> **Re-introduce Phase II** skills once each new level of discrimination is mastered.

Once a student has mastered Phase IIIA, immediately begin teaching him to "travel" with this level of discrimination. Set up a situation where the student will want something you have, arrange for the book to be away from the student (where it typically is kept) with a picture of the highly desired item and the distracter item on the cover. The objective for this lesson is for the student to travel to get his book, discriminate, then travel to the communicative partner. Remember, the teacher's role, now, is to arrange for opportunities to address new levels of discrimination AND arrange for incidental opportunities for requesting across the day.

If you are working with a group of children and are targeting a skill in addition to PECS, keep the PECS book available with the front cover arranged at a level the student has already mastered. This way the student will practice using PECS successfully across a variety of activities. When you are targeting a new discrimination level, then arrange the book accordingly. REMEMBER, teach one objective at a time!

TAKE NOTICE!

Requesting "Out-of-Sight" Items

Have you ever been sitting comfortably on the couch enjoying your favorite television show when your partner walks into the room eating your favorite chocolate bar? Your reaction, most likely, is a sudden intense craving for that chocolate, so you either ask for a bite or ask your partner to get you one of your own. Typically developing children learning to communicate initially request and comment on items in their immediate environment. Daddy walks in the room and Dominic squeals "Daddy!" Dominic sees his older brother Sam eating a cookie and he says, "Cookie!" At the store, Dominic and Sam each ask for their favorite cereal as Mom wheels the cart past the brightly-colored boxes in the cereal aisle. What often occasions a communicative exchange is suddenly seeing, hearing, smelling, feeling, or tasting something.

As children's communication skills mature and become more sophisticated, they learn to communicate about items or events that are not in their immediate environment. Allie is hungry, so she asks Dad to make her a sandwich. John comes in from playing outside and says to his brother, "Did you see that truck that just went by? It was fast!"

Students using PECS also must learn to ask for items or comment on activities that are not immediately present. We introduce this skill within the requesting format once the students have become persistent communicators and are discriminating between a variety of symbols. Begin to create opportunities for the student to do this in a variety of locations. Do this gradually by slowly putting items away.

- Put something away immediately after the student has requested and received it and then see if he will request it again.
- Stand at an open cupboard and entice the student with something you know he likes (eating the food item, or playing with one sample of the item is a good strategy). When he approaches you, put the item in the cupboard and close the cupboard.
- In your classroom or home, put curtains over shelves.
- Put toys in boxes.

Assessing the Trainers

Phase III involves one trainer working with the student. Various people should act as trainer, so staff or family members can assess each other's performance. The trainer continues to arrange the environment effectively so that many orpportunities are created across the day for the student to request in a variety of settings and activities.

Discrimination begins by contrasting a highly reinforcing and a non-preferred or contextually irrelevant item. The new behavior is choosing a picture, so the trainer must provide social reinforcement within 1/2 second of the student reaching for the "correct" picture, and then provide tangible reinforcement once the exchange is completed.

The trainer should assess all aspects of the lessons if problems occur, including whether the highly reinforcing item is still reinforcing and whether the non-preferred or contextually irrelevant item is evoking a negative response. When the student makes an error, the trainer responds using the 4-Step Error Correction Procedure.

PHASE IIIA- high vs. distracter discrimination
• Arranges effective training environment
• Entices with both items
• Socially reinforces as soon as student touches correct picture
• Appropriate reinforcement with requested item
• Uses a variety of distracter items and a variety of target pictures

• Conducts error correction procedures correctly- high vs. non-desired
    ▪ Gives non-desired item
    ▪ Elicits negative response
    ▪ **Model**
    ▪ **Prompt**
    ▪ **Switch**
    ▪ **Repeat**
• Second error correction if necessary

• Moves pictures around on book (diagonal, vertical, horizontal)
• No insistence on speech

Once the student is discriminating between a picture of a high-preference item and a picture of a distracter item, the trainer begins teaching discrimination between pictures representing equally reinforcing items using correspondence checks. The trainer entices with both items, waits for the student to give a picture, and then conducts a correspondence check. If the student does not reach for the item corresponding to the picture he gave, the trainer blocks access and conducts the 4-Step Error Correction Procedure ending with a correspondence check.

The trainer systematically increases the number of pictures the student must discriminate among and continues to conduct correspondence checks. Once the student can discriminate among 5 pictures, the trainer teaches the student to look inside the book for the needed picture.

Phase IIIB multiple preferred discrimination
• Arranges effective training environment
• Entices with both items
• Conducts correspondence check

• Conducts error correction procedures correctly- high vs. high with correspondence check
  ▪ Prevents student from taking non-corresponding item
  ▪ Model picture of item reached for
  ▪ **Model**
  ▪ **Prompt**
  ▪ **Switch**
  ▪ **Repeat**
• Second error correction if necessary

• Moves pictures around on book (diagonal, vertical, horizontal)
• Teaches 3, 4, 5-way discrimination
• Uses a variety of target pictures in the 2-, 3-, 4-, or 5-way mix
• Teaches looking inside book
• No insistence on speech

Cross-Reference with Additional Skills

As the student begins learning to discriminate between symbols in his communication book, begin teaching him to answer, "Do you want this?" Introduce requesting help and requesting a break -using symbols that are visually distinctive if the student is not discriminating between many symbols. Now that the bank account is very full, begin introducing the concept of "wait." Use a visual signal and initially expect no more than a couple of seconds! Continue teaching the student to respond to a variety of visual directions, and as he masters several of these, incorporate them into a visual schedule. Continue using the visual reinforcement system—as the student masters various pictures, replace the actual object on the work card with the picture of the item.

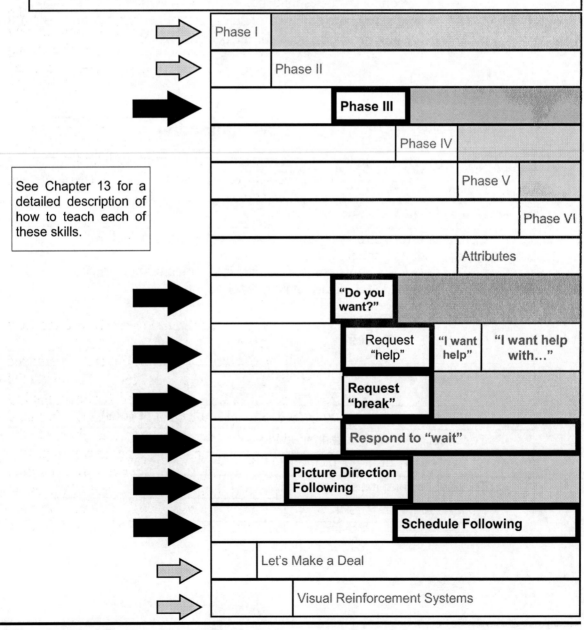

See Chapter 13 for a detailed description of how to teach each of these skills.

??..Frequently asked questions..??

1 **How do you determine when it is appropriate to begin the discrimination level (Phase III)?**

Because Phase II continues throughout all of PECS training, overlap between Phase II and Phase III will occur. For example, if a student has learned to go to the communicative partner to give the picture, but is still learning to go get his pictures, it is okay to begin the discrimination training. We begin discrimination training once the student has 5-10 pictures in his repertoire during Phase II. (Remember, these have been presented individually according to what currently is reinforcing!!). Each time a student masters a new skill throughout the rest of the protocol, reintroduce Phase II! Do NOT wait to begin discrimination training until the student is using 20 or more pictures singly. This will make introducing pairs of pictures in discrimination more "foreign" to the student, and, thus, too strange.

2 **How do you decide when to introduce new vocabulary?**

New vocabulary is added when the frequently conducted reinforcer assessment shows the need. The potential choices of pictures used in Phases I and II is unlimited as long as only one picture at a time is presented. In Phase III we continue to use these pictures but at the discrimination level at which the student is working. We find it helpful to conduct the reinforcer assessment and to use a vocabulary worksheet such as in Appendix D to get ideas for vocabulary for requesting. Remember to vary which pictures you present to the student during discrimination training!

3 My student "runs away" frequently in class, and I am concerned that if I allow him to get up during activities to go and get his communication book, he will actually try to run away. Can I skip this step to avoid this problem?

Remember, first of all, that you must determine *why* your student is running away and then teach a Functionally Equivalent Alternative Behavior. If running away continues to be a problem and is a threat to your student's safety, we suggest a compromise. We think being able to go and get your communication book is a crucial skill for ALL students to master. With students who have a history of running, though, we might have them carry their book from activity to activity so that they don't have to get up during an activity to get it. BUT! Because we must teach the student to "problem solve" arriving at a new activity without his communication book, we don't skip this skill. We teach it by arranging for a student to arrive at his activity without the book, and then having a physical prompter on hand to guide him to get his book. As a preventative measure, we keep the book in a location in the classroom on the other side from the exit door. This way, when the student gets out of his chair during an activity and heads in the direction of his book (not the door), we know we won't have to run after him.

4 How do you determine the number of symbols to be used during an activity?

If the student is in Phase I or Phase II of training, only one symbol is to be presented at a time. It is up to the trainer to determine, from the reinforcer assessment and from the natural routines, which picture should be made available at each point in an activity. If the child is in Phase III of training, the number of symbols is determined by the student's current discrimination abilities. Beyond Phase III, all pictures should be available to the student.

5 Do you use individual books or classroom-based systems?

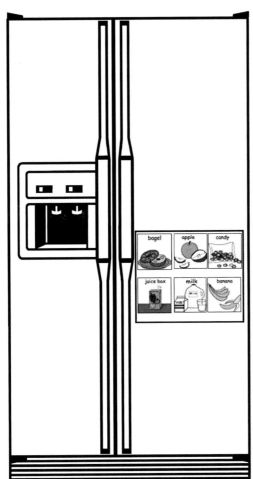

Each student should have his own communication book that goes with him wherever he goes. The teacher or parent should not be responsible for carrying the book from setting to setting—the student must learn to do so. Menus or room-based systems at home are extremely useful, too. These can be boards that contain vocabulary specific to the location. For example, in the bathroom, there might be a board containing pictures of soap, towel, and bath toys, etc. On the refrigerator, you could keep pictures of various food items. At school in the motor area hang a board containing pictures of the equipment. What is important to remember is that the student must have a system to take with him when he leaves the home or classroom where the center-based boards are located, so much of the vocabulary on these "menu" boards will be replicated in the child's personal vocabulary book.

One strategy we have found helpful in homes is to use pages within the communication binder as these "menu" boards that will be posted around the house. This way, when you leave the house, you merely have to collect the pages, snap them back in the book, and you're on your way!

Bright Ideas
(Phase III)

1. Even after a student masters discrimination, make sure that the board occasionally contains a picture of a non-preferred item. This functions as a periodic "check" on discrimination skills. If the student gives this picture and then reacts negatively to getting this item, you will know that he is not discriminating correctly.

2. Unless you are using commercially prepared pictures, making the pictures can be a time-consuming task. One strategy we have found helpful in a school or residential setting is to have monthly "Make and Take" parties. We gather family, friends, and staff in a central location, provide lots of materials (including printed pictures), and spend an hour or two putting pictures together. We take advantage of this time to talk about PECS and troubleshooting particular problems. In order for everyone to have access to these pictures, we do a "Make and Take" party one month and a "Make and Leave" party the next.

3. If you have more than one student in a classroom using PECS, assign each student a "PECS Manager." This person (any team member—teacher, para-professional, speech language pathologist, parent, etc.) is responsible for "maintaining" the PECS book by tracking which pictures it should contain, replacing lost or damaged pictures, and making new pictures as new vocabulary is being developed.

4. In order to keep up with the picture needs of students, in a classroom we find it helpful to establish a specific location where team members can jot down an idea for a new picture or a note about a picture that can be replaced. A unique spot on the blackboard, or a write-on/wipe-off board can serve this purpose. At the end of the day or week, the PECS Manager collects the information in order to make new pictures.

Monitoring Progress

D A T E	T R I A L	Discrimination Level (circle picture student gives)	negative reaction? Y or N	PICTURES
3/2	1	H + ⓓ	Y	cookie/stick
	2	Ⓗ + D		cookie/stick
	3	Ⓗ + D		cookie/stick
	4	H + ⓓ	Y	cookie/stick
	5	H + ⓓ	Y	cookie/stick
	6	H + ⓓ	Y	cookie/stick
	7	Ⓗ + D		cookie/stick
	8	Ⓗ + D		cookie/stick
	9	Ⓗ + D		cookie/stick
	10	Ⓗ + D		cookie/stick

H = Highly Preferred   D = Distracter

In this example the student is just beginning discrimination training so the trainer is probing his reaction to the distractor item (the stick). If this is the first discrimination trial lesson, the student essentially has a 50/50 chance of giving the correct picture, so it is important to see the negative reaction. The student initially gives the stick picture and reacts negatively when given the stick. His reactions are consistently negative when given the stick and by trial number 7, he begins to reliably give the correct picture.

Monitoring Progress

D A T E	T R I A L	Discrimination Level (circle item student gives)	negative reaction ? Y or N	PICTURES
3/2	1	(H)+ D		bubbles/ sock
	2	H +(D)	N	bubbles/ sock
	3	H +(D)	N	bubbles/ sock
	4	(H)+ D		bubbles/ clothespin
	5	H +(D)	Y	bubbles/ clothespin
	6	H +(D)	Y	bubbles/ clothespin
	7	(H)+ D		bubbles/ spoon
	8	(H)+ D		bubbles/ spoon
	9	H +(D)	Y	bubbles/ spoon
	10	(H)+ D		bubbles/ spoon

H = Highly Preferred   D = Distracter

In this example, the student is beginning discrimination training. The first time she exchanges the picture of the contextually inappropriate item, she does not have a negative reaction to receiving the sock. This happens again on the next trial, so the trainer selects another item (clothespin) to use as the contextually inappropriate distractor item. The second item does elicit a negative response, so the trainer continues to use it on the next two trials. The trainer then switches to a different distracter.

Monitoring Progress

Date	Trial	Discrim. Level	Correspon- dence check	Distance to Trainer	Distance to book	Item Selected
3/2	1	2 P	+	8ft	room	walkman
	2	2P	+	8ft	room	pretzel
	3	2P + D	+	8 ft	room	pretzel
	4	2P + D	+	5 ft	room	pretzel
3/3	5	2P	+	3 ft.	0	puzzle
	6	2P + D	+	0	0	puzzle
	7	3P	+	0	0	puzzle
	8	3P	-	0	0	juice
	9	3P	+	0	0	juice
	10	3P	+	0	0	juice

P= Preferred item   D= Distractor (non preferred/blank/negative/neutral)
For correspondence check: "+"= took same item as requested   "-" = took incorrect item

In this example, at the end of one day the student was discriminating between two preferred plus one distractor item with correct correspondence. The trainer was also incorporating some distance training due to the student's success. The next day the trainer initially simplified the task for the first trial and the student correctly discriminated between 2 preferred items with correct correspondence. He had one correspondence error when switching from puzzle to juice but was correct again on the next trial.

7

Phase IV

Sentence Structure

Phase IV - Sentence Structure

Terminal Objective: *The student requests present and non-present items using a multi-word phrase by going to the book, picking up a picture/symbol of "I want," putting it on a sentence strip, picking out the picture of what is wanted, putting it on the sentence strip, removing the strip from the communication board, approaching the communicative partner, and giving the sentence strip to him. By the end of this phase the student typically has twenty or more pictures on the communication board and is communicating with a variety of partners.*

Skinner (1957) referred to these requests as "**MANDS,**" to the comments as "**TACTS,**" and tones of voice, gestures, eye gaze, etc. as "**AUTOCLITICS.**" See Chapter 15 for more details.

Rationale: So far in PECS, students have learned to request a variety of desired items from a variety of communicative partners across various settings. The communication skill still to be addressed is **commenting.** As typically developing children learn language, they generally acquire comments at the same time as requests. The two functions co-develop and are used with roughly equal frequency. The typically developing speaking child who is using a single word a t a time (e.g. is not yet combining words into short phrases) lets the listener know whether he is commenting versus requesting by combining the spoken words with intonation and gestures. The requesting word is accompanied by a "demanding" tone of voice and reaching toward or pointing to the desired object. The commenting word is accompanied by an exclamatory tone of voice, pointing, and looking back and forth between the listener and the item of interest. Children using PECS, because they are not speaking, are unable to provide the listener with tone-of-voice cues. Also, these children, because of their social deficits, ordinarily do not develop the common reaching and pointing gestures or eye gaze. Consequently, in planning to teach commenting, we must anticipate that our students need to learn alternative methods of letting listeners know if the pictures being exchanged are to request or to comment.

In short, our students need to learn two very important skills: a new communicative function and a way to mark this new function and the original function as either a comment or a request. We will teach the students to use a simple phrase or "sentence-starter" such as "I want," "I see," or "It is" in order for their messages to be interpreted correctly. Because we teach one new skill at a time, we will teach the student to use a Sentence-starter within the already mastered communicative function; in Phase IV, we will teach the student to combine pictures to form the phrase "I want _____." We will use a single picture to represent "I want." Separating the "I" from the "want" at this point in time is not necessary because we are not teaching the concept of "I" vs. "you," "he," "she," etc. To maintain the physical approach and exchange, we will teach the student to build this phrase by putting the two icons onto a sentence strip and to exchange the entire strip.

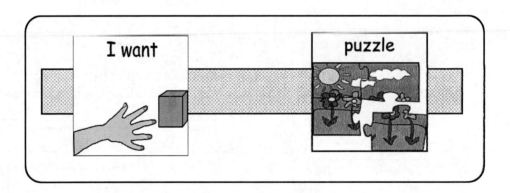

Sequence to be learned:

1. Get book
2. Remove "I want" icon from book
3. Put "I want" icon on sentence strip
4. Remove reinforcer picture from book
5. Put reinforcer picture on sentence strip
6. Remove sentence strip
7. Give sentence strip to communicative partner

The Structured Training Environment

Setting

For structured training, have available the communication book, a "sentence" strip" that can be Velcroed to the communication board and to which pictures can be attached, an "I want" picture, reinforcing objects/activities, and the corresponding pictures. Because the student's vocabulary is growing, the pictures on the communication board can be arranged in broad categories for easier retrieval.

notes

1. **No verbal prompts used during this Phase.**
2. **Use "Backward Chaining" to teach sentence strip construction.**
3. **In addition to structured training trials, create many opportunities for spontaneous requesting during functional activities each day.**
4. **Continue "correspondence" checks when adding vocabulary.**
5. **Simplify some aspects of the lesson while teaching the new behavior, then re-incorporate.**

Teaching Strategy

Backward Chaining: When the last step in a sequence of steps is most strongly associated with access to a reinforcer, that behavior is the most easily learned step. The Backward Chaining strategy teaches a chain, or sequence, of behaviors by reinforcing the last step, then the last two steps, then the last three steps, and so on. (See Sulzer-Azaroff and Mayer, 1991.) The trainer provides assistance to complete the sequence of steps and fades the assistance first at the "back end" of the chain.

The sequence in Phase IV is: get book, remove "I want" picture from book, place on sentence strip, remove reinforcer-picture from book, place on sentenced strip, remove sentence strip, and exchange sentence strip. The step that we initially will target, therefore, is exchanging the strip. We will provide the needed assistance at the beginning of the chain through the end, and fade this assistance from the end of the chain.

Step 1: Adding reinforcer picture to sentence strip.

The "I want" picture is attached to the left side of the sentence strip before the lesson begins. To simplify other aspects of the lesson, you might want to reduce the number of pictures on the front of the book. So far, when the student wants something, he will let you know by removing the corresponding picture from the book and reaching toward you with it. **This is an initiation and we must continue to wait for this!** Because the student has initiated, it is okay for the communicative partner to prompt the student by physically guiding him to put the picture onto the sentence strip next to the "I want" picture. Then guide the student to give you the sentence strip (now containing "I want" and a single picture). Respond by reading the strip to the student while providing access to the item. Turn the strip around to face the student, and point to each picture as you say it's name. Do this quickly, however! By the time the student reaches Phase IV, he is able to tolerate slightly longer delays in access

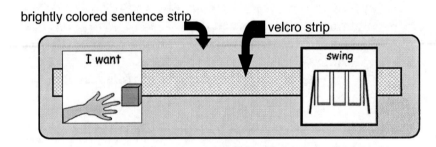

brightly colored sentence strip

velcro strip

I want

swing

to the reinforcer, but don't draw out the "read-back" too long at this point in training. Over several trials, fade your physical assistance—the goal is for the student to independently add the reinforcer icon to the strip and to then exchange the strip.

The new skill is to put the reinforcer picture on the sentence strip. Therefore, reinforce this behavior the moment the student engages in it. As soon as the student independently puts the picture on the strip, provide some social feedback (i.e., "Yes," "Uh-huh!"). Then once he exchanges the strip, provide further reinforcement by giving him the item he requested. Mastery of this step is reached when the student is able to attach the picture of the desired item to the sentence strip (which already contains the "I want" picture), approach the communicative partner, and give the entire sentence strip with no prompting.

Reinforcement Reminder

Step 2: Manipulating the "I want" picture.

Move the "I want" picture to the left side of the communication book. At this point, the student will initiate by attempting to remove the reinforcer picture from the book. In order to teach the student to construct the sentence in the correct order, we want to encourage him to put the "I want" picture on the strip first.   Therefore, when the child reaches for the reinforcer-picture (this is the **initiation!**), <u>block him from doing so</u>, and physically prompt him to remove the "I want" picture and put it on the strip. Once this has been completed, the book and strip look like it did in Step 1, so the student should complete the construction and exchange independently. Continue responding to the student by reading the sentence strip. Fade all physical prompts over time so that the student learns to construct and exchange the sentence strip independently.

The new skill now is independently picking up the "I want" icon first. The first time the student reaches for the "I want" icon before the reinforcer icon, praise him. Then, after he completes the sentence strip and the exchange, provide access to the requested item.

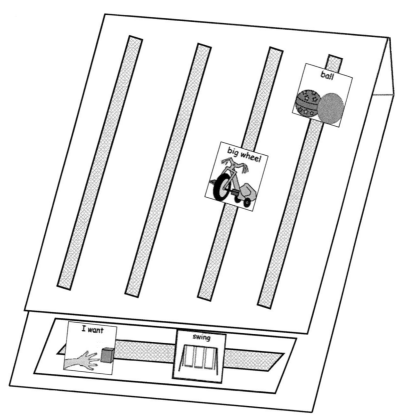

Step 3: "Reading" the sentence strip.

Sometimes, children develop a pattern whereby they construct the sentence strip, bring it to you, put it into your hand and walk away. The interaction between the student and the communicative partner becomes fleeting– the student rushes off as if waiting for "room service" now to be delivered! We think it is important for a student to continue hearing the words spoken, so teaching him to point to each picture while we read the strip is one way to do this.

We find it helpful to maintain the student's interaction if he points to the pictures on the sentence strip as you "read" them to him. We teach "reading" the strip with physical prompting using a backward chaining strategy. The communicative partner provides this assistance — a physical prompter is not necessary because the student's initiation is intact (he constructs and brings you the strip). When the student independently constructs and puts the sentence strip into the your hand, turn the strip around to him and physically prompt him to point to each picture while you "read" each picture. Over time, fade this assistance (from the end of the sequence) until the student independently exchanges the strip, waits for the communicative partner to turn it to him, and then points to each picture while the communicative partner reads.

> Do not attempt to teach this until the student has mastered constructing and exchanging the sentence strip.

Once the student has mastered pointing while you read the strip, a further step we add is providing the student with an opportunity to speak during the exchange. We teach this using a Constant Time Delay strategy.

Teaching Strategy

Delayed Prompting/ *Constant* Time Delay:
This strategy involves pairing a prompt with the natural cue you want to eventually control the final behavior. Present the natural cue and after a fixed, pre-determined length of time, if the student has not exhibited the desired behavior, provide the additional "helping" prompt. This "helping" prompt historically has been an effective prompt, so the student is likely to engage in the desired behavior. This strategy works when we differentially reinforce the behavior if the student engages in it prior to the delivery of the "helping" prompt.

Ideally, we want the student to construct and exchange the strip and then say the words with the communicative partner during the "read back." To encourage this, we take advantage of many students' desire to see familiar routines completed. If we pause while reading the strip, we often see children looking at us—waiting for us to say the next word. When we don't, many of the students "fill in the blank" by saying the word themselves! Using a pre-determined delay length (typically 3-5 seconds), the trainer provides the initial prompt, pauses to allow for the desired behavior, and then completes the sequence. Specifically, the communicative partner will turn the strip to the child, wait for the student to point to the first picture, read, "I want," wait for him to point to the next picture, and then pause. This is when we typically hear students begin talking. If the student does say or vocally approximate the word, have a party!! If he doesn't within the 3-5 second delay, the communicative partner says the word and reinforces the exchange by providing access to the requested item. Notice the use of *differential reinforcement* with this strategy. If the student speaks, he gets a larger "serving" of the reinforcer (more of an item, longer time with the item, or more social praise). If he doesn't, he still gets the reinforcer because he did effectively communicate with us.

Ideally, the communicative partner then "backs up" in the sequence to encourage the student to "read" the entire strip. Next, she would turn the strip to the student, wait for him to point to the "I want" icon, and then pause to allow an opportunity to say, "I want." What should come to control the speaking is first pointing to the picture, and later, having the strip turned to face him.

> Use differential reinforcement when the student speaks—he receives what he requests, but receives more if he also talks.

Never insist on speech within PECS. PECS is an acceptable communication strategy for the child, and withholding access to a requested item until the student attempts to say or imitate the word may undermine the student's communication. It may result in frustration on the part of the child and, most likely, in the child discontinuing communicating. USE DIFFERENTIAL REINFORCEMENT at this point in PECS! If a student makes an exchange but does not speak, he should get the item or activity he asked for. If, however, he does speak, give him MORE of the item or allow him to engage in the activity for a LONGER period of time.

Errorless Learning:

- When the backward chaining strategy is used to teach sentence strip construction, the student should not put the pictures on the strip in the wrong order. Don't worry if he infrequently does this early in sentence strip use, though. Unobtrusively switch them around for the student as you are turning the strip around to read. A student's age is important to consider. Left-to-right sequencing is developmentally difficult for very young children, so expecting correct placement would be inappropriate. This is an excellent functional context, however, in which to teach left-to-right sequencing.

- If the student frequently puts the "I want" and noun picture in reverse order on the sentence strip, when he hands you the strip with the pictures in the wrong order, pretend not to understand what he wants and put the pictures and strip back on the communication book. Often, this is a *natural cue* for the student to correct his error.

- If the student continues to make this error, it is an error in a sequential task. Consequently, we would respond to this using "**Backstepping.**"

Error Correction

Sequential error: Backstepping: This involves moving the child back into the sequence of assembling the sentence strip to the last point where he was correct and then prompting him through the rest of the sequence. For many students, this involves going back to the beginning of the trial—taking the strip apart, putting the pictures back on the book, and then prompting the student to reach for the "I want" picture first and put it into the correct location on the strip. Then differentially reinforce this construction by providing access to the reinforcer but on a smaller scale. On subsequent opportunities, provide enough physical assistance as described earlier to teach the student to assemble the strip in the correct sequence.

The lesson to be learned is that constructing the strip correctly the first go 'round is better!

The Relaxed Training Environment

Setting

Everywhere!! PECS should be in use, now, in virtually all environments, across a variety of activities and with many communicative partners. This should include the community—the "real world." Even very young children can learn to ask Mom or an instructor for french fries when at the fast food restaurant, and older children, adolescents, and adults should learn to order the fries on their own!

At this point during PECS training the student will have become quite independent at communicating with a wide variety of people—both trainers and "lay" people. Continue to assess the environment and create communicative opportunities. Continue the "STOP, DROP & TALK" opportunities across the day, and across a variety of activities.

Add pictures to the front of the book. If you simplified the front of the book early in Phase IV training, remember to "unsimplify" the front of the book once the student masters constructing the sentence strip. Continue keeping the most frequently used pictures on the front of the book and organizing the pictures inside the book.

Re-introduce Phase II issues. Don't forget to incorporate Phase II skills that you simplified. Make sure that the student can

- go get his communication book in order to construct the sentence strip
- go to the communicative partner
- communicate with a variety of communicative partners
- communicate in a variety of environments
- communicate within a variety of activities

See Chapter 12 for a detailed discussion on strategies for teaching communication across the day.

To conduct PECS during a variety of activities, assess the activity to determine what is reinforcing to the student within the activity. For example, during art, one student might like to use markers and another might like to cut and paste. These preferences can become vocabulary items if the trainer leading the activity "sabotages" the activity by arranging for a particular item to be missing.

Remember, though, that these sabotage strategies only work if the student actually wants the item within the task.

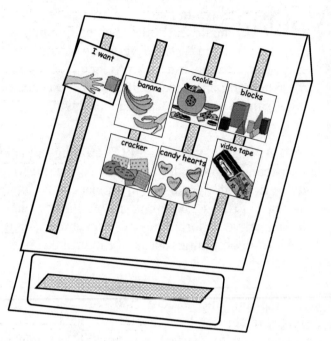

A concern professionals and families sometimes voice is the speed at which a student uses PECS. In order to facilitate the most rapid construction of the sentence strip, we find it helpful to arrange the student's communication book so that the "I want" sentence-starter is on the outside cover on the left side. We continue to keep the most frequently used pictures on the outside cover of the book, and we continue organizing pictures inside the communication book according to categories. The student should be able to flip through the pages in order to find the appropriate picture. We have designed communication binders that have an extension at the bottom where the sentence strip is kept. This allows the student to have access to the strip while he flips through the pages of the book rather than having either to hold the sentence strip while looking in the book for a picture or flip back and forth to the front cover if that is where the sentence strip is kept.

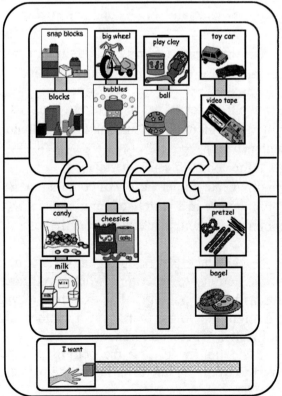

Requesting Multiple Items

Another time-saving strategy is requesting multiple items. During art, rather than making two separate requests—construct and exchange the strip, "I want paper," then construct and exchange the strip, "I want markers,"—the student could ask for both within one request— "I want paper markers."

This lesson does not have to be mastered before moving on in the training protocol, but, can be addressed as the student develops more vocabulary. For example, you might not teach this lesson until the student has begun using attributes (see next chapter) and is working in Phases V and VI.

As your student becomes more and more proficient with PECS, you also could teach the student to use the word or symbol for "and" in this request and to request more than two items!

Reducing Picture Size

You've probably noticed that your student's book is getting quite full! If this is the case, consider reducing the size of the pictures in order to put more in the same-size book. Begin by reducing the size of just a few picture—we typically start with the most frequently-used pictures. If the student uses these with no errors, continue reducing the remaining pictures. The types of errors you might see when you begin reducing the picture size include ignoring the smaller pictures or discriminating incorrectly between the smaller pictures. Create lessons during which the student is motivated to use the smaller pictures and conduct correspondence checks when he begins using the smaller ones to ensure that he is discriminating correctly. If your student makes continued errors, consider that you have reduced the pictures too much and try an intermediate step.

> You might even have to get your student a longer sentence strip!

Saying, "NO"

By now, many trainers are beginning to wonder if they can say "no" to a student's request. For example, during a trip to the mall, it is not always feasible or appropriate to provide a student with the "swings" he requests. Early in training, we stress trying to honor as many requests as possible so that the student learns the new behavior of communicating. At this point in training, though, it is perfectly acceptable to begin telling the student "no." This can be done in several ways, many of which involve the use of visual cues.

1. Empty containers: Showing the student that the bowl of chips is empty is a natural way of saying "no." Often the student who sees the empty bowl will find something else he likes. It might be useful to keep empty containers around so that if the student asks for bubbles, the trainer can show him the empty bottle.

2. Offer alternatives. Show the student what he **can** have at this point in time. Show him either the actual items or the pictures he has in his book.

3. "Let's Make a Deal" This strategy is one that we incorporate into all of our classrooms and homes from the beginning of training. It involves teaching the student that getting access to the requested item is often one-half of a deal that can be created between the student and the communicative partner. For example, if a student asks for a video, the trainer might first ask the student to complete a simple task such as putting the last piece of a puzzle into the puzzle board. Over time, these deals can be "stretched" so that the student learns to do more in order to access a particular reinforcer. We integrate the deals with use of a token-like system. Of course, it is important to remember that many requests should be granted immediately, with no deal-making, so as not to undermine the student's communication.

For more information on "Let's Make a Deal," refer to chapter 13 in this manual and to *The Pyramid Approach to Education in Autism* (Bondy, 1996, and Bondy & Sulzer-Azaroff, 2001).

4. "Not right now" This can be signaled to the student by putting the pictures of currently unavailable items on a special page in his communication book or by putting a universal "no" symbol on the pictures of unavailable items. Initially, the student may not understand what this symbol means. If you are consistent with your response to him when he makes a request using a picture with the "no" symbol on it, he eventually will learn that he can ask you hundreds of times for the item, but as long as the "no" symbol is on the picture, you won't give him the item.

5. Scheduling access to a reinforcer: If a student is using a picture schedule, the trainer could take the picture the student has used to request a currently non-available item and add it to the schedule so that the student will know when that item will be available.

Refer to Chapter 11 for a detailed description of teaching schedule following and responding to "Wait."

6. Teach the student to "wait." Of course, this will only work when you can definitely provide access to the item in a reasonable time frame! Don't use this strategy if you really can't give the item to the student.

7. Say, "NO!" This is a "real world" lesson and is one that all students have to learn! Of course, our students will most likely respond similarly to ALL students—that is, initially they won't respond well! So, be prepared for a tantrum or other inappropriate behavior. Remember, reinforce appropriate responding to "No," or any of the other strategies.

TAKE NOTICE !

Do not take pictures away from or hide pictures from students!!

We can't take words away from speaking students. Even when they nag us, we do not tape their mouths shut! Students using PECS have the same rights as speaking children! Taking pictures away from students using PECS is unethical.

Assessing the Trainers

During Phase IV, the trainer teaches two separate skills. Initially she teaches the student to construct the sentence strip using "backward chaining." Appropriate reinforcement is critical, so the trainer provides social reinforcement the moment the new skill is engaged in, and access to the requested item the moment the child completes the physical exchange. Second, the trainer teaches the student to "read" the sentence strip. Once the student has mastered Phase IV, the trainer immediately should make plans to begin teaching attributes.

PHASE IV
• Begins with "I want" already on sentence strip
• Waits for initiation
• Physically guides student to put R+ picture on strip and exchange
• Fades physical guidance to put R+ picture on strip and exchange
• Verbal praise + turns strip around and "reads" sentence
• Teaches assembly of entire strip- backward chaining
• Reinforces new behavior within ½ second
• Appropriately reinforces with tangible item
• Uses physical assistance to teach student to point while strip is being "read"
• Uses delay (3-5 seconds) in "reading" strip
• Differentially reinforces if student speaks
• Avoids verbal prompting
• Conducts error correction for incorrect picture sequence
• Organizes communication book appropriately
• Does not insist on or drill speech imitation/production during PECS

Cross-Reference with Additional Skills

When you begin sentence structure, continue addressing all of the skills previously introduced. The deals become more complex—expect more work per token or add more tokens to the total number to be earned. Continue teaching the student to indicate, "Yes," or "No," to "Do you want this?" Continue teaching requesting a break and perhaps visually representing to the student how many breaks he can take. Continue gradually increasing the amount of time the student waits, keeping in mind how long typically developing peers wait!

Once the student can construct a sentence strip independently, incorporate his "help" symbol so that he uses the sentence, "I want help" to request assistance.

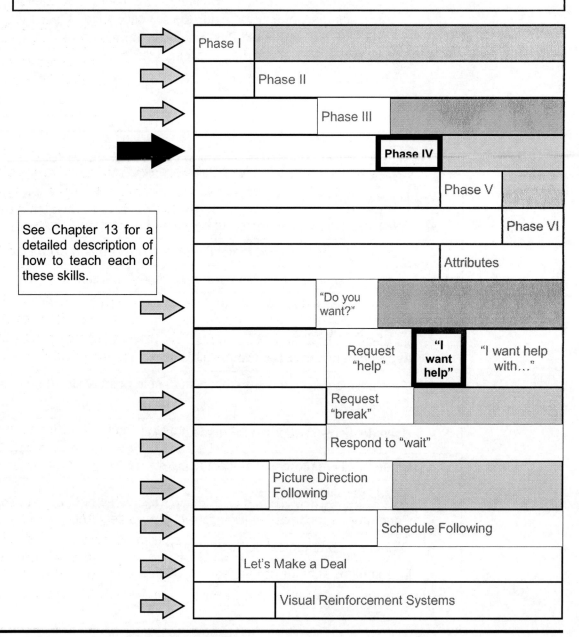

See Chapter 13 for a detailed description of how to teach each of these skills.

??..Frequently asked questions..??

1 Is it okay if my student puts the reinforcer-icon on the sentence strip before he puts the "I want" icon on the strip, but gets them in the correct order?

At this stage of training, we accept this response as correct as long as the student continues to "read" or point to the pictures in the correct order. Pay careful attention to this behavior later in the training protocol (attributes and beyond) when the student is using more than two icons. Then it will be important to put the pictures on the strip in the right order. If the student loses sight of this order as he adds more and more pictures to the strip, then he will need to be taught to put the pictures on the strip starting with the Sentence-starter icon. Remember, this is a sequential error and will require the Backstep Error Correction Procedure.

Putting the pictures onto the strip by beginning with the Sentence-starter icon also becomes important as literacy skills develop. If the student will be learning to write or type sentences, then he will need to do this from the beginning of the sentence in a left to right sequence.

Some students use both hands to create the sentence—they will pull the "I want" icon with one hand and the reinforcer icon with the other hand, but at the same time. They then add them to the sentence strip at the same time and in the correct order. This, too, is acceptable. In fact, it saves the student time and helps him to get the sentence strip into the communicative partner's hand that much more quickly!

2 I think my student has mastered Phase IV, but today he approached me with a single picture. Is this acceptable or should I insist that he use the sentence strip?

This is a debatable issue and one that will require your best judgment. On the one hand, at this stage in training, you know when your student approaches you with a single picture that he is requesting the item—there is very little chance of misinterpreting his message. On the other hand, we taught the student to use the sentence strip as a first step toward teaching longer sentences AND toward differentiating requests from comments. If your goal is to continue teaching longer sentences and to introduce commenting, your student must maintain the ability to request using the sentence strip. Accepting a simpler response from the student will undermine his future use of the more complex skill (use of the sentence strip).

One solution to this dilemma is to respond to your student as if you don't understand. When he approaches you with the single picture, look at him questioningly and then say, "I don't understand. What do you mean?" Ideally, he will realize his error and correct it on his own. If he does not do so, then Backstep him by putting the picture back on his book and providing extra assistance to make a complete request. If he reaches for the single picture again, block this response and gesture to the "I want" icon. Use differential reinforcement in responding to this assisted request.

Another solution is to purposefully misinterpret his message. When your student approaches you with a single picture, interpret it as a comment and respond accordingly ("Book? Yes, I see that book over there, too! It's one of my favorites!"). Again, if the student self-corrects, reinforce the correction. If he doesn't, use the Backstep procedure.

3 Do we teach PECS in order to teach speech?

Absolutely not!! We teach students to use PECS in order to teach them functional communication skills. These skills start with learning spontaneously to ask for things that are rewarding to the individual learning PECS. We believe it is important to teach everyone to initiate functional communication skills within a social context. For an individual who does not have these skills the communicative modality to be used is less important than the acquisition of the fundamental skill. Therefore, we do not teach PECS as a way to learn to speak; we teach PECS as a way to learn to communicate. We have been very pleased with the high proportion of young students who acquire speech after using PECS for a period of time. The acquisition of speech can be viewed as a wonderful by-product of the approach and not its direct focus. Even for children and adults who do not acquire speech, the acquisition of skills within PECS leads to a much more communicatively successful person.

We continue to conduct imitation and vocal imitation lessons at other times—we don't mix PECS at the same time, though!

4 When children begin to speak, when is PECS discontinued?

For those children who develop speech after being introduced to PECS, the general pattern is to see imitation of words and phrases while the student is using the sentence strip. Recall that we suggest using a delayed prompt procedure while "reading" back the sentence strip. This strategy tends to promote "filling in the blank." As the child begins to complete more of the phrase we have found that some of them begin to approach us with the sentence strip and say the entire sentence without exchanging the strip! The issue then becomes whether or not the student can effectively communicate without PECS. Essentially, we assess whether or not a student's spoken language has "caught up with" his PECS language. We do this across several criteria. **If you remove access to PECS before all current skills are replaced by speech, you take skills away from the student—this is unethical!**

See Chapter 14 for an in-depth discussion of "giving up" PECS.

5 Who takes the pictures off of the sentence strip and puts them back on/in the book?

Initially, the communicative partner should take the pictures off of the sentence strip, and return them and the strip to the board so that it is ready for the next use. Requiring the PECS user to do so unnecessarily slows the communicative process. Some children insist on being the ones to put their pictures back, though! This is fine. Eventually, as students become integrated into community activities, they will need to learn to take the sentence strip back from the "lay communicative partner," so that pictures and sentence strips don't get lost.

6 What about articulation training?

If your student is mispronouncing sounds or words as he speaks along with PECS, consult a speech-language pathologist who will assess whether or not your student would benefit from speech therapy. Do not drill on correct pronunciation within PECS, though! If the student mispronounces a word while "reading" the sentence strip, it's okay to provide an appropriate model and to pause for a second or two to see if the student attempts to imitate your pronunciation. If he does, use differential reinforcement. If he does not do so, however, do not withhold the requested item!

Many speech language pathologists who conduct articulation therapy with students using PECS inventory the current PECS vocabulary and teach sounds that are frequently used (keeping in mind the typical age and sequence for sound development). Sometimes articulation lessons are difficult for the student, so to avoid any negative association with PECS use, do not use the same symbols or pictures in articulation therapy as you do in PECS.

Bright Ideas
(Phase IV)

1. Use a sturdy sentence strip! It will be used for virtually every communicative interaction from this point forward, so it will be subject to much wear and tear. Make or buy a sentence strip that will survive this frequent use. We use sturdy plastic strips rather than laminated strips of paper that tend to curl and peel after a few days of use.

2. Make the sentence strip a different color than the student's PECS book. This helps distinguish it when the child is learning to put the strip together.

3. Continue using "activity boards" or mini-communication boards throughout your classroom or home that contain vocabulary specific to a particular lesson. For example, we might use an activity board during Morning Circle for the students to request a favorite song. We might use another activity board during art. This board would have pictures of the various materials available for the particular art activity. Remember to include a sentence strip and "I want" icon on each of these activity boards if your student once your student begins Phase IV.

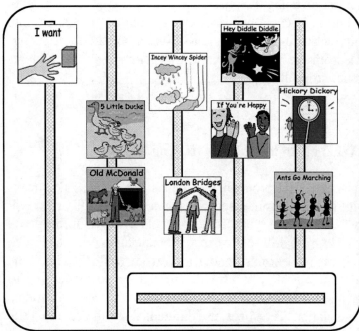

Monitoring Progress

Date	Trial	Put picture on strip	Put "I want" on strip	Exchange strip	Point to pictures	Correspondence Checks
12/12	1	NA	FP	FP	NA	NA
	2	NA	FP	FP	NA	NA
	3	NA	PP	+	NA	NA
	4	NA	+	+	NA	NA
	5	NA	+	+	NA	NA
	6	NA	+	+	NA	NA
	7	FP	+	+	NA	NA
	8	FP	+	+	NA	NA
	9	PP	+	+	NA	NA
	10	PP	+	+	NA	NA

These data are from a student's first Phase IV lesson. The sentence strip has been added to the bottom of the book, and an "I want" picture has been Velcroed to the left side of the sentence strip. When the trainer created a communicative opportunity, the student picked up the picture of the item and began to reach to the communicative partner. The communicative partner intercepted the reach and physically prompted the student to put the picture on the sentence strip. She then physically prompted him to exchange the entire strip. Note that "NA" (Not Applicable) is marked in the "I want," the "point" and the "correspondence checks" column as these skills are not addressed at this time. Over the course of trials 2-4 the communicative partner was able to fade the physical assistance, and the student independently attached the reinforcer picture to the strip. On trial 7 the communicative partner moved the "I want" picture off the sentence strip and when the student reaches for the reinforcer picture, she physically prompts him to first remove the "I want" picture and put it on the strip. Once he has done this, the student independently completes constructing the sentence strip and exchanges it.

Phase IV

Monitoring Progress

Date	Trial	Put "I want" on strip	Put picture on strip	Ex-change strip	Point to pictures	Correspon-dence Checks
2/12	1	+	+	+	P	NA
	2	+	+	+	P	NA
	3	+	+	+	+	NA
	4	+	+	+	+	NA
	5	+	+	+	+	+
	6	+	+	+	+	+
	7					
	8					
	9					
	10					

This student has mastered assembling the sentence strip. He is learning to assist in the "read back" of the strip. During trials 1 and 2, he needed physical assistance to point to/tap each picture while the communicative partner read it back. The teacher did not require a correspondence check at the end of this trial, as the delay to the reinforcer would have been too long. On the third trial the student independently completed the assembly, the exchange, and the pointing. On the next trial he did so again, so the teacher added a correspondence check to assess discrimination skills now that the student has mastered sentence strip construction

Once the student has mastered Phase IV, the training protocol divides along two paths. Along one, the student continues through Phases V and VI leading to commenting. The other path, however, teaches the student to use descriptive vocabulary and vocabulary regarding things other than highly preferred items and activities. **The two paths should be taught concurrently!!** We first will describe teaching attributes, but keep in mind that while you are creating and implementing lessons to teach attributes, you also should be creating and implementing lessons to teach Phases V and VI. So, the objective for some lessons is Phase V and then Phase VI skills, while other lessons during the day are devoted to teaching attributes and additional vocabulary. In the future, new lessons will combine the skills learned along each path. The student eventually should be able to incorporate attributes into these additional communication skills.

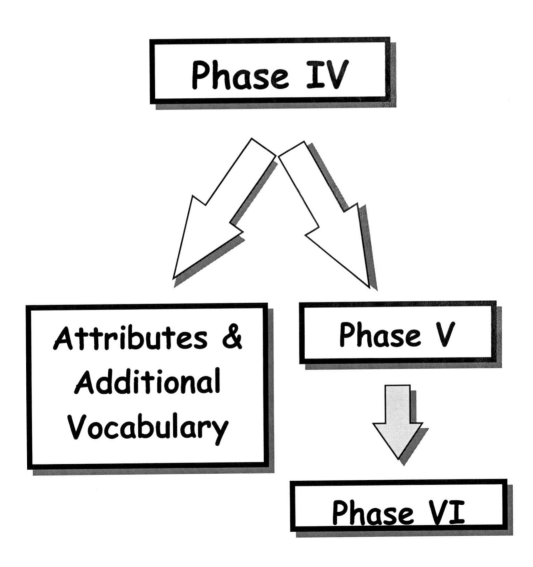

8

Attributes

Attributes

> **Terminal Objective:** *The student requests present and non-present items by going to his communication book, constructing a sentence strip containing an "I want" icon, an attribute icon and a reinforcer icon and then exchanging the strip. The student uses a variety of attribute icons and combines attributes to formulate sentences containing more than three icons.*

Rationale:

We often have observed many students to be very selective in what they want. When offered a handful of candies, one student meticulously picks out the red ones. When offered a long pretzel stick versus a short one, another student always selects the long pretzel. While building a tower of blocks, the student carefully selects a square block to place next on the tower. Each of these students is indicating awareness about certain features of various objects- features that can be thought of as attributes of the object. The student who picks out red candies may never have had a single "color" lesson, yet he is responsive to colors. In such situations, we take advantage of the student's skill in using PECS to make requests to teach the student to use attributes to refine or clarify his request.

Must the student have mastered/learned these concepts "receptively" prior to using them "productively" within a PECS request? <u>NO!</u>
There is no evidence that a student must be able to respond to the direction, "Touch blue" before he can learn to ask for something blue. Teaching a student to respond to "touch blue" is not teaching the concept of color. If you have observed that a student always builds his block tower by beginning with blue blocks, then you have observed a student who "knows" or sees color differences. Touching blue in response to "touch blue," OR asking for a blue block are both ways a student can **indicate to us** that he can see the difference between colors. Especially for children with autism, asking for "blue" is a more motivating way to indicate that he can see the difference between colors, so we begin with this task.

The Structured Training Environment

notes

1. No verbal prompts!
2. Conduct reinforcer assessments frequently.
3. Use a variety of trainers.
4. In addition to structured training trials, create many opportunities for spontaneous requesting during functional activities each day.
5. Teach multiple exemplars of each concept.

Teaching Strategy

Backward Chaining: The first skill learned in using attributes is to construct a three-icon sentence. This is a sequential lesson, so use Backward Chaining to teach this. The sequence is: get book, remove "I want" picture from book, place on sentence strip, remove attribute icon from book, place on sentence strip, remove reinforcer picture from book, place on sentence strip, remove sentence strip, and exchange sentence strip. We provide the needed assistance at the beginning of the chain through the end, and fade this assistance from the end of the chain.

Teaching Strategy

Discrimination Training within a Discrete Trial Format. Use this strategy to teach the student to discriminate between icons representing the specific attributes being taught. This will involve creating lessons similar to those used in Phase III in which the initial discrimination involves icons representing a preferred item and a non-preferred item. Over time, we use correspondence checks to teach discrimination between icons representing a variety of preferred items.

Reinforcer Assessment: Determine which attributes are important to the student.

The critical first step in teaching attributes is identifying when a particular attribute is important to the student. If the student does not care which color cookie he gets, then he is not going to be motivated to learn how to get a particular color of cookie. Survey the student's current vocabulary and determine whether a particular size, color, shape, etc. item is more reinforcing. Think back to Phase III when you conducted correspondence checks for a particular item. When one item on the tray was Fruit Loops® did the student specifically take only purple ones? When conducting correspondence checks with markers, did you notice that the student always took the green one? If so, then that is a good indication that color, in regard to Fruit Loops® or markers, is important to the student. Because the student is motivated to get a specific color of Fruit Loops® or marker, we begin teaching the student about colors in the context of requesting a specific Fruit Loops® or marker.

We don't necessarily begin attribute lessons by teaching about colors. Some children demonstrate to us that size is important to them. Have you noticed that a student always reaches for the biggest piece of cookie to eat or the biggest ball to play with? In this case, size would be important and motivating within a communication lesson. Some students prefer a specific texture of item, a specific temperature of food, or a particular shape of cookie.

When we begin teaching attributes, we must use items that are identical except for the targeted concept. For example, Fruit Loops® look alike except for their color, so this would be an appropriate item. We would not use items that vary along two dimensions such as an Oreo® cookie and a Lorna Doon® cookie because these two items vary along two dimensions—color and shape. Also, we would not use two items such as a green marker vs. a blue crayon. In this case, the student would only have to ask for marker vs. crayon. When teaching attributes, the following chart might be helpful to complete when determining which attribute to begin teaching.

Concept	Current Reinforcers						
	Wagon/ scooter	Massager	Cookies	Legos	Shoelace licorice	Ball	Cereal
Size	Prefers child –size (big) to doll size (little)		Prefers big	Prefers big ones (Duplo)	Prefers long ones	Prefers playground ball to super ball	
Color			Likes black (Oreos)		Prefers yellow and green		Prefers purple (Fruit Loops)
Shape			Round	Prefers rectangle ones			Circle (Fruit Loops)
Texture						Likes the "bumpy" ball in OT	
Speed	Likes to be pushed or pulled fast	Likes the fast speed setting				Likes to have ball rolled slowly to him	
Body Parts		Likes it on his arms/ legs, but not on his tummy					
Action						Likes to roll, kick, catch. Does not like to throw	
Position			Chips Ahoy vs. Oreo cookie in target location			Preferred vs. non-preferred ball in target location	Preferred vs. non-preferred in target location

Step 1. Three-picture sentence construction (No discrimination between icons).

Create a situation during which the student is likely to want a particular item. Simplify the front of the communication book to contain only the "I want" picture, the target attribute picture, and the desired item picture. Entice the student with two samples of a specific item. Ideally, one of these items should be a preferred example of the target item and the other should be a non-preferred example. For example, if the student likes blue candy and dislikes orange candy, then candy would be an appropriate initial lesson. Once the student requests "I want candy" move these two icons apart on his sentence strip and then hold out both types of candy, indicating, "Which one?" As he reaches for his preferred candy, don't let him take it, but rather physically prompt him to take the icon for that color and put it onto the sentence strip between the "I want" and the "juice" icon. Now read it back to him ("I want BLUE candy.") and give him the blue candy.

> Begin with a high-preference vs. a low-preference example of the attribute if available.

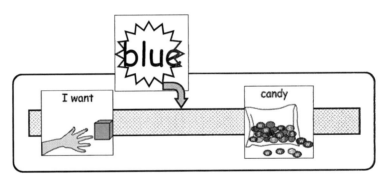

On the next trial, allow the student to put the "I want" icon on the sentence strip, and, as he is reaching for the reinforcer picture, block this response and physically guide him to pick up the attribute picture and put it on the strip. Then allow him to add the reinforcer picture to the strip. Once he gives you the strip, read it back to him and give him the candy.

Continue this backward chaining sequence until the student independently constructs and exchanges the sentence, "I want blue candy." Provide positive feedback ("Ahhh" "Yes!") the moment he engages in the new behavior –when he reaches for the attribute picture having just put the "I want" picture on the strip. Using this backward chaining procedure, the student should learn to construct the three-picture sentence in the correct sequence.

Reinforcement Reminder

If the student hands you a sentence strip with the pictures in an incorrect sequence, respond to this sequential error using the Backstepping procedure.

Step 2. Discriminating between high-preference vs. low-preference attribute icons.

Add a second attribute picture to the book so that the student must discriminate between it and the target attribute. Ideally, this attribute icon should represent an item the student does not like, as long as it is from the same class as the initial item (e.g., blue candy vs. orange candy or blue marker vs. orange marker). The task for the student, now, is to discriminate between "blue," and "orange," etc.

If the student uses the icon representing the high-preference candy, praise him the moment he reaches for the icon and then give him the preferred candy once he constructs and exchanges the strip.

If he starts to choose the icon representing the non-preferred item, provide no feedback as he reaches for it. Allow the student to make an exchange, then read the strip to him, and give him the non-preferred item. Wait for a 'negative' reaction just as we did in Phase III, and then proceed through the 4-Step error correction procedure to teach the correct color icon.

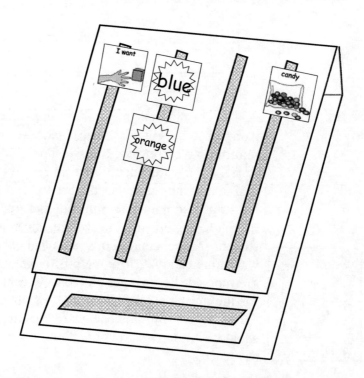

4-Step Error Correction Procedure with attributes

Step	Teacher	Student
	Entice with preferred and non-preferred	
		Exchanges strip with incorrect attribute icon
	Give corresponding item	
		Reacts negatively
	Put attribute icon back on book	
MODEL or SHOW	Show/tap/ target picture (get S to look at it)	
		Looks at target picture on book
PROMPT	Hold open hand near target picture or physically prompt or gesture/prompt S to put target picture on sentence strip	
		Adds target picture to sentence strip
	Praise (do not give item). Put attribute icon back on book	
SWITCH	"Do this," or pause, etc.	
		Performs switch
REPEAT	Entice with both items	
		Adds correct picture to sentence strip
	Read strip, praise and give item	

This is a discrimination error, so we do not require the student to reconstruct the entire sentence strip. The error correction involves the attribute icon only.

If on the Repeat the student uses the incorrect icon, go through the error correction procedure a second time. If he is correct on this round, reinforce appropriately. If not, simplify the task by going back to the previously mastered step (in this case, having one color icon on the book), so that the student has an opportunity for a correct response.

REMEMBER!

Step 3.   Discriminating between icons representing two or more preferred examples of a preferred item.

Add another color icon representing a color of candy the student likes. The student must now discriminate between three color icons, two representing preferred colors of juice and one a non-preferred color.

Once the student requests a specific juice ("I want red juice"), conduct a correspondence check to determine that he is using the correct icon. Indicate "Take it" to him. If he reaches for the correct candy, allow him to have some. If he reaches for the incorrect candy, block his access and use the 4-step error correction procedure.

When you read the sentence strip to the student and then conduct a correspondence check, do not say the attribute in order to assure that the student's actions correspond to the picture he used rather than the word you said. Say something like, "I want that candy," or "I want hmmm candy." Then once the student has completed the correspondence check correctly, you can name the attribute "(I want blue candy," or "Blue candy!").

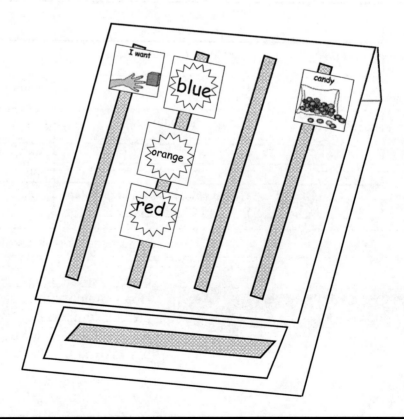

Step	Teacher	Student
4-Step Error Correction Procedure with attributes and correspondence checks		
	Entice with 2 or more preferred examples of the attribute	
		Exchanges 3-icon strip with attribute icon
	" I want hmmm candy," "Take it."	
		Reaches for incorrect item
	Block access to item	
	Put attribute icon back on book	
MODEL or SHOW	Show/tap target picture (get S to look picture)	
		Looks at target picture on book
PROMPT	Hold open hand near target picture or physically prompt OR gesture to empty spot on sentence strip	
		Adds target picture to sentence strip
	Praise (do not give item). Put attribute icon back on book	
SWITCH	"Do this," or pause, etc.	
		Performs switch
REPEAT	Entice with both items	
		Adds picture to sentence strip
	"I want that candy." "Here."	
		Takes corresponding item
	Read strip and praise.	

REMEMBER: When you use the 4-Step error correction procedure after an incorrect correspondence check, you must end the error correction sequence with another correspondence check.

Step 4. Increase complexity of attribute discrimination task.

Add additional attribute icons (e.g., to represent more colors of candy) and offer additional preferred items related to this category.

Increase the number of items you offer when you do correspondence checks. Remember not to name the item when reading back the sentence strip if you are doing a correspondence check.

As in Phase III, conduct frequent correspondence checks when introducing a new icon and fewer once the student progresses.

Step 5. Introduce additional exemplars for this attribute.

Asking for and then taking blue candy does not mean that a child has "mastered" colors. Asking for and taking a specific color of a VARIETY of items is crucial, so very quickly introduce other items for which the attribute is important.

If you began teaching your initial attribute by teaching the student to request a variety of colored candies, find another reinforcer for which color is important. Perhaps the student likes a specific color of marker, juice, or blocks.

Simplify the lesson initially by including the "I want" icon, the color icons and the reinforcer icon only on the front of the communication book.

Probe the student's performance when you offer 2 or 3 examples (different colors) of the new item by conducting a trial with a correspondence check. If the student completes correspondence checks correctly on several trials, great! If not, teach the attribute with these new objects using the steps just described.

Add the picture of the initial item (candy), so that the student now must choose the correct attribute icon AND the correct reinforcer icon.

Continue this sequence, adding additional examples of reinforcers for which the attribute is relevant. As you add icons, conduct correspondence checks in which several colors of blocks, candy, markers, etc. are offered. The student's task, then, is to discriminate attribute icons and reinforcer icons.

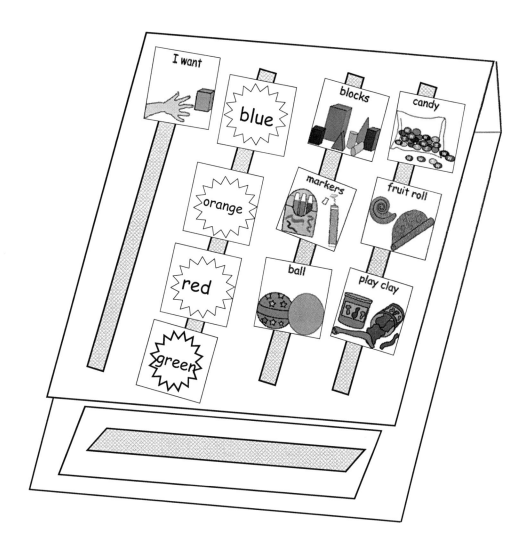

Teaching Additional Attributes

Continue probing additional attributes by determining whether current reinforcers lend themselves to lessons. If the first attribute you taught was color, try teaching a size attribute (big/little), a shape attribute, or a position attribute next. Some examples of attributes and materials could include:

Attribute	Example	Sample
Color	Skittles Playdough M&M's Licorice Fruit rolls Crackers Markers Juice Paint Cookies	
Size **Big/little** **Long/short**	Food Miniature toys Licorice strands Pencils	
Shape	Cookies Crackers Cookie cutters Blocks Parquetry blocks	
Position **In, on, under,** **next to, behind,** **first, second,** **near, far**	Any "generic" reinforcer for which one exemplar is pre-ferred and one is not-preferred. The preferred item is put in the target location.	
Body parts	Mr. Potato Head Band Aid where? Massager where? Stickers where? Ink Stamps where?	

Attribute	Example	Sample
Temperature **Hot/cold**	Foods Ice/heat pack Drinks	
Speed **Fast/slow**	Wagon rides Toy cars Swing Dance Run	
Texture **Rough/smooth** **bumpy**	Potato chips (with or without ridges) Pretzels (salted or unsalted) Paper	
Quantity **1,8,10,** **a lot**	Any favorite item	

Polar Concepts

With some of the "polar" concepts such as big/little, long/short, full/empty, it may be difficult to motivate the student to ask for the non-dominant concept. For example, when offered a large vs. small cookie, most students would choose the large each time (who wouldn't?). When a student learns to ask for "big cookie," he may not really "know" big vs. little; he may just have new label for the cookie he wants. In order to use the concepts "big" and "little" comprehensively, we must find situations in which the child can describe the same cookie as either "big" or "little" depending on the relative value of one item vs. another. In other words, the student must learn to change the attribute label according to the qualities of the item to which we are comparing it.

For example, a student loves chocolate sandwich cookies. He learned early in PECS to ask for these. When we introduced attributes, we offered both regular and mini-chocolate sandwich cookies. The student learned to ask for "big" cookie. When all of the big cookies were gone, he reluctantly would eat the mini-cookies, but needed only to ask for "cookie" because there was only the one size left. We then found a large plastic toy sandwich cookie. In this comparison, his preferred cookie was the relatively "little one" because the "big" cookie was now just plastic.

With other polar concepts, we must teach the student to switch attributes in the same manner. For example, one student loved shoelace licorice and has learned to ask for the "long licorice." In order to make the "short licorice" appealing to him, we left the "long licorice" unwrapped for a day or two so that it became dry and brittle. When offered this licorice and the fresh (but shorter) licorice, he was motivated to ask for the "short licorice."

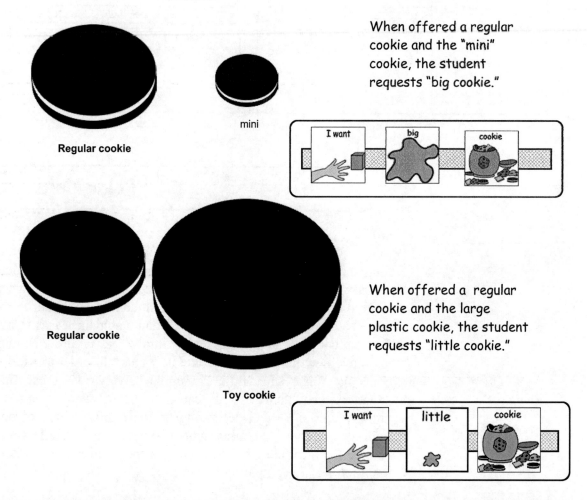

mini

Regular cookie

When offered a regular cookie and the "mini" cookie, the student requests "big cookie."

I want | big | cookie

Regular cookie

Toy cookie

When offered a regular cookie and the large plastic cookie, the student requests "little cookie."

I want | little | cookie

Combining Attributes

A sophisticated communication skill is describing a desired items along many dimensions. For example, while building a block tower, a student might want a specific color of block to add next, but also a specific size. Asking for a "big block" might result in access to the wrong color block, and asking for a "blue block" might result in access to the wrong size. Asking for a "big, blue block," however, results in access to the perfect block.

Perhaps there are two "big red" blocks—one triangular block and one rectangle block. In this case the student must ask for the specific block using three attributes.

Maybe the student is an expert tower builder and not only wants big, red, triangle blocks, but wants more than one at a time!

The Relaxed Training Environment

The students are acquiring a manner in which to *describe* what it is they want or to ask for a very *specific* item. A great activity to begin at this point in training is to periodically offer the child an item for which he has no picture. Once you have determined that the item is one that the child would like (remember the "First One's Free" strategy), entice him with it. Then, wait and see which picture(s) he uses to ask for the item. Many students will come up with interesting ways of describing what they want. For example, during snack one day, we offered a group of preschool children an iced toaster pastry. All of the children liked it, none had a specific symbol for it in his or her book, and when we then offered more, the requests they made were very creative:

1. "I want cracker" (the cracker picture looked a lot like the toaster pastry)
2. "I want rectangle cookie"
3. "I want flat cake"
4. "I want brown rectangle"

These requests surely reflect the creativity and versatility these children are acquiring in their language skills!

Continue using PECS in all environments! Once a student can use attribute concepts, the vocabulary he or she can develop is limitless! In art, imagine the possibilities:

- **Color:**   markers, paint, crayons, paper...
- **Big/Little:** paper, scissors, markers, crayons...
- **Shape:**   stencils, paper...
- **Long/Short:** pencils, crayons, tape, ribbon...

When attributes are not important...

What can you do when you cannot identify any attributes that are important to the student? Some students don't have a preference for a specific color of candy or shape of cookie, etc. If this is the case, you can create requesting lessons in which the only way to access a preferred item of any kind is by using a specific attribute. One way to do this is to find containers that are identical in all aspects except one attribute. Initially, fill one of these containers with a favorite item and teach the student to request the container. Once the student can request the container, then introduce a second container identical to the first except for the target attribute. In one of the containers, put a favorite item. Leave the other container empty. In order to gain access to the preferred item, the student must request the container according to the specific attribute. One of our favorite items is the plastic eggs you can buy at many stores. These eggs are available in a variety of colors AND a variety of sizes.

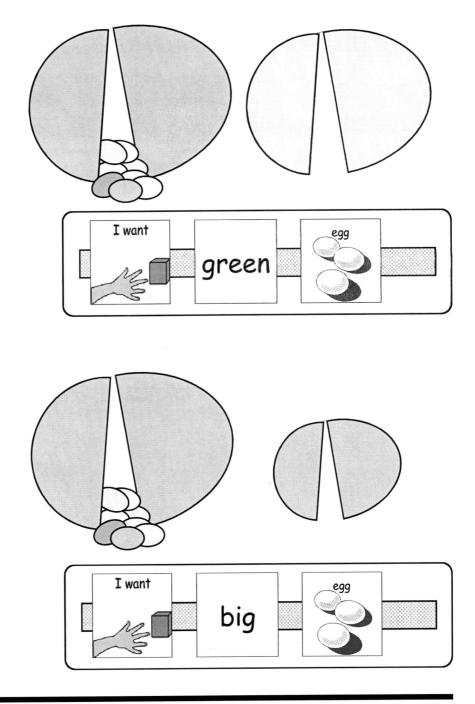

Another "container" strategy is to use boxes that are identical except for the targeted attributes. We find many such boxes at craft stores or stores that specialize in organizational containers. Initially, the student must understand that a desired item is in the box. To demonstrate this, begin with two boxes. Show the child the boxes with the lids off. Then, while the child is watching, put a desired item in one box and put the lid on it. If the child opens the box to retrieve the item, and can do this several times as you switch between boxes, then you can teach the child to request "container" in order to access his preferred item. Once the child can do this, then begin teaching the child to track which box the desired item is in and to request that box according to the specific attribute.

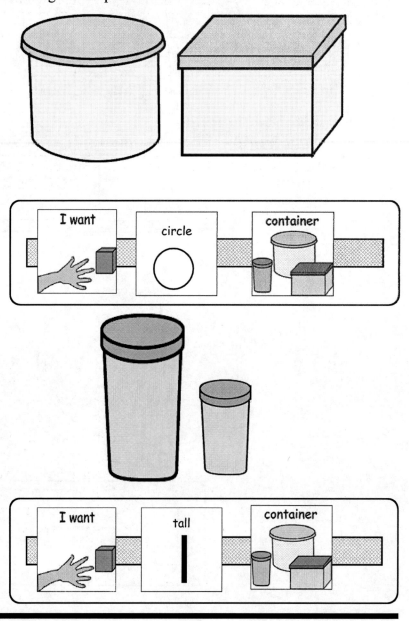

Assessing the Trainers

Attribute training must begin as soon as the student masters Phase IV. Begin by assessing the student's current picture vocabulary to determine which attributes will be motivating to the student. Teach a variety of attributes with a variety of objects.

Attributes
• Assesses current reinforcers for potential attributes
• Teaches three-picture construction
• Reinforces new behavior within ½ second
• Teaches discrimination between attribute icons
• Conducts correspondence check with attributes
• Conducts error correction for attribute icons
• Conducts error correction for incorrect picture sequence
• Teaches variety of attributes within same class (several colors, variety of sizes)
• Teaches multiple exemplars of each attribute (several "red" items)

??..Frequently asked questions..??

1 Wouldn't it be easier for the student to learn these concepts if he or she had already learned them receptively (e.g., touch blue)?

First, communication is a two-way street- we communicate to others and we try to understand the communication from others. Even for typically developing children, these skills are actually learned independently at first, and then generalize once a large repertoire is acquired. Therefore, 'knowing' something receptively may not automatically transfer to 'using' that skill- just as being able to say a word does not automatically indicate that someone can understand that same word whcn uscd by another person.

Many programs for young children with language difficulties focus on receptive skills early in programming. They do so NOT because it is required prior to working on productive skills but because these programs focus on teaching the child to speak (or sign) usually via imitation. If a child is learning to imitate actions, single sounds, blended sounds, etc., then that child cannot yet request or name things. Therefore, the program must put emphasis on skills that are possible- receptive skills. There is NO theoretical reason to require receptive acquisition before expressive use. Furthermore, we think it is clearly more motivating to learn to request something (i.e., "I want RED crayon") than to learn it receptively (i.e., "Touch the RED crayon").

Bright Ideas (Attributes)

1. Shop 'til you drop! Finding materials to teach attribute lessons can be a challenge. For initial attribute lessons you will need to find items that are identical except for the attribute being taught. We keep PECS in the back of our minds whenever we are out shopping. Imagine the grocery store: the snack food aisle contains materials for dozens of attribute lessons. Crackers and cookies come in a variety of sizes, shapes, colors, textures, etc. Snack-size cheese crackers, for example, can be found in at least three sizes of circle-shaped crackers. The cheese crackers, depending on the brand, can be found in a variety of shapes. Pretzels can be found in the "crooked" format or the "straight" format. The "crooked" pretzels are available in a variety of sizes. The "straight" pretzels can be found in the short, thin variety or the long, fat variety. Potato chips are either smooth (plain) or rough (ridged). Discount stores, party supply stores, "dollar" stores, and drug stores are great places to find a variety of inexpensive toys: big/little cars that are various colors, different colors of molding clay, etc. Look through your own children's abandoned toys for

ideas to teach attribute lessons.

2. Teach "generic" vocabulary to create the desire to use attributes. Yes, we would like our children to learn to ask for an Oreo® versus a Lorna Doon® versus a Vienna Finger®. Before teaching these specific labels, though, teach an attribute to use to modify a request for "cookie." Oreo® cookies are "circle cookies." Lorna Doon® cookies are "square cookies." Vienna Fingers® are "oval cookies." Once a child is able to use attributes to describe specifically what he or she wants, he will be able to let you know about new items he wants so that you can get that item for the child and eventually add a specific symbol to his communication book.

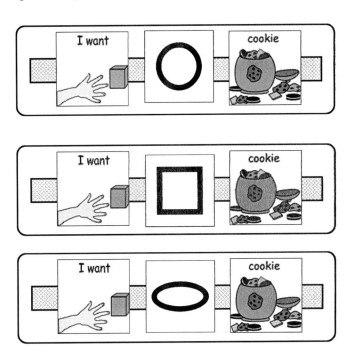

Monitoring Progress

Date	Trial	Constructs 3-picture sentence strip	Target Attribute	Number of available:		Uses correct attribute	Corres. Check
				Icons	Items		
5/15	1	PP	red	1	1	NA	NA
	2	PP	red	1	1	NA	NA
	3	PP	red	1	1	NA	NA
	4	+	red	1	1	NA	NA
	5	+	red	1	1	NA	NA
	6	+	red	2	1	+	NA
	7	+	red	2	2	NA	+
	8	+	red	3	3	NA	+
	9	+	red	4	4	NA	+
	10						

This is this student's first attribute lesson. The trainer identified that the student liked red Skittles. The initial goal is to teach the student to construct the 3-picture sentence strip. The student needed physical prompting on the first three trials. On the fourth and fifth trials, she independently constructed the sentence strip. On the sixth trial, the trainer added a second attribute to the communication book and continued to offer only one color of skittle. The student independently constructed the sentence strip using the correct icon. On the 7th trial, the teacher offered two colors of Skittle with their corresponding color icons on the communication book. Because the student now had a choice of Skittles, the teacher conducted a correspondence check to determine whether the student used the correct icon. She did so. On the 8th and 9th trials, the teacher increased the number of Skittles she offered and the number of icons on the communication book. Note that on the 7th, 8th, and 9th trials we are not able to determine if the child used the correct attribute icon until the correspondence check has been conducted, so no data point is reported.

9

Phase V

Responding to "What do you want?"

Phase V- Responding to "What do you want?" (Responsive Requesting)

Terminal Objective: *The student spontaneously requests a variety of items and answers the question, "What do you want?"*

Rationale: We continue to teach functional skills that are immediately useful, and we continue building toward the commenting we will teach in Phase VI. Children with autism and related disabilities who are at this Phase in PECS generally remain more responsive to the tangible consequences that follow a request than to the social consequences that follow a comment. Therefore, we anticipate that teaching spontaneous commenting will be difficult. Bondy, Ryan, and Hayes (1991) found it more effective to teach commenting initially in response to a simple question ("What do you see?"). So far in the PECS protocol, students have not answered questions. So, we have identified two new skills that our students must learn—answering a question and commenting. We initially will teach answering a question, but will teach a question related to tangible outcomes—"What do you want?"

 This is the first time that we are directly asking, "What do you want?" Once we begin asking this, it is quite easy to forget about spontaneous requesting, the skill the children originally learned in PECS. Therefore, at this point in training, it is extremely important to remember to continue creating many opportunities for the child to request spontaneously.

The Structured Training Environment

Setting Have available the communication book with the "I want" picture, the sentence strip, and pictures of items on the cover. Have several reinforcing items available but inaccessible.

notes

1. Continue to verbally and tangibly reinforce each correct response.
2. Use "delayed prompting" to train during this phase.
3. Create opportunities to answer, "What do you want?" *and* to spontaneously request.
4. Continue creating multiple communicative opportunities across the day.

Teaching Strategy

Delayed Prompting– Progressive Time Delay

When the natural cue does not reliably elicit the desired response, a second "helping prompt" is added. This "helping prompt" is known to elicit the behavior that can then be reinforced. Initially the natural cue and the "helping prompt" are presented simultaneously. The delay between presentation of the natural cue and the helping prompt gets longer and longer across successive trials until the student performs the desired behavior in advance of the "helping prompt." The trainer uses differential reinforcement—more if the student engages in the target behavior independent of the helping prompt.

The natural cue in Phase V is the question, "What do you want?" The goal is for the student to learn to answer this question as soon as it is asked. The initial "helping prompt" we will use in Phase V is the trainer pointing to or touching the sentence-starter picture —the "I want" picture. We choose this cue because the student was exposed to our pointing to or gesturing to the "I want" icon in Phase IV.

"What do you want?"

Step 1. Zero second delay. With a desired object present and with corresponding pictures and the "I want" card on the communication book, *simultaneously* (zero second delay) points to or tap the "I want" card and ask, "What do you want?" Because requesting desired items is a familiar task, the child should pick up the "I want" picture and complete the exchange. If he does not, physically guide him to the "I want" picture. Use this more effective physical prompt as the "helping" prompt on successive trials.

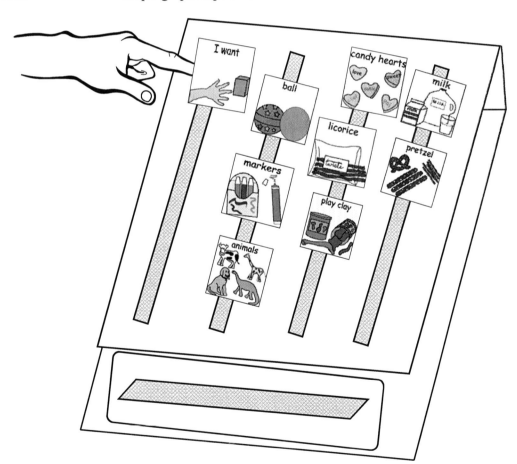

Step 2. Increasing delay interval. Begin increasing the time between asking, "What do you want?" and pointing to the "I want" card. Initially, ask, "What do you want?" and pause 1-2 seconds before pointing to the "I want" icon. The time intervals should be increased by about one or two seconds over a series of trials. The goal is for the student to be able to "beat" the helping prompt consistently.

Each time the student answers the question, provide the requested item. If the student answers the question before you point to the "I want" icon, provide *more* reinforcement (differential reinforcement). Give him a larger serving of an item or allow him to play longer with the requested item, or give him several of the requested items, as well as more enthusiastic praise.

Step 3. Switching between responsive requesting and spontaneous requesting. Now that you are asking the student, "What do you want?" remember to create opportunities for spontaneous requesting. Within structured activities, pause during "What do you want?" trials and entice the student with some of your available items. The student should spontaneously request the item if it is something he truly wants.

Error Correction

Delayed Prompting should be an *errorless learning* strategy. If the student does not answer the question at the zero-second delay, then your "helping prompt" is not effective and you should choose another type of prompt.

The Relaxed Training Environment

Setting

All settings, all environments! The student should be quite a proficient communicator. He should be able to go get his book and find a communicative partner in all environments and across all activities. Continue creating communicative opportunities all day and expecting communication all day.

By now, the student should be using PECS to request a variety of items across the entire day. Continue assessing functional activities and introducing vocabulary for PECS within each. Within these activities create opportunities for answering "What do you want?" and spontaneously requesting. See Chapter 12 for a detailed discussion of communication training within functional activities.

Re-introduce Phase II issues such as traveling to the communication book and to the communicative partner. Throughout the day, ask the student, "What do you want?" related to specific items within an activity or task. Ensure that you also are creating many opportunities for the student to request spontaneously.

As we imbed communication opportunities in more and more of our daily activities and conduct less structured training, monitoring a student's use of PECS can become more difficult. Because every person with whom the student regularly interacts should expect communication all day, we find using the "PECS Spot Check" form to be helpful. Staff within a classroom or other staff coming into the classroom even for only a moment can quickly assess the overall "communication

PECS Spot Check			
Date:			
Observer:			
1. PECS books available to all.			
2. Students involved in functional activities.			
3. Environment "engineered" to elicit communication.			
4. Staff expect communication.			
5. Spontaneous requesting occurring.			
6. Functional direction following training occurring.			
7. Appropriate prompting strategies used.			
8. Appropriate error correction used.			

environment" in order to determine if communicative opportunities are being created and that staff are expecting communication.

This type of tracking system can be used for staff to track their own behaviors across time. We often set up staff incentive or reinforcement systems based on this type of data. Staff can track their own or each other's behaviors within a class or staff can track the team's behavior and compare it to another team's behavior.

Assessing the Trainers

The trainer must manipulate the delay interval between the natural cue and the "helping cue" so that the student makes no errors. This could require that the trainer lengthen the delay on one interval and shorten it on another. Once the student has mastered asking, "What do you want?" the trainer must begin mixing opportunities for answering this question and spontaneously requesting.

PHASE V
• Uses delayed prompting to teach "What do you want?"
• Uses differential reinforcement if student "beats" the second prompt
• Reinforces new behavior within ½ second
• Creates multiple opportunities for spontaneously requesting AND answering, "What do you want?" within the same lesson.

Cross-Reference with Additional Skills

Phase V and Attribute training both are begun after Phase IV. Some lessons should address Phase V and others should introduce attributes. As the student masters answering, "What do you want?" integrate the question in lessons involving all communication skills addressed thus far. As the student learns to use attributes, integrate this with other skills. For example, create a situation during which you ask, "What do you want?" and the student must use an attribute to answer. Continue creating opportunities for the student to request assistance, and introduce vocabulary for specific requests ("I want help open," etc.).

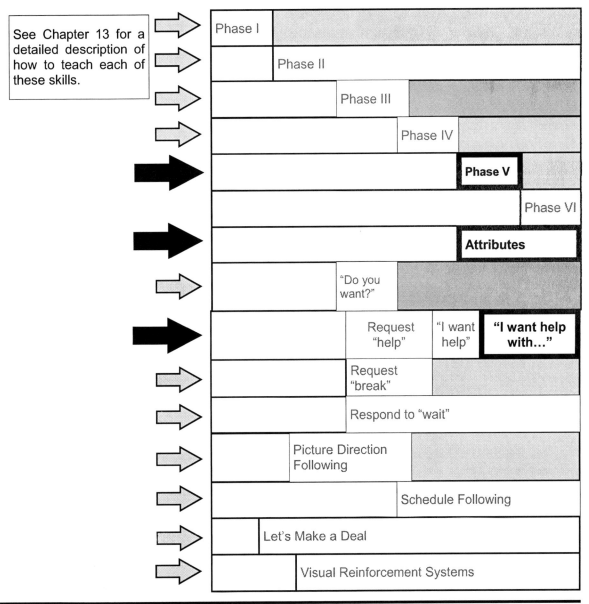

See Chapter 13 for a detailed description of how to teach each of these skills.

Phase I
Phase II
Phase III
Phase IV
Phase V
Phase VI
Attributes
"Do you want?"
Request "help" — "I want help" — **"I want help with…"**
Request "break"
Respond to "wait"
Picture Direction Following
Schedule Following
Let's Make a Deal
Visual Reinforcement Systems

??..Frequently asked questions..??

1 We're not perfect! I'm sure that my student has heard us ask, "What do you want?" at some point in so far. Why do I need to teach this skill as a formal Phase? Even though you think that your student might have heard and perhaps responded to, "What do you want?" plan on teaching this formally. While we have concentrated so far on spontaneity in PECS training, we also want to ensure that our students can respond to questions as this is the strategy we will use in Phase VI. We teach this "responding" behavior in Phase V within the requesting function in order to enhance the likelihood that our student will be successful. Remember, we are building toward the next step in our communication program—commenting, and the training strategies that we are using in Phase V are the same as we will introduce in Phase VI. When we begin Phase VI, we use the same progressive time-delay procedure to teach responsive commenting.

2 Is there another way to eliminate the pointing to the "I want" icon at the beginning of this Phase? You can combine the progressive time-delay strategy with physically fading your pointing prompt. During the early trials, you may fully tap on the icon but as trials continue, you can start to point but stop short of touching the picture. Over time, reduce how much you move your finger—as long as the student continues to respond! Eventually, you should be able to ask the question, not move a muscle in your arm, and the student will respond by constructing and exchanging the sentence strip.

3 Now that we are allowed to ask a direct question, my team seems to ask all the time—rarely setting up opportunities for spontaneous requests—what can I do? It may be hard during a typically busy day to informally keep track of how many spontaneous versus responsive requests occur each day. In general, it is less critical to keep track of how many responsive requests occur, but it is very important to set a minimum goal for spontaneous requests. That is, the student may be responsive 10 or 20 times per day depending on what activities are taking place. However, you want to ensure that at least 10 times per school day, he can be spontaneous in enticing situations. You may find it helpful to post a sheet in the room so that everyone has open access to it to record the number of spontaneous requests.

Helpful Hints
(Phase V)

1. Try to avoid inserting additional prompts that the student can use to respond to your question. For example, if you picked up the student's communication book to bring to him each time you got ready to ask, "What do you want?" he might learn to start a request even before you've asked the question! Therefore, make your approach unpredictable by avoiding personal routines and rituals and by introducing surprises in the midst of an activity or lesson. Mix up situations when the student sees something he likes with ones during which he only hears your question. Of course, be ready to respond to requests that may not seem to fit the situation. That is, if you are sincere in your question, be prepared to earnestly reply to his request! Also, be sure that the student can respond to the question from everyone at home or at school.

Phase V

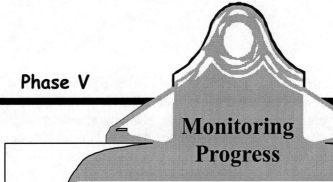

Monitoring Progress

Date	Trial	Delay Interval	Answer question	Beat prompt ?	Spontaneous Request	Correspon-dence Check
5/25	1	0"	+	n		
	2	0"	+	n		
	3	0"	+	n		
	4	2"	+	n		
	5	3"	+	n		
	6	3"	+	y		
	7	3"	+	n		
	8	4"	+	y		
	9		+	NA		
	10				+	

During this initial Phase V lesson, the student answered the question, "What do you want?" in response to a simultaneous presentation of the "helping" prompt and question on trials 1 through 3. On trials 4 and 5, he answered the question when the gestural prompt was provided after a two-, then three-second delay. On trials 6 he beat the prompt, bud did not do so on trial 7. On trials 8 and 9 he answered the question before the trainer provided the additional prompt. On trial 9, the trainer provided no prompt and the student answered the question. On trial 10 the trainer did not ask a question, and the student spontaneously requested an item.

Monitoring Progress

Date	Trial	Delay Interval	Answer ques-tion	Beat prompt?	Spontaneous Request	Correspondence Check
5/25	1		+			
	2		+			
	3				+	
	4				+	
	5		+			
	6				P	
	7				+	
	8				+	
	9		+			
	10				+	

Key: + = independent response   P = prompted response

This lesson took place after the student had mastered answering, "What do you want?" The purpose was to mix opportunities for answering the question and spontaneously requesting.   The student was able to switch back and forth until trial 6 when he did not respond to a subtle enticement.   The communicative partner signaled to another staff person to physically prompt the student to make a request. After that, he again was able to switch back and forth independently. On trial 8, the communicative partner did a correspondence check to ensure the student was using some of his newer pictures correctly.

10

Phase VI

Commenting

Phase VI: Commenting

Terminal Objective: *The student answers "What do you want?" "What do you see?" "What do you have?" "What do you hear?" and "What is it?" and spontaneously requests and comments.*

Rationale: Thus far in PECS we've taught our student to use a Sentence-starter to initiate a request and to answer a request question. Our goal for the completion of Phase VI is for the student to demonstrate both responsive and spontaneous commenting. Even when we reach this point in training, many students with autism remain less responsive to social reinforcement than to tangible reinforcement. Therefore, rather than beginning Phase VI with spontaneous commenting, we begin by taking advantage of the previously learned ability to respond to simple questions. We move from asking, "What do you want?" to "What do you see?" After the student learns this responsive commenting, we will introduce strategies to promote spontaneous commenting.

Remember, the difference between commenting and requesting is twofold—
* commenting occurs in response to some interesting event or occurrence in the environment, while requesting occurs in response to a need or desire of the speaker.
* commenting results in social reinforcement and requesting results in tangible or direct results.

	In Response to:	Results in:
Commenting	An interesting environmental event	Social or environmental reinforcement
Requesting	A need/desire	Tangible or direct reinforcement

The Structured Training Environment

Setting

Have available the communication book, the "I want" icon, an "I see" icon, and pictures of various familiar items. Have available objects or photographs corresponding to these communication board pictures. These objects should be ones with which the student is familiar, but not items that are the most reinforcing items.

notes

1. Reinforce each communicative act appropriately: *tangible and social* for requests and *social only* for comments.
2. Use "delayed prompting" to train responses to each new question during this phase.
3. Use discrimination training to teach discrimination between sentence-starter icons.
4. Create at least 30 opportunities per day for the student to request or comment during functional activities.

Teaching Strategy

Delayed Prompting-Progressive Time Delay
Use the same strategy introduced in Phase V. Begin by simultaneously pointing to the "I see" picture and asking, "What do you see?" Over successive opportunities, increase the time interval between asking "What do you see?" and pointing to the "I see" picture. Remember the goal is for the student to "beat" you to the prompt.

Step 1. Answering the First Comment Question.

In planning your first training session, consider the type of activity in which to teach commenting. Because our goal is for the student to comment spontaneously, we should create activities that are similar to those during which typically developing communicators comment. Think about a small child learning to comment to her parents. At the dinner table, she is not likely to comment on such items as the tablecloth, the wall, the ceiling, or the chairs. She is likely to comment on the clock chiming the hour, the dog running to the door to bark, or the juice pitcher that gets tipped over. These types of "environmental events" elicit comments because they:

- are novel (a new toy appears)
- violate an expectation (instead of play clothes, Mom gets out pajamas to wear for the day)
- are startling or surprising (the dog barks)

When we create our first commenting lesson, we need to remember to include at least one of these elements. If we line several items up on a table and systematically ask the student "What do you see?" or "What is it?" about each one, the student might learn to answer in order to comply with your "lesson," but he is not likely to comment spontaneously during such a lesson. Potential lessons include:

- The mystery box or bag—fill with familiar objects and pull out one at a time.
- Looking through a photo album containing pictures of familiar items.
- Watching a favorite video or CD program.
- Looking through a familiar book- "Pop-up" books are great!.
- Going for a walk (on a route that you have previously arranged to contain surprises, etc.).
- Listening to favorite sounds.

Once you have created an appropriate activity/ environment, simplify the front of the communication book so as to enhance the potential for success. Take the "I want" icon off the book and most reinforcer icons off and place them inside the book. Place the commenting sentence-starter icon on the left side of the cover of the communication book   The first sentence-starter you use is based on what you know about the interests of your student. It could be "I see," "I hear," "It is," etc. Also on the front of the book, place a few pictures of items you will use in your lesson.

Create the environmental event (draw a familiar object out of a box, etc.) and then simultaneously point to the "I see" icon and ask, "What do you see?" Your gestural prompt to the "I see" icon should be the effective prompt for the student to remove the "I see" icon and place it on the sentence strip. Because he recognizes the other item and knows about its associated icon, he likely will put it on the strip and then exchange the strip.

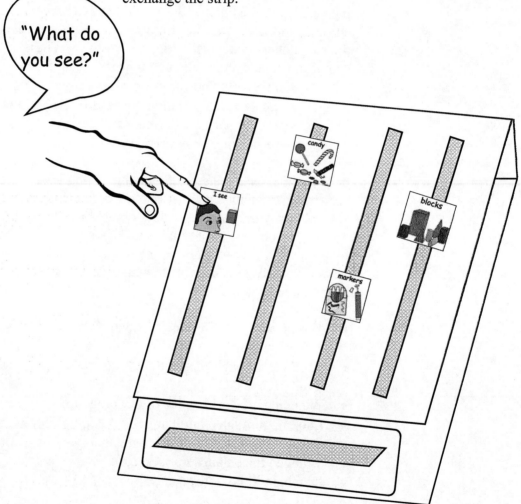

Your reaction to this *comment* is crucial!!!! Provide only social reinforcement at this point ("Yes, that's a ball!!"). Do not give the item to the student. Your student might react in a less-than-happy fashion, so remember to begin this lesson with an item the child is familiar with but that is not the most reinforcing item in the whole world.

- If the gestural prompt to the "I see" icon is effective, the student should make no errors. If he is making errors, then the gestural prompt is not effective! You might have to use a physical prompt.

- As the student successfully answers this question several times (using a variety of items), begin adding a delay between asking, "What do you see?" and providing the prompt to the "I see" icon. Again, the goal is for the student to "beat" you to the prompt! If he does, remember to use differential reinforcement (more social praise, hugs, etc.) The student has mastered this level when he no longer needs the prompt in order to answer the question using the correct sentence-starter.

Step 2. Discrimination between Sentence Starters.

Teaching Strategy

Discrimination Training: Use the discrete trial format to teach the student to discriminate between the various question forms and sentence starters. Begin by randomizing "What do you want?" and "What do you see?" Reinforce appropriate responses and use error correction for incorrect responses. As you add additional questions and sentence-starters, add these to the randomization.

Arrange the cover of the communication book with both sentence-starter icons on the left side. Add pictures of familiar items that you will use in the lesson. These items should be those that you used in Step 1 that also are items the student is likely to want. Create the environmental event and ask, "What do you see?" On the next trial entice with the item and ask, "What do you want?" The student now must discriminate between the questions by using the corresponding sentence-starter to answer. So, the new behavior is choosing between the

Reinforcement Reminder

"I want" and the "I see" icons. The moment the student reaches for the correct sentence-starter, begin providing the positive social feedback. Once he constructs the sentence strip and then exchanges it, provide the appropriate social (for comments) or tangible (for requests) reinforcement.

If the student reaches for the incorrect Sentence-starter icon, provide no feedback and allow him to complete the exchange. Then react to this *error during a discrete lesson* using the 4-Step error correction procedure.

Error Correction

Discrimination error– Discrete lesson– 4-Step

Use the 4-Step error correction procedure if the student answers incorrectly by using the wrong Sentence-starter icon (e.g., uses the "I want" icon when you have asked, "What do you see?"). The student should have placed the two icons on the sentence strip in the correct order, so respond to the discrimination error by putting the Sentence-starter icon back on the student's book and then:

- **Model:** Point to the correct sentence-starter icon.

- **Prompt:** Ask the original question ("What do you see" or "What do you want?") and prompt the student to use the correct sentence-starter icon.

- **Switch:** to the unrelated task.

- **Repeat:** (put the sentence-starter icon back on the book) and ask the original question.

For many children with autism spectrum disorder, commenting, even in response to a question, will remain difficult when it leads to social reinforcement only. If this is the case with your student, try adding an "unrelated" tangible reinforcement—not the item on which he commented! This could be a token (See Chapter 13) or a small toy or snack. Analyze your activity to ensure that it is interesting to the student, and use a portion of the activity as an incentive during the lesson. Examples include:

1. While reading a pop-up book, you open the first surprise. If the student appropriately comments on it, he can open the next one.
2. Comment on sounds heard via the Language Master. You run the first card through and, if the student appropriately comments on the sound, "I hear a cat!" he can run the next card through.

With these and similar activities, incorporate answering "What do you want?" to allow the student to request "turn page," within the pop-up book, or "I want dog" in order to hear the dog sound on the Language Master.

Step 3. Maintaining spontaneous requesting.

Remember the original skill the student learned– *spontaneous requesting*! Create opportunities within your lessons for the student to spontaneously request. For example, in the midst of randomly asking "What do you see?" and "What do you want?" pause and allow the student to spontaneously request something!

Step 4. Spontaneous commenting.

Our ultimate goal in Phase VI is for the student to comment spontaneously. So far he comments in response to a question. We want him to comment, however, in response to some environmental event in order to gain access to a social response from a communicative partner. Continue to create interesting environmental events and eliminate the question in order to achieve spontaneous commenting. Perhaps the easiest way to do this would be to fade the question. If the student is able to participate in an activity where you successively create a series of interesting environmental events, then you should be able to replicate this activity and systematically fade your question.

For example the following sequence might occur:

Environmental event	Teacher says...	PECS sentence
The teacher dramatically pulls an item out of a mystery box.	"OH!!! What do you see?"	"I see a dog"
The teacher dramatically pulls an item out of a mystery box	"OH!! What?"	"I see a rabbit"
The teacher dramatically pulls an item out of a mystery box	"Oh!!"	"I see a penguin"
The teacher dramatically pulls an item out of a mystery box		"I see a monkey"

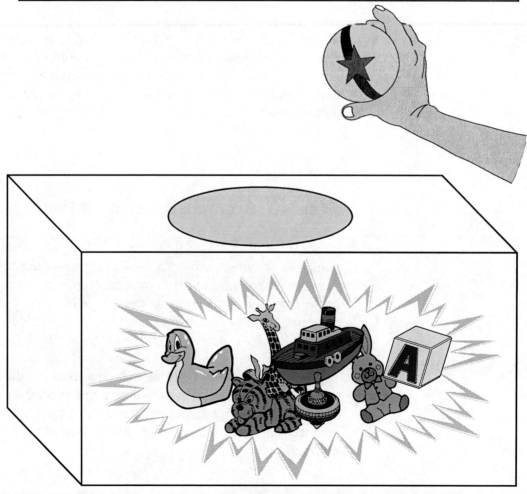

Teaching Additional Comments

Add additional Sentence Starter icons to the cover of the student's communication book and teach these comments. Follow the same format as described in teaching "What do you see?" This should include specific lessons that are designed to teach the discrimination between the various Sentence Starter icons. Examples of additional Sentence Starter include:

- **"It is"**
- **"I hear"**
- **"I have"**

During these commenting lessons and while making requests, if the student uses an incorrect picture of the target item (responds, "I hear a dog," when he heard the cow "moo"), respond to this discrimination error using the 4-Step Error Correction procedure just as in Phase III.

The **Relaxed** Training Environment

Setting

Everywhere! Once Phase VI is introduced and the student is making progress, additional vocabulary can be taught. Assess ongoing activities and lessons for opportunities for commenting and teach the vocabulary for those activities. Continue taking the student to new environments and new communicative partners (don't forget peers).

Once your student learns to comment, either spontaneously or in response to a question, many new vocabulary lessons are now available. Begin teaching vocabulary related to specific "units." For preschool and early elementary-age students, these units would include vocabulary related to seasons, holidays, field trips, morning circle, and playtime etc. Older students might participate in lessons related to job skills or specific academic subjects.

This is a wonderful time to create PECS Activity Boards related to a specific activity or unit. We use a separate communication board or book for each activity and include the various sentence starters and pictures of the vocabulary items. These boards are great to use during group activities—sharing the vocabulary can help promote waiting and turn-taking. If the vocabulary items on a particular activity board become vocabulary used at times in addition to these lessons, replicate it in the student's own communication book.

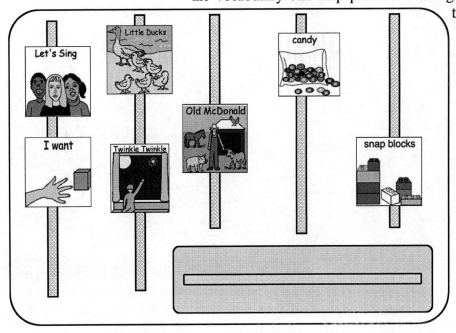

Continue introducing additional Sentence Starters to correspond to specific activities. For example, if you address "personal information" during your morning meeting or morning circle time, teach your students to use Sentence Starters such as "My name is," "My address is," "My birthday is," etc.

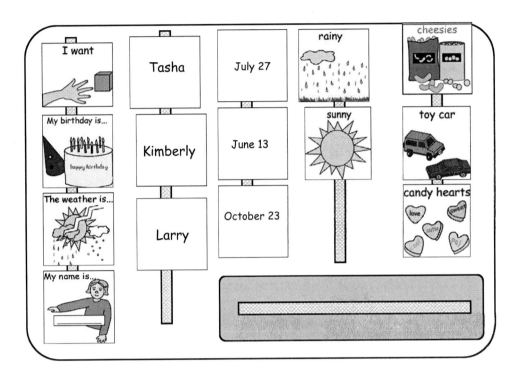

Assessing the Trainers

Phase VI involves Delayed Prompting to teach use of the new Sentence Starters and Discrimination Training to teach the discrimination between various Sentence Starters. The trainer must pay special attention to using the appropriate reinforcement for a comment versus a request. Once the student can use the comment Sentence Starters, the trainer must continue to create opportunities for spontaneous requesting. The trainer uses a prompt fading strategy to elicit spontaneous comments. Finally, the trainer must incorporate previously learned vocabulary into the comments (including attributes).

PHASE VI
• Uses delayed prompting to teach commenting in response to comment question
• Continues to create opportunities for spontaneous requesting
• Differentially reinforces commenting/requesting
• Teaches "comment question" vs. "What do you want?" discrimination (sentence
• Uses error correction for incorrect discrimination between sentence starters
• Teaches "comment question" vs. "What do you want?" vs. spontaneous
• Creates lessons to elicit spontaneous commenting
• Fades "comment question" to elicit spontaneous comment
• Incorporates attributes into comment lessons
• Teaches additional comments and/or "comment" questions

Cross-Reference with Additional Skills

When the student begins Phase VI, all additional critical communication skills have been introduced. Continue expanding on these additional skills and incorporate concepts learned into commenting training. For example, have the student comment using an attribute or ask for help with a specific item ("I want help with green ball.").

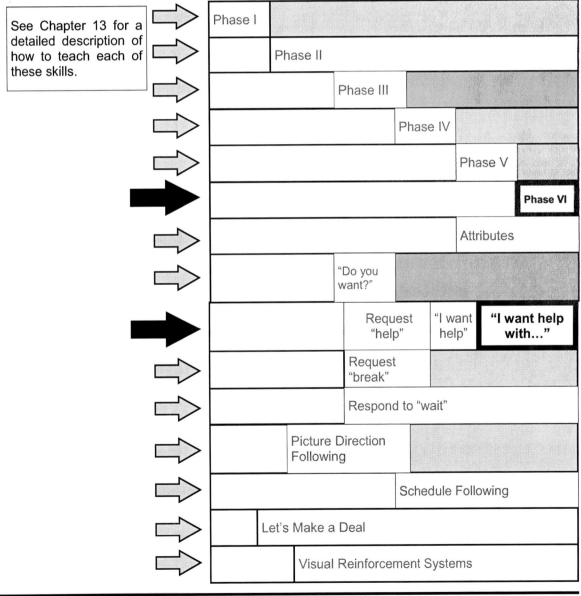

See Chapter 13 for a detailed description of how to teach each of these skills.

Phase I
Phase II
Phase III
Phase IV
Phase V
Phase VI
Attributes
"Do you want?"
Request "help" | "I want help" | **"I want help with…"**
Request "break"
Respond to "wait"
Picture Direction Following
Schedule Following
Let's Make a Deal
Visual Reinforcement Systems

??..Frequently asked questions..??

1 I know that my child/student is not responsive to social reinforcement. Should I even attempt this phase?

This is a complex question to which there is no single answer. Your student's team must discuss the issue and make the decision. Consider your student's current placement and future "learning environment." Is your student currently or will he soon be learning in a "typical" environment? If so, consider the teaching strategies to which he will be expected to respond. Most lessons taught to groups of students put the students in a "responsive" mode. The instructor talks, demonstrates, etc., and then asks questions to encourage discussion or to assess the students' understanding of the lesson. Even in preschool classrooms, this teaching style predominates. Teachers ask, "What day is it?" "Where are we going?" "What's this?" "What did you do?" If this is the type of environment your student is or will be in, then the beginning of Phase VI will teach a useful, functional skill. You might teach the responsive commenting and then consider whether or not to address spontaneous commenting.

Bright Ideas
(Phase VI)

1. When you create lessons for commenting, make PECS Activity Boards for each lesson. Store these boards in a common location (a large binder or folder), or store in a container with the lesson's materials.
2. Watch typically developing children and note the circumstances surrounding their comments.

Monitoring Progress

Date	Trial	What see? SS	What see? pic	What want? SS	What want? pic	Spont request SS	Spont request pic	_____ SS	_____ pic
10/23	1	P							
	2	P							
	3	P							
	4	P							
	5	P							
	6	+							
	7	+							
	8			-					
	9			+					
	10		-						

Key: + independent response   **P** prompted response   − Incorrect response

This was the student's first Phase VI lesson. Initially, the goal was for the student to learn to use the "I see" Sentence Starter with familiar items. He needed prompting on the first 5 trials before he "beat the prompt" and answered the question independently. He made no errors using the correct picture of the item on which he was commenting. The instructor next switched between asking "What do you see?" and "What do you want?" and the student made errors discriminating between the sentence starter icons.

Monitoring Progress

Date	Trial	What see? SS	What see? pic	What want? SS	What want? pic	Spont request SS	Spont request pic	_____ SS	_____ pic
6/13	1	−	+						
	2	+	+						
	3			+	+				
	4			+	+				
	5					P	+		
	6	−	+						
	7	+	+						
	8			−	+				
	9					+	+		
	10	+	+						

Key: **+** independent response   **P** prompted response   **−** Incorrect response

The objective of this lesson was switching among answering, "What do you see?" "What do you want?" and spontaneous requesting. On the first trial, the student used the incorrect Sentence Starter to answer, "What do you see?" He was correct on the second trial. When the instructor asked, "What do you want?" on the next two trials, the student answered independently. When the instructor paused (trial #5) and enticed with a desired item, the student needed prompting to request it. On trial #6, the student again used the incorrect Sentence Starter to answer, "What do you see?" He answered independently on trial #7. When the instructor then switched to "What do you want?" the student used the wrong Sentence Starter icon. He then was able to spontaneously request a desired item and on trial #10, independently answered, "What do you see?" Overall, this student's main weakness is using the correct Sentence Starter.

Monitoring Progress

Date	Trial	What see? SS	pic	What want? SS	pic	Spont request SS	pic	<u>What hear?</u>	
6/13	1							+	+
	2							+	+
	3	+	+						
	4			+	+				
	5							+	+
	6			+	+				
	7	-	+						
	8	+	+						
	9	+	+						
	10							+	+

Key: **+** independent response   **P** prompted response   **-** Incorrect response

The objective for this lesson was using the correct Sentence Starter icons to answer, "What do you hear?" "What do you see," and "What do you want?" and to spontaneously request. The student had one error when switching from using the "I want" Sentence Starter to the "I see" Sentence Starter.

Monitoring Progress

Date	Trial	What is it?		What hear?		Spont request SS	pic	Spont comment SS	pic
11/1	1	+	+						
	2			+	+				
	3							P I hear	+
	4							+ I hear	+
	5							+ I hear	+
	6	+	+						
	7					+	+		
	8							P It's a	
	9							+ It's a	
	10					+	+		

Key: **+** independent response   **P** prompted response   **–** Incorrect response

During this activity, the instructor used various small stuffed animals that, when squeezed, made their corresponding animal sound. The instructor either:

- showed the student the animal, and asked, "What is it?"
- hid the animal, squeezed it, and asked, "What do you hear?"
- showed the student the animal and said nothing.
- hid the animal, squeezed it, and said nothing.
- played with one of the animals and said nothing.

The objective was for the student to answer the questions, spontaneously comment using the appropriate sentence starter, or spontaneously request. This student initially answered "What is it?" and "What do you hear?" independently. He then needed a prompt to spontaneously comment when the instructor hid and squeezed the animal. The instructor continued switching among the various tasks. The student needed one prompt to use the "It's a" sentence starter in order to comment spontaneously.

11

Additional Critical Communication Skills

Additional Critical Communication Skills

When we began our discussion of functional communication, we identified a list of critical communication skills. Mastery of these skills is essential for independence in a home, community, and work setting. Requesting was the first skill described, and is what we teach early in PECS. The additional skills should be taught concurrently with PECS. For example, while Phase II and III are introduced during some lessons and activities, teaching a student to request assistance or a break are taught during other lessons the same day.

Additional Critical Communication Skills

√ **Request assistance**
√ **Indicate "no" to "Do you want?"**
√ **Indicate "yes" to "Do you want?"**
√ **Request "break"**
√ **Respond to "Wait"**
√ **Follow functional directions**
√ **Transition between activities**
√ **Follow schedule**

The following time line will help you to plan for teaching both PECS lessons and additional communication skills lessons. You saw portions of this timeline highlighted at the end of each Phase description. Remember, as with PECS lessons, you must use specific prompting strategies and error correction strategies when teaching these additional skills. Skills that involve INITIATION are taught most effectively with the two-person prompting procedure. Sequential lessons typically will involve backward chaining. Errors involving discrimination require use of the 4-Step error correction procedure and sequential errors require use of the Backstepping procedure or anticipatory prompting when Backstepping is not feasible. Generalization will be planned from the beginning of each of these lessons.

Communication Training Timeline

	Acquisition		Maintenance		
Phase I					
	Phase II				
		Phase III			
			Phase IV		
				Phase V	
					Phase VI
				Attributes	
		"Do you want?"			
			Request "help"	"I want help"	"I want help with…"
			Request "break"		
			Respond to "wait"		
		Picture Direction Following			
			Schedule Following		
	Let's Make a Deal				
		Visual Reinforcement Systems			

Step 1: Exchanging a single symbol for "help"

Prompting Procedure: 2-Person
Error Correction Procedure: Backstepping

Choose a symbol:

Note on the communication skills timeline that we begin teaching "help" before the student has mastered discrimination. When we initially create these "help" lessons, we simplify other aspects of PECS, so the "help" icon is the only one available. In order to make discriminating it from among others easier for the student, we choose a "help" icon that is very different from the other symbols. Use one that is a different shape, size, texture, etc. It is the use of the symbol that will teach its meaning, not its visual configuration.

- The communicative partner sets up a situation involving a preferred item with which the student will require help. For example she gives the student an item he really likes in a container that he cannot open (the item should be visible).
- The moment the child has difficulty with the item, or when he tries to give it back to the communicative partner (but before a tantrum develops) the physical prompter assists the student to give the "help" icon to the communicative partner.
- As soon as the communicative partner receives the icon, she says to the child, "Oh, I'll help you with this," (or a comparable response) and fixes the problem.
- Repeat this scenario using a variety of items.

TAKE NOTICE!

Ensure that the "help" symbol is available at all times and plan to incorporate Phase II issues by teaching the child to go get the symbol from his book and go find the communicative partner across distances.

- Teach this lesson in a variety of environments, with a variety of trainers, across a variety of troublesome items. Use a variety of "obstacles" in addition to containers.

For example:

- opening/inserting a straw for a juice box
- winding up a toy
- tying shoes
- zipping a coat
- shaking a tornado bottle
- blowing up a balloon
- unwrapping cheese slices

- peeling a banana/orange
- swinging
- opening a milk carton
- blowing bubbles
- opening a door
- putting in a puzzle piece
- opening a bag of food
- putting in a tape or video

Alternatively:

- At a very early age, a typically developing child often brings Mom or Dad a troublesome item. Many of our students also do this. Depending on the student's age, you may have determined that this is an appropriate response for the student to use to access help. You might not initially teach him to use a "help" icon.
  - When you do begin teaching use of the icon, the student's *initiation* would take the form of reaching to the communicative partner with the troublesome item. In this case, as soon as the student does this, the physical prompter then guides the student to give a "help" symbol to the communicative partner. The partner immediately provides the appropriate assistance and gives the item back to the child. Over successive opportunities, the physical prompter fades assistance to give the "help" symbol so that the student learns to hand the item and then the symbol or just the symbol.

Step 2: Requesting help using the sentence strip

Once the student has mastered PECS Phase IV (Sentence Structure), teach the student to ask for help using the "I want" sentence starter. Teach this using the same backward chaining strategy described in Phase IV.

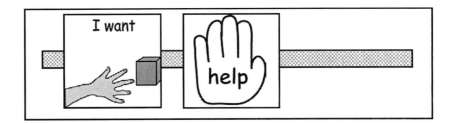

Step 3: Requesting help using a sentence

- Next, teach the student additional symbols to use in order to request help with specific items ("I want help straw." "I want help tornado bottle.").

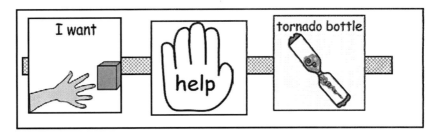

- If the student is learning to use some printed words, introduce the word "with" and teach him to incorporate this into his requests ("I want help **with** shoe.").

- As you introduce vocabulary to include actions, teach the student to request even more specific forms of help ("I want help tie shoe." "I want help open juice box."

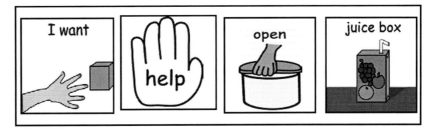

Answering "No" to "Do you want _____?"

Answering "Yes" to "Do you want _____?"

Earlier, we described two types of "yes/no" questions. Answering "Is this a _____?" leads to social reinforcement-"You're right, it is a _____!" Answering "Do you want _____?" leads to tangible reinforcement in that the student either gains access to a desired item, or avoids a non-preferred item. Because the latter reinforcement likely is more reinforcing for our students, we teach this question first.

Stimulus	Response	Consequence
"Is this an apple?"	"yes"	
"Do you want an apple?"	"yes" or "no"	or

Step 1: Choose a response form

Determine what specific response you want your student to use when answering this question. Because these students do not speak, the options are either a picture of some sort or a gesture. Because pictures of "yes" or "no" are abstract, we prefer to teach the child to gesture in order to indicate "yes" or "no." Head nodding and head shaking are generally universally understood gestures, so we teach these.

Step 2: Decide whether to teach "no" or "yes" first

Next, determine whether you are going to teach the "no" or "yes" response first. Typically developing children learn both at essentially the same time, but our students initially will need lessons to teach each separately and then together. We typically choose to teach the "no" response first, only because the inability to calmly indicate "no" usually leads to more severe behavior outbursts than does the inability to indicate "yes."

REMEMBER! Before beginning this training, you must know what your student does and does not like. You most likely have learned this through your PECS implementation. Continue your reinforcer assessment to determine both what the student likes and does not like.

Prompting Procedure: 2-Person

This skill does not strictly involve the student initiating a communicative exchange in response to an environmental or internal state; rather, the student is responding to a question. We have found, though, that using the 2-person prompting procedure results in quicker acquisition of an independent response. When the communicative partner asks the question, "Do you want _____?" and provides the physical prompts for the student to nod/shake his head, these prompts can be very difficult to fade. We have observed students being asked this question take the communicative partner's hands and place them on their own heads—these were children who were not taught with the 2-person prompting procedure, but learned that the communicative partner's hands touching their own heads was part of the response!

Error Correction: errorless learning or 4-Step Procedure

Because the physical prompter is providing physical prompts, these should be faded systematically, using an *errorless learning strategy*. Once the child has acquired an independent head shake/nod, he sometimes makes errors during which he might nod his head ("yes") but really doesn't want the item. This is a discrimination error, so the error correction procedure would be the 4-Step procedure.

Step 1: Head shaking to indicate "no."

- The communicative partner sits/stands in front of the student and shows him a non-preferred item while asking, "Do you want _____?" The physical prompter immediately and gently prompts the student (from behind) to shake his head back and forth. The communicative partner immediately responds with, "Okay, we'll put it away," or, "Okay, you don't have to," etc. and removes the item.

- Repeat this sequence over several opportunities, using other non-preferred items. Do not offer the same item on consecutive opportunities. Doing this is not sensible—from the child's perspective it would seem that you didn't understand or remember his previous response when he indicated, "no!"

- Fade physical prompts until the student independently shakes his head back and forth when asked, "Do you want this?"

- Vary your questions between "Do you want this?" and "Do you want (cheese curls) ?"

- Phase II issues—switch roles as trainers; introduce additional trainers; vary activities, offered items, locations; incorporate traveling; do this across the day!
- To create multiple opportunities for the child to spontaneously request these same items via PECS!

Step 2: Head nodding to indicate "yes"

Follow the same procedure as above, but physically prompt the student to nod his head up and down to indicate "yes."

- Phase II issues— use a variety of items, trainers, activities, times of day, and locations, distances.
- To create multiple opportunities for the child to spontaneously request these same items via PECS!

Step 3: Mixing "yes" and "no" opportunities

Begin this step as soon as the child independently shakes and nods his head.

- Using a variety of both preferred and non-preferred items, show the student a single item and ask either, "Do you want this?" or "Do you want _____?"

- If the child makes an error that you recognize (he nods "yes" when you are offering an item that you know he does not like), use the 4-Step error correction procedure. The "prompt" step will involve you gently physically prompting the correct response.

- To create multiple opportunities for the child to engage in ALL communication skills you are teaching.

Step 4: Answering when items are not present

Because we cannot always hold out the item we are offering (e.g., the swings on the playground, the swimming pool, a fast-food hamburger), we must teach the student to answer "Do you want _____?" when the item is not visible.

- Begin by offering items that are in sight. Over several opportunities, begin covering the items up. One strategy we use is to put items in a clear container and then begin putting masking tape around the outside of the container so that it is more difficult to see into.

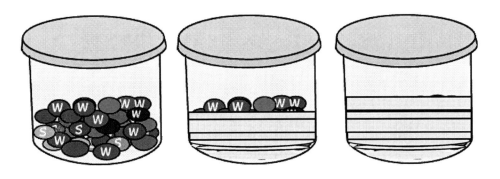

- Continue training by offering items that are not in your immediate presence but are nearby.
- Gradually begin to ask this question regarding items that are not nearby, but are in sight (the swings that you see through the window).
- Ask the question regarding items that are not in sight. If the student does not understand your spoken language, use a visual signal when asking the question.

Future Directions:

Children and adults reject and affirm for a variety of reasons and in response to an array of conditions. Analyze your student's current and future environment to determine what additional training you should complete. Suggestions include:

- Indicating "No" when given a direction to begin a non-preferred activity.
- Discontinuing an ongoing activity- indicating "I've had enough!" Alternatively, you could teach the student to indicate "All done," or "No more."

> For an excellent, in-depth discussion on teaching rejecting, see, Sigafoos, O'Reilly, Drasgow, and Reichle (2002).

- Indicating "No" when offered a preferred item that is contextually inappropriate or that the student does not want at this particular time.
- Indicating "No" to a requested item when a more attractive item is seen.
- Indicating "No" when offered more of an item the student currently is enjoying. Again, teaching "No more," or "All done," would be appropriate.

Also: A natural extension of answering "Yes" to "Do you want _____?" is to answer appropriately when given a choice- "Do you want _____ or _____." In this circumstance the student would need to respond with a specific request by using either a single picture or a sentence. When teaching this, you must create lessons during which the object is for the student to answer "Yes" or "No," or make a specific request.

Teaching "Yes" or "No" to "Is this _____?" As described in Chapter 2, answering "Yes" or "No" when asked, "Is this _____?" is a skill that is tied to the overall commenting function. Remember, answering this question should result in social reinforcement. This skill should be addressed but not until the student has learned to answer a variety of "comment" questions in Phase VI.

Requesting a Break

In our daily lives, we take frequent breaks from our work. We might take a formal break during which we leave the work area, or we might just pause for a few moments. Another type of break we take is in the form of vacation days! Requesting a break is a different skill than indicating, "No!" A person who rejects an item or activity is indicating that he or she does not want the item or activity at all. A person who requests a break is indicating that he or she will return to the activity.

"Break" ≠ "No thanks"

Before you can begin teaching a student to request a break, you must determine when the student is likely to need or want a break. You probably have observed a sequence of behaviors that the student engages in when he wants to escape from an activity. This sequence often ends in a temper tantrum. The situations from which students want to escape typically involve:

- Boring activities
- Difficult activities
- High demands
- Low reinforcement rates

break

Our goal is for the student to spontaneously request a break rather than engage in the inappropriate behavior or respond to a prompt to request to take a break. Therefore, we must be familiar enough with the student's behavior patterns so that we can teach the lesson *before* the inappropriate behavior occurs rather than *in response to* the inappropriate behavior.

Taking a break involves spending time in a demand-free situation. Break-time should be a period of time in which no demands are placed on the student, and should involve a "neutral" or "calming" activity. Asking for a break is not the same as requesting a preferred activity, so the student taking a break should not be accessing highly preferred items or activities. The symbol you choose for "break" is your choice.

Because this concept is hard to represent in a picture, we typically use the printed word on a card of a different color and shape.

Prepare an area in the home or classroom where break-time will be spent. We typically designate a specific area as the "break area," and furnish it with a chair, a beanbag, or a mat, and a timer. We sometimes label the area with the icon that is identical to the icon the student will be using to request the break.

The student's reward for asking for a break is temporary escape or avoidance. It is not access to reinforcing items in the break area. When you teach a student to request a break, you must be prepared to honor the request. This means that you will be able to stop what you are doing, take the student to the break area, and then take the student back to the current activity at the end of the break. We typically set a timer in the break area for 2 minutes and teach the student to respond to the timer signaling that break-time is over so that he does not have to rely on us to tell him that it is over.

Prompting Procedure: 2-Person

Requesting a break is an act of initiation, therefore, the 2-Person prompting procedure will be used.

Error Correction: Backstepping

Step 1: Initiating a request for a break.

- Create a controlled situation from which the student is likely to want to escape. For example, begin giving the student a rapid series of demands.

- The moment the student begins the behavior sequence you previously have observed in this situation, but **BEFORE** the full tantrum begins, the physical prompter guides the student to pick up and give a "break" icon to the communicative partner.

- As soon as she receives the icon, the communicative partner responds with, "Yes, you can take a break," and then accompanies the student to the break area. Physically prompt the student to activate the timer and then leave him alone.

- Once the timer rings, approach the student, signal to him the next available reinforcer, and accompany him back to the original activity. Do not approach the student and signal to him that he must go back to "work" without first signaling the reinforcer!

- If the student leaves the area before the timer rings, take him back to the original activity. We interpret this choice as indicating that the break area (escape from the activity) is no longer reinforcing.

- Because this activity is stressful, the student will likely want another break. *Before* the student engages in inappropriate behavior the physical prompter should again prompt him to exchange the "break" icon.

- The communicative partner again takes the student to the break area and repeats the sequence.

- Our goal is for the student to learn that he must stay in the break area during break time!

- The physical prompter fades assistance to exchange the "break" icon so that the student spontaneously asks for a break.

- Teach the student to start/stop the timer on his own. Many students can learn to do the entire break sequence independently!

- Practice this lesson across the day, across activities, across environments, and with a variety of trainers.

REMEMBER!

- Don't confuse "break" with "time-out." If you use a time-out procedure, do not use the same area for it as you do for break-time. Time-out is teacher-imposed, whereas requesting a break should be student initiated.

"Break" ≠ "Time out"

- If the student engages in inappropriate behavior prior to asking for a break, do not then prompt him to take a break! This prompt will teach him that he can escape an activity by acting inappropriately.

- If the student is attempting to "break" from all activities, assess the situation by reviewing your Pyramid. Is the reinforcement effective? Is the activity a functional one? A happy student shouldn't want out of an activity!

- If the student asks for a break and then attempts to gain access to a specific item, consider that he is now using the "break" icon as a generic requesting icon. Determine if he can ask for that item during times other than "break." If so, signal to him when that item is available. If not, teach him to ask for those items.

> Requesting frequent breaks is an indication that the reinforcement associated with the activity is not effective.

Step 2: Limited breaks

Once the student is independently *initiating* requests for breaks and is taking breaks appropriately, consider gradually placing some limits on the number of breaks that are available at any given time. Typical adults in the workforce average taking a break (formal and "informal") every two to two and one-half, hours so we should not expect our students to go longer than this. Options for limiting breaks include:

- Allowing a specific number of breaks per activity.
- Allowing a specific number of breaks per day or portion of a day.

- Visually signal to the student how many breaks are available to him. You can do this by giving him a number of break cards that he "spends." Each time he exchanges a card, that card disappears.

- To determine how many breaks with which to begin, first determine how many breaks the student takes, on average, per activity or portion of the day. Then give the student *more* break cards than this, so that he does not run out of cards. For example, if you collect information across 5-10 days, and determine that, on average, you student takes 6 breaks per day, give him 7 break cards to begin with. If the number of breaks taken per day varies greatly from day to day, consider offering even more than 7.
- Over time begin gradually reducing the number of break cards available to the student at a time by presenting him with one less card, then one more less card, and so on, as long as the original target behavior remains infrequent.

- Make sure the student can ask for a break in a variety of environments, including the community.
- If the student's escape-motivated behavior increases, reconsider how many breaks per time period he should be allowed.

TAKE NOTICE!

Be nice to your students! We do not limit giving treats to our students to when they have asked or 'earned' them. Just as we sometimes approach a student and give him a cookie or an extra turn on the swing, sometimes we suggest that he go take a break! As when teaching the student to request a break, though, be careful when doing this not to suggest a break once a student has begun behaving inappropriately. For example, if you've had a particularly hectic day, but your student is doing relatively well, offer the opportunity for a break.

Responding to "Wait"

All children, those who are typically developing and those with disabilities, encounter situations during which they must wait before accessing something they like. All children occasionally have difficulty waiting. We have all seen children at home or in public who are not enjoying waiting. Do you remember a particularly dramatic temper tantrum? Adults, too, spend hours and hours each year waiting for a variety of activities, and sometimes we, too, find this difficult.

To teach "wait" you must control:

Access to the reinforcer
The time the student must wait

We can guarantee failure if we teach our first "wait lesson" while in line for lunch at a fast food restaurant because we do not control the reinforcer in this environment. Rather, we begin these lessons in a structured environment when we are sure we will not be distracted by other demands for our attention, and with a "wait interval" that is literally a couple of seconds long! Just as we respond to a variety of visual cues to remind us to wait (a red stop light, a clock, the length of a line), we will provide our students with a visual reminder to wait. This reminder is something tangible that we give to the student when it is time to wait. Because the concept of "wait" also is hard to picture, we use a uniquely shaped/colored card with the word "wait" printed on it. The student holds or keeps the "wait card" with him, and then gives it back to us when the waiting period is over.

We begin teaching "wait" once a student has mastered Phase I and much of Phase II in PECS. At this point in time, the student is proficient at getting a picture, finding a communicative partner, and exchanging the picture. He is doing this in many environments, and has learned to tolerate slight delays while the communicative partner goes to get the requested item. In Phase I we try to reinforce EACH request that the student makes while he is learning to exchange a picture. Remember the coin bank we referred to and how we are making deposits to it during Phases I and II each time we reinforce a PECS exchange. When we ask a student to "wait" we are withdrawing coins, so we can gauge how frequently and for how long we can ask him to wait based on the current level of coins in the bank.

Step 1: Waiting less than 30 seconds

- Arrange a lesson during which the student requests a desired item. As soon as he gives you the picture, give him the "wait card," and tell him, "Wait." Within two to three seconds, take the wait card back from the student, saying, "Great waiting," and give him the requested item (do not require another request). This interval is so short the student will barely have time to look at this unfamiliar item you have given him before the wait period is over.
- Continue this type of training across the day, in a variety of situations. Each time you ask the student to wait, give him the wait card.
- Gradually begin increasing the wait interval by one or two seconds at a time.
- If the child behaves inappropriately while waiting, this is your signal that the wait interval is too long. Simply take the wait card, redirect the child to a different task, and try the lesson again later. DO NOT give the child the item for which he was waiting! Shorten the length of the **next** "wait" period and begin again increasing the time for each lesson.
- Once the student can wait for 20-30 seconds (keep in mind what is appropriate based on his age!), proceed to Step 2.

We give the student the wait card to hold so that he has something to keep his hands busy with. But! Over time, as the student's waiting is appropriately reinforced, this wait card comes to serve as a promissory note—the student learns that as long as he holds it, good things are sure to follow.

Also, teach the student to wait in response to environmental events—not just when he has asked for something that is not available at the moment. For example, when approaching the bathroom, give the student the "wait" card to indicate that he must wait his turn.

- Conduct this lesson in interspersed opportunities across the day. Do not create one "wait lesson" after another—this will lower the level of coins in the bank too quickly!
- Create opportunities for the student to request desired items and respond to this request so as to add more coins to the bank!

Step 2: Waiting for longer intervals

As adults, when we know ahead of time that we are going to have to wait, we plan to do something during the waiting time. If we are going to the dentist, we take a book or a magazine along. We shouldn't, therefore, expect our students to do nothing but sit quietly while waiting.

- Once the student is waiting for 30 seconds, when you tell him, "Wait," give him the wait card, and also give him something to do to occupy his hands during the wait time. This item should not be the item the student requested or a highly desired item, but an item that will keep him busy. We often keep a "wait box" on hand. This box contains items that can occupy the student while waiting. Then, when we tell the student to wait, we offer the box from which he can choose an item.
- Over several days, or even weeks, gradually increase the wait interval to a minute, then two minutes, and so on, keeping your student's age in mind when you determine what is an appropriate amount of waiting time.
- If the student is waiting for a specific item or activity, it is sometimes helpful to put a picture of that activity on the wait card as a reminder of the "payoff" for waiting.
- As the interval gets longer than a minute, help the student predict how much longer he must wait by adding additional visual cues. We do this by adding Velcro® dots to the wait card and by then giving the student small objects to put on the dots. Initially, we have one dot on the card. Just as he gets to the end of the wait interval, give him the small object, guide him to attach it to the Velcro®, and then point to the "full circle" while you say, "We're done waiting! Here's your _____." Over time, add a second Velcro® dot. Give the child the first object about 3/4 of the time into the interval. He most likely

will try to give you the wait card, thinking that waiting is over. Indicate to him that he has another "circle to fill," wait a few seconds, and then give him the final object. Over time, increase from two to three, four, and then five Velcro® dots. The student does not have to give you the tokens at the end of the wait period.

- As you conduct more and more successful wait lessons, the wait card becomes a "promissory note" to the student. He learns that as long as he has the wait card, he can trust you to follow through with your end of the "deal."
- If your student "fails" a wait lesson, do not reinforce the failure by giving the student what he was waiting for—change activities, and try again later with a shorter the interval.
- Never say, "Wait" to the student if you really mean, "No."

Step 3: The "real" world

- Venture out into the community where you don't know exactly how long your student will have to wait.
- Take along all of your waiting supplies—the wait card, the tokens, something for the student to do while waiting, and your confidence! Your student should be carrying his PECS book.
- Begin in an environment where you are fairly sure the wait interval will be relatively short. For example, go to McDonald's® for frenchfries at 2:00 PM after the lunch crowd has gone.
- Expand the environments where the student must wait so that he experiences waiting opportunities across a variety of activities and settings and intervals that are longer.

TAKE NOTICE !

- Continue creating opportunities for the student to use ALL of his communication skills. By this time, your student should be requesting with a great deal of persistence, asking for "Help," answering "Yes" or "No" and discriminating from among a few symbols at a time.

Following Functional Directions

Sometimes, we give directions because they help us, the speaker, in some way. For example, Mom might say to her son, "Bring me that book." The outcome from Mom's perspective is that she gets the book she wants. The outcome from the son's perspective, however, is that Mom says, "Thanks!" Remember, though, that many students with disabilities do not find this type of outcome rewarding. Recall in our discussion of functional communication that we noted children learn to communicate because the skills are useful in their everyday lives. Therefore, in order to teach students to follow directions, we must teach directions that are useful to them. In other words, we need to arrange lessons in which naturally-reinforcing consequences follow the directions. For example, telling the student to "Sit down," should result in a pleasant activity that works best while seated (e.g., snack time, drawing with markers, etc.). Responding to "Go to gym," should result in being able to participate in an enjoyable activity such as playing with a favorite ball. Attributes like size can become important within directions we give if following the direction results in access to a good outcome (e.g., "The juice is in the big pitcher.").

Just as people use various modalities to convey their messages, students need to be able to understand communication sent in different ways. Therefore, regardless of whether they speak, sign, or use pictures to express themselves, we also must plan to teach students to respond appropriately to a range of pictorial, written, and spoken instructions.

Following Visual Directions

When we begin to teach instruction following with pictures or symbols, we first need to assess that the student understands the picture by itself. That is, while there may be times when we want to combine speech with visual cues, if a student responded to this combination then we would not be able identify if he reacted to the spoken words alone, the picture alone, or to the combination. Given the need in our society to respond to visual cues in isolation from auditory cues, this lesson is important for all students. Thus, we suggest teaching the instructional use of visual cues without also saying the direction.

Prompting Procedure: Backward Chaining
Error Correction: Backstepping

Identify a set of directions to teach. Choose directions that will involve objects or locations that are familiar to the student and ones that the student either enjoys (like a ball) or ones that the student knows what to do with (e.g., put plates on the table before a meal).

locations and associated items

Gym— ball, swing, jump rope
Table— pencil, markers, plates, cups
Sink— cup, plate, spoon
Circle— items for songs, weather, etc.
Music— musical instruments
Play area— toys
Door— shoes, playground toys, book bag

> Do not introduce a picture unless its associated item or activity is familiar to the student- he must know what to do with the item, where to go with it, or what happens during the activity.

Symbol type: For students using PECS, use the same symbol type that the student is accustomed to within PECS. However, to avoid confusion, we find it helpful to differentiate between pictures the student will use to communicate with us and those we will use when communicating with the student. Generally, we do this by making the pictures we use to communicate with the student larger than those he uses within PECS. As with PECS, you should use any symbol that the student can understand- that is, photographs, product logos, miniature or full sized items, 3-dimensional representations or similar symbols.

Step 1: Full Physical Prompting

Begin by showing the student the symbol and then gently guiding him to where that item is kept. For example, assume that your student is familiar with playing with toy cars in the play area. He likes the cars and associates those cars with the play area. Show him the "toy car" picture and physically guide him to the play area where he can see the toy cars. He should pick up the car and begin to play with it. Throughout other times of the day, do this activity with a variety of pictures. When you show the student the picture, remember not to name the location or item! You can say, "Go here," or "Get this," or similar phrases, or you can remain quiet. Sometimes, the student takes the picture from you and carries it to match it to an identical symbol in the appropriate area. At other times, we just show the student the picture and we keep it.

Step 2: Fading physical assistance

With each symbol you are teaching, begin fading your physical assistance from the end of the sequence. Physically guide the student through the beginning of the sequence, stop a foot or two short of the target location, and let the student complete the sequence on his own. Continue fading your assistance until the student independently completes the sequence when you show him the symbol.

The goal is for the student, upon seeing the symbol, to go to the pictured location or get the pictured item and use it appropriately.

REMEMBER!

At some point in time, your student might make an error. On the way to the target location or item, he might get distracted by something and stop, or he might see something across the room and detour in that direction. When this error occurs, respond to it by *Backstepping*. Take the student back to the place in the sequence where he was last correct, physically help him to complete the sequence, and then provide differential reinforcement (e.g., less time to play with the cars, a not-so-favorite car from the box of cars, etc.). You might be tempted when the student detours or stops, to go to him and redirect him to the correct location. Resist this temptation! Using re-direction will teach the student to head out into the middle of the room and then wait for you to catch up and take him to the correct location!

Following spoken directions

The sequence for teaching a student to follow a spoken direction is identical to the sequence we use to teach following a visual direction. The only difference is the stimulus—now the student must respond only to the spoken cue. Some students with disabilities have difficulty responding to an auditory cue alone. These are the students who either don't respond at all when given a direction or respond incorrectly despite many opportunities to respond. For these students, several issues must be considered:

1. **Do you have the student's attention?** When showing the student a visual direction, it is natural for us to approach him with the direction. When we deliver an auditory direction, however, it is easy for us to forget to ensure that we have the student's attention because we assume the student can hear from across the room. So, before giving the auditory direction, approach the student and touch him to get his attention. If the student responds to his name being called, always call on him before giving the direction.

2. **Review the Pyramid!** Is the direction a functional one? The direction should be meaningful to the student. Saying, "Go to the door," with no associated 'reason' is not a functional direction. Saying "Go to the door," with an associated 'reason'- we're leaving the classroom- is a functional direction. Is the reinforcement associated with the task signaled to the student before the direction is given? If not, both of these elements must be adjusted.

3. **Review how you are delivering the message.** The message should be delivered simply and concisely. For example, if you want the student to line up at the door, you might simply say, "Door" and then physically prompt the student to the door. For a student who can respond to slightly more complex language, you could say, "Go to the door." Most students will not respond to something like, "We're getting ready to go to gym and that's why we put our gym clothes and shoes on, and on the way there we're going to stop at the office and drop of the attendance form, so please line up at the door." If this is how we typically talk to our students, they most likely are responding as if "white noise" were playing in the background. Remember that what we say to the students needs to be the relevant words! If we imbed the direction in the midst of a long comment or explanation, the student most likely won't respond!

4. **Consider your student's history.** Has the student been in an environment where spoken directions are repeated and repeated and repeated and repeated...? If so, then most likely he has learned that he doesn't have to respond the first time you say something to him—maybe even not the second

or third or fourth! **DON"T REPEAT YOUR DIRECTIONS IF THE STUDENT DOES NOT RESPOND IMMEDIATELY!!** Remember the teaching strategy we are using for direction following is backward chaining. That means that the first time we give the student the direction, we don't allow time for a mistake— we immediately physically prompt the student to respond. Over time, we fade those physical prompts.

Can I use a visual signal to teach responding to auditory directions?

If your student has learned to respond to visual signals, you can take advantage of this skill to teach him to respond to auditory signals. Remember, the long-term goal is for the student to respond to just a spoken direction- the natural cue. If we use visual signals as prompts, then we must plan to eliminate that prompt! One effective strategy is to use delayed prompting as discussed in teaching Phases V and VI. Specifically, use a *progressive time delay*. Begin by giving the auditory direction while simultaneously providing the visual prompt (either a gesture or a picture). Over time, increase the delay between saying the direction and providing the visual prompt until the student responds to the auditory signal alone.

Long-Term Visual Support

Some student have a long history of difficulty responding to auditory stimuli. These students have made limited progress in training during which visual prompts were added to auditory stimuli. Peterson, Bondy, Vincent & Finnegan (1995) worked with two such students and concluded that, even over time, the students made better gains in direction following when communicative input made up of both auditory and visual stimuli was used than they did when directions contained only auditory input. If this is the case with your student, consider that he might always require visual support for direction following.

Responding to Transitional Cues

We described in Chapter 2 that many students appear to have difficulty transitioning from activity to activity. When told or signaled in some way to end one activity and move to another, these children react poorly— crying, tantruming, or refusing to comply. Although some of these children are reacting to not knowing what is expected of them, many more are reacting to the loss of their current reinforcer. When you tell a student move to another activity, you also have told him to stop the activity he is enjoying. Suddenly losing a reinforcer elicits negative reactions in all of us. Furthermore, the instruction may be vague in that it does not assure the student that another reinforcer will be available to him in the next activity.

The key to successful transitions for these students is to remember our **"reinforcer first"** strategy, and signal what reinforcer is available next before signaling that it is time to switch activities. This signal should be visual, either by showing the student the actual reinforcer that is available next or

showing a picture of that reinforcer *before* signaling the next activity.

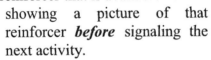
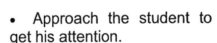

- Approach the student to get his attention.
- Show him the next available reinforcer.
- If he shows interest in it, withhold it while signaling the next activity.
- Once the student has transitioned successfully to the next activity, provide the reinforcer.

If you are at a point in training where you have begun to teach visual direction following, you can approach the student, show him the next reinforcer, and then show the picture direction he is to follow. This combination of signals can be expanded further when you begin schedule following by pairing a picture of the next available reinforcer with the schedule picture.

Following a Visual Schedule

Once your student can follow 6-8 visual directions when individually presented, the next logical step is to combine those pictures to form a schedule he can follow. We arrange the pictures vertically because vertical discrimination is developmentally acquired before left-right sequencing. The purpose of teaching a student to follow a schedule is for him to learn to transition *independently* from activity to activity across the day. Generally, the student should learn that upon arriving at school (or home), he immediately goes to his schedule to find the first activity. He should participate in that activity, and then independently return to the schedule to find what's next. To act in ways similar to adults going through our day, students must learn to independently do this entire sequence. In order for this independence to develop, we must teach the student the *sequence* of steps involved in schedule following. Because the student is not likely respond to verbal prompts about these steps (e.g., "Take the picture off the top of the schedule"), or to modeling prompts, we use physical prompts to teach this skill.

circle

puzzle

bathroom

snack

finished

Prompting Procedure: Backward chaining

Error Correction Procedure: Backstepping

The steps in schedule following are:

1. **Go to schedule**
2. **Remove top picture**
3. **Put picture on "current activity" location**
4. **Go to activity area**
5. **At end of activity, return to schedule**
6. **Place "current activity" picture in "finished" box**

Repeat Steps 2-6 for each activity/symbol.

When the student arrives at school (or home), meet him at the door and immediately physically prompt him to walk to his schedule, remove the first picture and put it on the "current activity" space. At this point, because the student learned to respond to these pictures during direction following training, he should immediately respond to this picture (not our spoken direction!) by going to the designated area and beginning the activity. Once the activity is complete, physically prompt the student to return to the schedule, remove the current picture, put it in the "finished" box, remove the top picture, place it on the "current activity" section, and respond to that picture. You should not verbally prompt any of this sequence- you will have to fade the physical prompt, so don't add a second prompt to fade!! Do reinforce each independently completed step. Over time, fade your physical assistance (from the end of the chain) until the student independently completes the sequence for each activity across the day.

Signaling the end of an activity:

Because the goal of schedule following is independent sequencing from activity to activity, the student must learn to respond to natural cues that signal the end of the activity. We avoid phrases such as, "Check your schedule," or "See what's next," etc. We adults do not have someone on hand telling us that an activity has ended and that we must go on to the next. We do not want our students to come to rely on those types of prompts, either. Examples of natural cues that signal the end of an activity include:

- A project is complete
- Lunch items have all been consumed
- The last page of a book has been read
- A teacher says to everyone, "That's it!"
- A teacher says, "We're finished!"
- A bell rings
- A video ends
- The dishwasher is empty
- Throwing away a paper towel after hand washing
- Putting a toothbrush away after tooth brushing

Note that some of these are environmental signals and several are teacher originated signals. The teacher signals are not *prompts*, though, because they are ones that children without disabilities are likely to hear at home or school. We don't intend to fade these signals, so they are natural *cues*.

Additional Schedule Components:

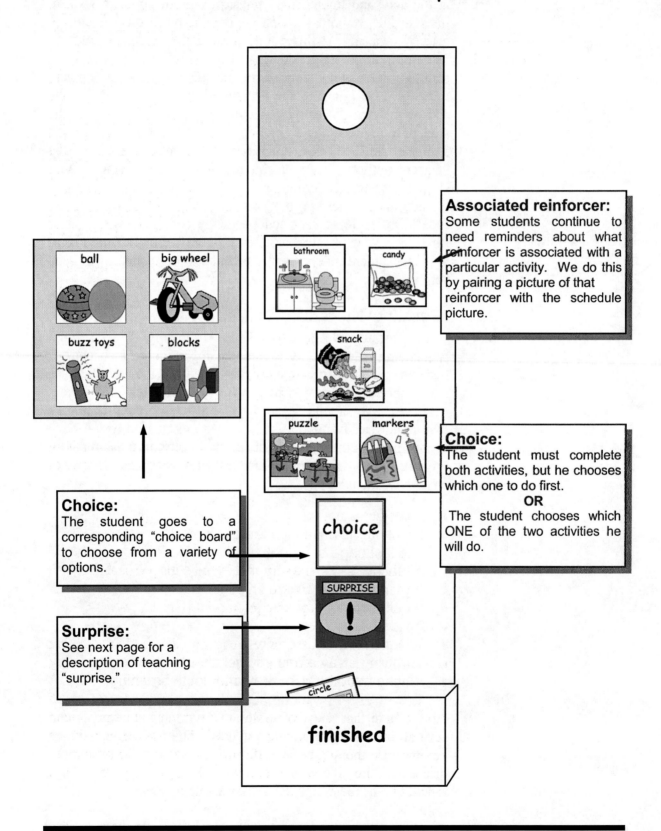

Associated reinforcer:
Some students continue to need reminders about what reinforcer is associated with a particular activity. We do this by pairing a picture of that reinforcer with the schedule picture.

Choice:
The student must complete both activities, but he chooses which one to do first.

OR

The student chooses which ONE of the two activities he will do.

Choice:
The student goes to a corresponding "choice board" to choose from a variety of options.

Surprise:
See next page for a description of teaching "surprise."

Teaching "Surprise!"

Children with autism characteristically have difficulty dealing with change. Often, we try to avoid the negative behaviors that these children might demonstrate in response to changes by arranging for their days to be as unvarying as possible. Unfortunately, life presents many unavoidable changes, so we must teach children to deal with surprises. We teach the students to respond to an icon that represents, **"SURPRISE!"** Oftentimes, the changes we encounter in our daily lives are favorable ones. We play with the blocks instead of the toy cars, we go to the steak-and-lobster restaurant rather than the fast-food restaurant. We can't always predict when unexpected circumstances will arise, though, and we can't always expect them to be pleasant ones! For this reason, we teach students to respond to a generic "surprise" icon on their schedules. The "surprise" icon is unique in that the student does not independently go to some activity upon seeing that icon as he does with his other schedule icons. Rather, he waits for the teacher to describe what the surprise is at that particular moment.

Initially, these surprises are pleasant ones—
-We are playing outside for an extra ten minutes.
-We are having an ice cream party.
-We are watching a video instead of taking the math test.

Once the student begins anticipating something "different" in response to the surprise icon, the surprises sometimes are more neutral events—
-We are having Cheerios® instead of Rice Krispies®.
-Mrs. Kohli is teaching art today rather than Mrs. Johnson.

Eventually, some surprises include less pleasant ones—
-We're going to the dental screening.
-It's raining, we can't go outside today.

Plan for these surprises to occur at different times during the day, and make each day's surprise different. Vary among pleasant, neutral, and unpleasant surprises. Sometimes, put the surprise icon on the schedule the moment it is to be used (even more of a surprise!). Eventually, you can use the surprise icon on a schedule when you plan a specific time for the activity, or you can use the surprise icon at a moment's notice during for direction following when events such as a fire drill arise. Always reinforce your student's calm response!

Each of these additional communication skills has been presented separately. When you complete the "Initial Critical Communication Skills Checklist," you may find you need to quickly teach one of these skills. It may be tempting to hold off teaching a particular skill until problems arise related to its absence. That is, only when we see a child who is waiting to go outside begin tantruming do we introduce the "wait" lessons. Our advice is to systematically plan to teach all of these skills to all of the children and adults you work or live with. Everyone encounters situations wherein they will need help, must wait for something, or must understand what someone else is trying to communicate. Therefore, everyone eventually needs to acquire the skills noted in this chapter. Using the timeline presented in this Chapter (and in Appendix F) you can review guidelines as to when to start these lessons relative to lessons within PECS. While there is some independence between skills, we do believe there are certain priorities. We want children to follow our instructions but it is more important to teach children to express their own needs. Starting all interactions with a "do this" orientation puts compliance at the top of the teaching list. We see no reason that this emphasis must be in place before beginning to teach other communication skills.

Our goal in teaching these communication skills is for the student to be able to use any or all of them depending on current circumstances. We must create opportunities during which students must use the appropriate communication skills to obtain a desired outcome. This does not mean that one communication skill will be more appropriate than another in a given situation. For example, a student on the playground might indicate, "No," when directed (visually and/or auditorally) to play ball, OR he might request the slide to let you know that he'd prefer that activity. It would not be appropriate to request a break in this circumstance. A student asked, "What do you want?" should respond with a request, and a student asked, "Do you want this?" should respond with a "Yes" or "No." Our interventions must teach the student to make the conditional discrimination of which skill to use at which time.

REMEMBER!

Create lessons in which the goal is discriminating which communication skill to use.

In the next chapter we will show how we can take advantage of a child's communication skills to promote cooperation between a teacher and a student so that lessons can be completed in a mutually beneficial manner.

12

Teaching Communication Across the Day

Teaching Communication Across the Day

The communication skills students learn and use in structured activities both at home and school are important skills. However, only when a student uses these new skills across the entire day and across all activities are we confident that he has truly "mastered" the skill. This chapter is designed to help parents and teachers select routines or activities in which communication can be taught, and to describe strategies that can be used to elicit communication when the students are participating in the routines.

The initial Phases in PECS teach students to request highly desirable or reinforcing items. We have discussed teaching PECS across all activities, and therefore, teaching the student to request items that are highly desired within a variety of activities (e.g., snack, free play, recess, etc.). But, what happens if a student is engaged in a particular activity for which there are only a couple of items he likes? Is it sufficient to teach only those items within the activity? What about activities for which you have not identified any reinforcing items? Is it acceptable not to expect spontaneous requests within these activities? For example, during art class a particular student may only like the markers. He might not enjoy other materials. We can teach him to ask for the markers, but this is a rather limited vocabulary for such a regular activity. Perhaps a student is learning how to brush his teeth. You might logically assume that if, one day, a toothbrush is missing, he would be motivated to ask for it. But, if the student does not like brushing his teeth, he won't be motivated to ask for the toothbrush. Another student is learning how to set the table. He might not particularly care for spoons and forks by themselves, so we probably have not taught that vocabulary.

When we consider teaching vocabulary related to routines, we have two options:

1. Vocabulary associated with related items

2. Vocabulary related to the routine itself

Teaching Vocabulary for Associated Items

Many of the following items are likely to be ones that your student has learned to request:

- drinks
- juice box
- cereal
- ice cream
- pudding

- music
- videos
- markers
- paint

These items require additional components in order for the student to use or enjoy them:

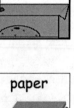

REINFORCER	ASSOCIATED ITEM
drinks	cup
juice box	straw
cereal	spoon
ice cream	spoon
pudding	spoon
music	tape, tape player
videos	VCR, remote
markers	paper

Once the student has learned to request the reinforcing item, try giving him that item without its associated item. This strategy, sometimes called the "Blocked Response" strategy, capitalizes on the student's history with the item. Having each component has been necessary for the student to enjoy the activity, so he will be motivated to obtain the missing item. If he is accustomed to drinking from a cup and is given a whole pitcher of juice, he likely will be motivated to ask for the cup. If he likes to paint and you give him only paint, he will be motivated to ask for the brushes.

Conduct an inventory of all the items your student has learned to request by looking through his PECS book. Once you have determined if particular reinforcers have associated items, you then can teach the student to request those items.

Teaching Communication in Functional Routines

Routines are activities or sequences of actions within an activity that are performed in the same manner at a predictable time of day. There are two types of routines:

After school:
☐ Empty book bag
☐ Fix snack
☐ Eat snack
☐ Play
☐ Set table
☐ Eat dinner
☐ Clean up
☐ Homework
☐ Bath
☐ Brush teeth
☐ Video
☐ Bed

Set table:
☐ Put out plates
☐ Put out forks
☐ Put out spoons
☐ Put out knives
☐ Put out napkins
☐ Put out cups
☐ Put out salt/pepper

1. The first type involves groups of activities done across the day. These activities generally occur in the same order or sequence each day. For example, a typical after-school routine might begin with emptying a book bag, and progress through snack, playing, dinner, evening work, bath, brushing teeth, video and bed. These activities are performed in the same sequence each day so that once a particular activity is completed, what comes next is predictable and expected.

2. The second type of routine involves the *steps* in each of the activities in the daily routine. For example the steps for dressing might involve removing pajamas, putting on underwear, socks, pants, shirt, and shoes. In an educational setting, the specific steps in the routine are delineated by conducting a ***task analysis***.

In order to identify potential routines for teaching communication, all team members who live and/or work with the student should analyze a typical day. In a school setting, a classroom teacher typically organizes her day around a set of activities or routines that generally are repeated from day to day. For each activity, the teacher has specific goals (e.g., academic, fine motor, self-help, etc.). In addition to these goals the team also targets certain communication skills to teach. We find it helpful to use the following form to analyze a daily routine. This worksheet helps a team look at each activity to determine the full range of communication skills that can be taught.

Time	Activity	Functional Objectives	Communication Goals	Who	Direction Following	Who
8:45	Arrival Free-time	unload book bags toileting free play	request help/toy Answer "Do you want?"	all	Follow simple directions "go to bathroom" "give it to me"	all cf, ks, ab, lr
9:00	circle	social interaction communication fine motor skills group direction-following	request songs/reinforcers request items to complete fine motor task answer "What do you hear?" answer "Do you want?"	all all Lr sf	respond to group directions: "stand up"	all
9:20	gym	transition to gym gross motor-kick/throw ball run/jump	request desired activity request help comment on environment	all all lr	respond to kick vs. throw respond to run vs. jump	all all
10:00	snack	transition to classroom set table communication appropriate eating	sit appropriately pour liquids into cup request desired item ask for help answer "Do you want?"	all	"throw away" "give me your cup" "get two/three…" "clean up"	all all lr all, sf
10:30	group table work	complete assembly tasks	request reinforcers signal "all done" request help	all lr, jd, sm all	"give it to me" "throw away"	all all

How can we teach communication within a routine?

We teach communication within a functional routine by using various "sabotage" strategies. Sometimes these strategies are referred to as "Interrupted Behavior Chain Strategies" (Halle, 1984). These procedures involve introducing an obstacle into the routine that will make finishing the routine impossible unless the student overcomes that obstacle. For example, within the table setting routine, some of the obstacles that could occur include:

We are creating an "establishing operation."

While I

I need

- The student goes to get the forks and discovers that they are missing.
- The student goes to get the forks and finds something unrelated in place of the forks- socks in the fork drawer!!
- The student can't reach the forks that have been stacked in the dish drainer.
- The student can't open the drawer to get the forks.
- The student doesn't have enough forks to set one beside each plate.

In order to teach the student to request a needed item within a routine, two elements must first be in place:

1.   Reinforcement: The student must want to participate in the routine. If he does not like participating in the activity, when we create an obstacle he is likely to celebrate ("My toothpaste is missing, so I don't have to brush my teeth!!"). This motivation can come from either of two sources:

a. If the routine is one the student enjoys because of the activity itself (e.g., recess, watching a video, etc.), then the actual ***participation*** in the routine is what is reinforcing.

first

then

b. If the student does not like a particular routine (e.g., tooth brushing, cleaning up toys), then the student's daily sequence of routines should be arranged so that the activity/routine that follows the non-desired routine is one that he likes. Over time, if parents and staff consistently allow the student access to the follow-up routine only if he completes the non-desired routine, he will learn that ***finishing*** the disliked routine provides access to the desired routine. The student will be motivated to participate in and finish the non-desired routine.

2. Mastery of the steps in the routine: The student must be able to perform the routine independently. If not, he will not know what item to request. For example, if a student is brushing his teeth and has not mastered the step during which he puts toothpaste on the toothbrush— if the toothpaste is missing, then he will probably just put the empty toothbrush into his mouth.

For example, Mary, who is 7 years old, uses a spoon appropriately but never asks for one or communicates anything about spoons because spoons in and of themselves are not interesting to her. Let's assume that Mary likes Fruitloops®. At breakfast time (or afternoon snack time) Mary's mother gives her the box of Fruitloops®. Her mother then brings Mary to the kitchen table and gives her an empty bowl. Mom then helps Mary pour cereal and then some milk into her bowl. Finally, Mary's mother hands her a spoon and Mary begins to eat. As her mother establishes this routine, it is important to go through each step in the same order every time. Also, as Mary's mother establishes this routine, she will not expect Mary to go through the each step independently. Rather, she will help her daughter at each step and give her the spoon at the proper time. Over several days, Mom gradually helps less and less until Mary can complete the sequence independently. While going through the routine, Mary's mother avoids asking questions or describing what she is doing using a lot of words. In fact, to help the activity become more of a predictable sequence of actions, it is best to basically say the same thing each time the routine is performed or to say nothing at all. Remember, what you say could inadvertently become a prompt!

One way to be consistent in performing your routines is to write a task analysis for each routine. This job involves analyzing the routine for each step and writing each step in a numbered, sequential list. For example, with Mary's cereal routine, her Mom came up with the following steps:

1. Get cereal
2. Get bowl
3. Get spoon
4. Get milk
5. Go to table
6. Pour cereal into bowl
7. Add milk
8. Eat cereal

Let's assume that Mary's parents have used this routine for a whole week and Mary is now able to independently fix herself a bowl of cereal. In looking at the requirements for teaching communication within a routine, we see that both are in place:

1. Reinforcement: Mary enjoys the routine itself because she loves Fruitloops!

2. Mastery of the routine: By the end of the week, when given all of the materials, Mary is able to make a bowl of cereal on her own.

To begin sabotaging the routine, one morning Mary's mother "forgets" to give Mary the spoon. She will have Mary's communication book available with a picture of spoon on the

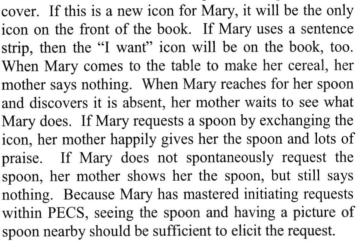

cover. If this is a new icon for Mary, it will be the only icon on the front of the book. If Mary uses a sentence strip, then the "I want" icon will be on the book, too. When Mary comes to the table to make her cereal, her mother says nothing. When Mary reaches for her spoon and discovers it is absent, her mother waits to see what Mary does. If Mary requests a spoon by exchanging the icon, her mother happily gives her the spoon and lots of praise. If Mary does not spontaneously request the spoon, her mother shows her the spoon, but still says nothing. Because Mary has mastered initiating requests within PECS, seeing the spoon and having a picture of spoon nearby should be sufficient to elicit the request.

Over several days, Mary's mother will sabotage the routine in **different** ways. One day the spoon is missing, another the milk is missing. BUT!!! <u>On some days the routine is intact</u>. We have known students who have been taught to request within a routine who ask for items whether or not the item is present. They essentially have learned a new sequence for the routine— requesting an item at some point. These students have not learned to discriminate between when the routine is intact versus when it is not.

As a generalization lesson, if Mary becomes accustomed to having cereal every day **after** getting dressed, her parents could create a different opportunity for Mary to request something she wants by *interrupting* the daily routine. In the cereal example, Mary's cue that it is time for cereal is finishing dressing. So, while she still is in the bedroom, Mom or Dad could say, "It's time for breakfast." Because Mary is used to making her cereal following getting dressed, she will go to the kitchen expecting to be given her cereal. But, when Mary goes to the kitchen, her parents "set the stage" for Mary to communicate by not offering the cereal box at all. Instead, they *delay* offering the box and *wait* for Mary to ask (in this case by giving a picture of cereal) for the cereal. Once Mary has asked for the cereal, her parents immediately give it to her and enthusiastically praise her for a job well done. The parents' role in this lesson is not to anticipate and provide what Mary is expecting (her morning cereal), but to teach Mary a vital skill by arranging what is happening in the routine so that Mary is highly likely to ask for something she wants.

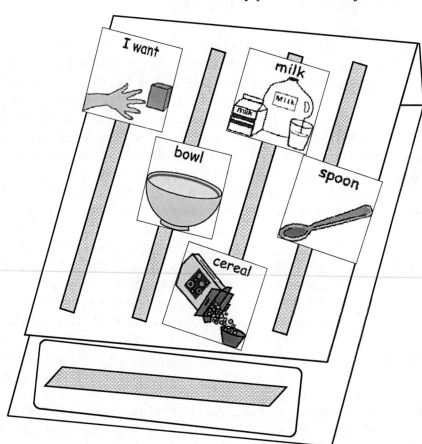

We suggest that parents and teachers select sequences of activities according to the time of day. For example, a common sequence on a school day morning may be: remove pajamas, get dressed, eat breakfast, wash up and brush teeth, put on a coat, and get on the school bus. After school, the sequence may be: put away the coat, have a snack in the kitchen, put on coat, go outside and play, come inside, put away the coat, wash hands and face, set the table, eat dinner, clean up, etc. During school, the routines are related to school activities. It is very helpful for parents and teachers to sit down together and write out these sequences. We know that families rarely follow the same exact routine each day. However, the more systematic are your routines, the faster will your student be able to learn to communicate to you about those routines. Once you have written down the sequence of activities, select one activity within each area in the house. Next, choose which step and its associated material you want to teach your student to communicate about. Then, establish the routine for at least one week (two if necessary) before interrupting the routine to use the *sabotage* strategy. **The student must have mastered the routine and participating in or finishing the routine must be reinforcing before the routine can be used to teach communication!** You may find it helpful to use the worksheets that follow.

The initial worksheets are used while "brainstorming" to list all of the routines the student participates in. List each routine by name. Next, assess the reinforcer that currently is available to the student for participating in the routine. If you note that no reinforcers are available, then assess whether or not that routine can be adjusted in order to become more reinforcing. If not, then you must teach the student that finishing the routine is reinforcing because of what follows. The form includes information on where in the home, school, or community the routine takes place so that you can plan to have the communication book or an activity board available. Finally, list the materials that are needed for this routine. These items are potential vocabulary items to teach.

The next worksheet is for analyzing a specific routine for its individual steps. List each step separately and any materials (vocabulary) for each step. Note the reinforcer available for the routine, and describe the sabotage strategies that will be used once the routine is mastered. Once the student masters the routine and you begin teaching communication, you can track from day to day the student's progress on using vocabulary that is specific to that routine.

Remember the important discrimination the student must learn to make— whether or not any communication is necessary within the routine. So, across several days, sabotage the routine in different ways so that the student requests a variety of items. But, on some days, leave the routine intact so that the objective is finishing the routine in a timely fashion.

Routine	Steps	Vocabulary for Requesting
	1. 2. 3. 4. 5. 6.	1. 2. 3. 4. 5. 6.

Location: _____ Time: _____

Routine	Reinforcement (routine itself or	Area of House/	Materials

Sabotage strategy once routine is mastered:

Routines and Communication in the Home and Classroom Worksheet©
summary of routines

Sample

Home MORNING

Routine	Reinforcement (routine itself or finishing routine)	Area of House/ class	Materials
get dressed	finishing - gets 5 minutes of video	bedroom	underwear, pants, shirt, socks, shoes
video	routine is reinforcing	family room	videotape, VCR
wash hands	finishing - gets breakfast	bathroom	water, soap, towel
eat breakfast	routine is reinforcing	kitchen	cereal, bowl, milk, spoon
brush teeth	finishing - gets 5 minutes of free play	bathroom	water, toothbrush, tooth-paste, towel
free play	routine	family room	train (specific cars), tracks, other currently favorite toys
get ready for bus	finishing - likes to ride school bus	family room	shoes, coat, backpack

Routines and Communication in the Home and Classroom Worksheet©
summary of routines

Sample

School MORNING

Routine	Reinforcement (routine itself or finishing routine)	Area of House/ class	Materials
arrival – unload book bag, etc.	finishing– gets to go to free play	classroom	book bag, basket for home/school log
free play	routine is reinforcing– loves toys in free play	classroom	toys
morning circle	routine is reinforcing– likes to sing songs	classroom	carpet squares, props for songs, song titles
academics/table-top activities	finishing – gets 5 minutes of free play	classroom	manipulatives, pencil, paper, etc.
motor group	routine– likes therapy ball, tunnel, etc.	all-purpose room	therapy ball, ramps, balls, tunnel
wash hands	finishing - gets to have snack	bathroom	water, soap, towel
snack	routine– likes snack foods	snack	snack foods, cup, plate, napkin, spoon, chair

Routines and Communication in the Home and Classroom Worksheet©
steps within routines

Name: _____ | Sample

Routine	Steps	Vocabulary for Requesting
washing hands	1. enter bathroom	1.
	2. turn on water	2. water
	3. get hands wet	3.
	4. put soap on hands	4. soap
	5. rub hands	5.
	6. rinse hands	6.
	7. dry hands	7. towel
	8.	8.
	9.	9.
	10.	10.
	11.	11.
Sabotage strategy once routine is mastered: prior to child arriving in bathroom, vary: turn water off tightly, hide soap, hide towel	12.	12.

REINFORCEMENT: finishing the routine for the next activity (snack or meal)

The routine was intact—no requesting was necessary.

Date	11/6	11/7	11/8	11/9	11/10	11/13	11/14	11/15	11/16	11/17
Item	soap	soap	towel	none	none	absent	towel	water	water	none
Response	+	+	+	-	+		+	-	-	-
Staff	lf	lf	lf	sr	sr	lf	lf	lf	jr	jr

Routines and Communication in the Home and Classroom Worksheet©
steps within routines

Name: _____ | Sample |

Routine	Steps	Vocabulary for Requesting
Cafeteria line	1. enter cafeteria	1.
	2. Get on line	2
	3. Move with line	3.
	4. Get tray	4. tray
	5. Pick up plastic ware	5. Fork/spoon
	6. Take tray from staff	6. food
	7. Add drink to tray	7. Juice/milk
	8. Pay cashier	8.
	9. Get straw and napkin	9. Straw/napkin
	10. Go to table	10.
Sabotage strategy once routine is mastered: various items are not available, cafeteria staff give empty tray.	11. Sit down	11. chair
	12. eat	12.
	REINFORCEMENT: finishing the routine – gets to eat lunch which he likes	

Date	12/6	12/7	12/8	12/9	12/10	12/13	12/14	12/15	12/16	12/17
Item	straw	straw	straw	straw	none	straw	milk	napkin	napkin	fork
Response	-	-	+	-	+	+	+	-	+	+
Staff	lf	sr	jr	lf	jr	sr	sr	lf	lf	lf

13

Tying it All Together

Visual Reinforcement Systems

Visual Reinforcement Systems

PECS enables students to consistently let us know what they want. This knowledge, in turn, allows us to make "deals" with the student— "Do this and I'll give you that." The foundation for all of our lessons- whether at home, school, or in the community- is our "Let's Make a Deal" orientation. When we plan a lesson for a student, we look at the "big picture"- what we want the student to do differently in the immediate and distant future. We plan for the activity to be a functional one during which we teach appropriate communication skills, some of which are chosen to replace inappropriate behaviors. We choose a lesson format based on the type of skill we are teaching, and we plan to use specific teaching strategies which involve appropriate prompting and error correction strategies.

All of this careful planning, however, is futile if we don't consider motivating the student to participate in the lesson. We described earlier that the relationship between a teacher and a student is analogous to the relationship between a boss and an employee. When we work for an employer we want to ensure that certain elements are part of our contract. We want to know if the "payoff" we receive is going to be sufficient for us to stay at the job. We want to know:

- What the reinforcer will be (paycheck!)
- When the reinforcer will be delivered
- What "time off" is available
- What job is to be done

In spite of our own excellent oral communication skills, we don't expect to remember all of the details spoken at our job interview, therefore, we want each element of the agreement to be described in a written contract. Another way to think about a written contract is to see it as a <u>visual</u> <u>representation</u> of the deal between the employer and the employee.

When a teacher expects a student to learn a lesson, the teacher actually wants him to do something differently at the end of the lesson (e.g., change his behavior in some way that indicates that the lesson was learned). This expectation is analogous to an employer wanting the employee to do a specific task. Just as we know **before** we accept our job assignment what the reinforcer will be, so too should our students. As noted in <u>The Pyramid Approach to Education </u>(Bondy & Sulzer-Azaroff, 2001), teachers should arrange for "Let's Make a Deal" with a student prior to all lessons. This deal should indicate the same basic elements our job contracts indicate, and should be visually represented.

When beginning PECS, reinforcing each request is central to mastery of the new communication skill. We discussed the idea of a "coin bank" that we begin to fill during Phases I and II. Each time we reinforce a PECS request, we are adding to the coin bank. However, over time, immediately reinforcing every request becomes impractical. We want our students to become increasingly independent which means we want them to do more "work" for us before they obtain their reinforcers. We suggest starting to teach deals as soon as our student has demonstrated persistence in exchanging a picture— typically a few days after beginning PECS.

Creating Deals

Step 1: Simple Deals— Reinforcer in sight

The lesson about setting deals starts with a student approaching an adult to make a request. Rather than immediately rewarding the student, the teacher gives him a small "task" to do. For example, while keeping the reinforcer in sight, she might have him put the last piece in a simple puzzle or put one spoon in the dishwasher. This task should be one that is simple to do, not one that he is still learning. Once he completes this simple task, the teacher says, "Nice work!" and gives the requested item. The student does not need to initiate another PECS exchange— he already did so. The "work" in this situation is very simple and very quickly completed. Over time, the teacher expects a bit more work of her student. She can have him do the last two, then three, then four pieces of the puzzle and so on. The teacher *gradually* increases the amount of work he must do from deal to deal.

> The initial "deal" involves a desired item and a task that the student can do easily.

The key to effectively using this strategy is understanding that the interaction- the deal- starts with the student indicating what is wanted before the teacher issues an instruction. Remember that we, as employees, would not take a job if the boss said, "Hey, I want you to do this job for me and in a year or so, I'll tell you what you've earned." We would only accept the job if we knew our salary- the reinforcer- before doing the work. The same should be true for students- they need to know what they can earn before they learn about the lesson. The entire time the student is participating in these early "deals" the soon-to-be-earned reinforcer remains in sight.

Sometimes, students are content to take it easy— they are comfortable sitting and doing nothing and don't make requests from us. For these students or for students who are not yet making frequent spontaneous requests for other reasons, the deal begins with the teacher approaching the student and holding out several preferred items. If the student reaches for one, the teacher sets the deal at that point. No language (spoken or picture) is necessary—the teacher offers, the student reaches, and the deal begins.

Each deal is successful only if the reinforcer is effective.

Step 2: The Visual Contract

Once the student successfully completes the short deals described above, begin using a picture to represent the reinforcer for the next deal.

- To begin the deal, rather than immediately issuing an instruction, place the picture on a special card (about the size of an index card) that includes a written phrase such as, "I am working for..." This card also contains one circle (with a Velcro® dot inside).
- After placing the icon on the card, signal the work to be done.

- As soon as the student completes the task, praise him, give him a token (a penny, a sticker, a trinket that is age-appropriate, etc.) and physically guide him to place it on the circle. This action is equivalent to "paying" the student.
- Next, physically prompt him to remove the token and give it to you. Immediately give him the item corresponding to the picture on the card. In this manner, he is taught to "buy" the item. We suggest keeping this strategy in place throughout the day for several days, or until it is clear that the student independently and quickly cashes in the token upon receiving one.

- **Next**, add a second circle to the card.
- Again, the sequence begins with a the student indicating what he wants.
- When the student completes a portion of the task, give him one token.
- At this point, the student probably will try to "cash in" the token. In that case, calmly point to the remaining open circle and indicate that he should continue to work.
- The remaining work should be very short and very simple—more so than the initial bit or work. As soon as he completes it, give him the second token.

- The student puts it on the reinforcer card. Having filled in all the circles, he can now cash in for the selected reward.

Over time, gradually increase the number of circles on a card to three, then to four, and then to five. We usually do not add more than five circles because keeping up with more becomes cumbersome. To encourage the student to do more work or to work for longer periods of time, the amount of work for each token gradually is increased (keeping in mind age-appropriate goals). Determine from activity to activity which card to use. For example, for a brand new, potentially difficult activity, use a one– or two-circle card, while for familiar activities, use a five-circle card.

How frequently to dispense the tokens can be determined in a couple of ways. First, the token intervals can be time-based. The student must work for a pre-determined length of time in order to earn each. We often set a timer as a reminder about the "deal." This timer can serve as another visual cue to the student during the work interval.

The tokens also can be dispensed based on a specific amount of work. For example, a student who is learning to put silverware from the dishwasher into the drawer initially gets one token for every couple of utensils. Over time, the teacher gradually increases the number of utensils he must put away before receiving each token. This shift in expectations should occur gradually!

Just as we sometimes get tired toward the end of a long day or a long activity, so too do our students. In this case, it is appropriate to require more work for the first several tokens and less work for the last tokens.

A final element to add to the visual contract is the opportunity to take a break. We put a single break card on the contract that the student can use and re-use, or we add a specific number of cards to the contract to indicate how many breaks he can take during this contract time. When he uses the break card, it is not returned to the contract until a new deal is negotiated.

At one time or another, many students lose their focus on the lesson. Typically, when such behaviors occur, we remind the student about the work that needs to be done- "You need to do your work!" or "Hey! Pay attention!" Rather than a sophisticated teaching strategy, these prompts simply rely upon 'nagging.' However, with a visual reinforcement system depicting what the student can earn, if his attention waivers, the teacher simply points to or gestures to the icon representing the next reward. Such reminders help the student focus on the potential reward. Most often, he will get back to work to earn the reward. Occasionally, the student will continue to be distracted. This means that the current reinforcer is no longer effective, so the lesson must end until the teacher and student renegotiate the deal. When this happens, we reset the deal to zero tokens earned toward the new reward. That is, there should not be a carry-over of tokens earned between rewards. This tactic eliminates the possibility that students will learn to switch reinforcer preferences frequently (which often serves as an escape-motivated behavior).

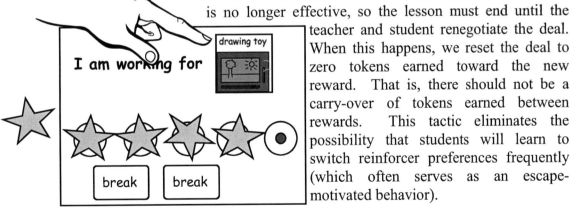

TAKE NOTICE!

Not every request must result in a deal!! We anticipate that students will make dozens and dozens of requests every day. We should respond to most of these immediately. Remember the coin bank and balance the number of requests you respond to immediately with those that begin a deal.

As students use these visual reinforcement systems more and more, the "work period" will become longer and longer. As is typical with adults in the work force, we generally stretch these "deals" to about two hours in duration. Sometimes, when the interval is this long, students really do change their mind in the middle of the deal. When this pattern begins to develop, rather than have the student choose a specific reward before beginning the deal, teach him to request the opportunity to choose from a "reinforcer menu" at the end of the deal. This approach is similar to when we earn a paycheck and then determine how we will spend it once we cash it.

I am working for: choice

break   break

Choice Board

apple · buzz toys · puzzle · juice box · cookie · markers

"What happens if..."

1. ...he has not mastered discriminating between pictures when I introduce the visual contract? The boundaries indicated on the timeline are not written in stone—some variability is fine! Notice on the timeline that we begin "Let's Make a Deal" toward the very end of Phase I. If your student masters Phase I in a matter of a few minutes, it might be better to wait a day or two before beginning "Let's Make a Deal," so that you have sufficient communicative exchanges to add many coins to the bank account. At the beginning of our deals, we typically hold the reinforcer while we indicate to the student what he is to do. Once he has done the work, we hand him the reinforcer. When you introduce the Visual Contract, you might do so, but delay using the picture of the reinforcer until the student can discriminate from among pictures of his favorite reinforcers. You can put the Visual Contract near the student and either still hold the reinforcer (keeping it in sight), or put it on the Visual Contract (just out of reach!).

2. ...I can't find anything that my student wants? Remember our firm rule— "No reinforcer, no deal." If you cannot identify a reinforcer, you cannot place demands on the student. Doing so would put you in the position of coercing your student rather than teaching your student. Review the strategies described in Chapter 3 on conducting a reinforcer assessment, and continue looking! Sometimes, we devote the entire first several days we work with a student to searching for reinforcers—during this time we place no demands on the student.

3. ...my student and I are in the middle of a deal and I decide that I've set a deal that is too difficult for the student? If you are in the middle of a 4-token deal and decide that 4 tokens really is too many to expect the student to earn, adjust your expectations for how much work the student has to do to earn each token. If he's earned only two of the four tokens, give him the third, then fourth tokens very quickly, and then adjust your standards when you set the next deal.

4. ...my student does something absolutely wonderful in the middle of a deal? Give him a bonus!! We all love to receive bonuses at work, and our students will, too. If your student surprised you in the midst of a deal by engaging in a behavior that has been difficult for him, give him a couple of tokens—you could even give him the remaining tokens so

that he quickly accesses the "pay-off." For example, if your student has earned one of three tokens needed to complete a deal and he spontaneously greets someone entering the room (a skill you've been working on but that he has not learned to do without prompting), praise him enthusiastically AND give him the remaining two tokens!

5. ...my student doesn't seem to be "catching on" to use of the Visual Contract? Visually representing a deal can be accomplished in a variety of ways. One way is based on the notion of putting together a puzzle. If the student wants to earn jelly beans, the teacher uses a picture of the jelly beans to represent the deal. Initially, as with the one-circle card, the student completes some work and earns the entire picture of the jelly beans that he then "cashes in" for jelly beans. Over time, the picture is cut into two, then three, then four, and finally five pieces. The student must earn each piece to complete the puzzle which he, in turn, trades in for the reward.

For a more comprehensive description of managing inappropriate behaviors, refer to Bondy and Sulzer-Azaroff 2001, The Pyramid Approach to Education in Autism

Caution!

These visual reinforcement systems are designed to promote positive changes in learning. It can be very tempting to take away tokens when a student behaves inappropriately. Once a token is earned, if an inappropriate behavior occurs, we deal with that behavior separately. We do not fine or punish the student by taking away earned tokens. Rather, we develop a separate system to address the behaviors we are trying to reduce or eliminate.

14

PECS Outcome

Transitioning to Other Modalities

PECS Outcome
Transitioning to Other Modalities

There are two broad questions regarding the use of PECS. The first is whether PECS works- does it help children acquire function communication skills? The second question looks at how use of PECS impacts upon other behaviors- social skills, behavior management, speech development, etc.

Does PECS Work?

Our initial report on PECS (Bondy & Frost, 1994) described the protocol and several outcome measures involving students from the Statewide Delaware Autistic Program. The report was not based upon a formally designed study- that is, it did not report data from children randomly assigned to PECS and non-PECS conditions. It reported outcome reliably observed by staff following the use of PECS by children involved in a comprehensive, behaviorally-oriented public school program. Each of the decisions we made for each child was predicated upon the data collected regarding specific educational goals as outlined in an IEP. No group designs were used.

In terms of the acquisition of skills within PECS, we observed rapid skill growth even with children with autism as young as 24 months. Since then, others interventionists have noted successful use of PECS by children as young as 18 months. Many have provided data-based reports of successful acquisition of skills within PECS, including Schwartz, Garfinkle, & Bauer (1998) and Charlop-Christy (i.e., Carpenter, Charlop-Christy, LeBlanc, & Le, 1998; Carpenter & Charlop-Christy, 2000).

We also observed a strong positive correlation between use of PECS and speech development in children with autism who were 5 years or younger when they entered the school program. Follow-up observations of 67 children aged five years and younger who used PECS for more than one year showed that 59% developed independent speech (Bondy & Frost, 1994). That is, these children stopped using PECS and used speech as their sole mode of communication (although often with continued language delays). Another 30% spoke while simultaneously using PECS. Schwartz, Garfinkle, and Bauer (1998) also found strong support for the use of PECS with preschoolers with various communication deficits and noted a positive correlation regarding the development of speech.

Marjorie H. Charlop-Christy from Claremont McKenna College and several graduate students from Claremont Graduate University have presented a series of studies regarding PECS and its impact during several recent conferences. In addition to providing strong empirical evidence for the effective use of PECS by a variety of learners, they also have presented data regarding:

1. **A decrease in maladaptive behaviors** following the introduction of PECS (Carpenter, Charlop-Christy, LeBlanc, & Kellet, 1998).
2. **Improved social behaviors** (Le and Charlop-Christy, 1999; Le, Charlop-Christy, Carpenter, & Kellet, 1999).
3. **Improvements in speech development** following the acquisition of PECS (Carpenter, Charlop-Christy, LeBlanc, & Le, 1998; Carpenter & Charlop-Christy, 2000).

Another phenomenon observed with children using PECS while acquiring speech is that their speech output improved in number of words spoken and the complexity of their communication when given access to their PECS books (Frost, Daly, & Bondy, 1997).

Throughout this manual, we have stressed that PECS is introduced to children to help them acquire functional communication skills. We do not implement PECS in order to make children speak. Of course, we want children to speak but not at the risk of inhibiting the development of functional communication. We see issues associated with vocal development as independent of communication development. For many children, given time and adequate reinforcement, these two areas merge.

To foster improvements within vocal development, children should be taught a number of skills and reinforced for a variety of actions. Imitation skills should be addressed including:

1. Large and small motor actions
2. Selection of objects
3. Actions with objects

We would suggest that the above list is not a required order of teaching. That is, some children will more readily acquire the 2nd and 3rd types of imitation skills than the first type. Vocalizations, especially novel ones, should be reinforced enthusiastically. To promote such behaviors, games involving vocal imitation and delayed-prompting (i.e., completion or fill-in-the-blank type of games) should be frequently arranged. As noted in our discussion of Phase IV and beyond, children who do vocalize should receive more/better reinforcement than when they remain silent. However, we cannot stress enough that a child who has properly used a sentence strip has engaged in effective functional communication and should be appropriately rewarded. A child who uses PECS but does not speak should not be treated as a failure.

Many parents and professionals are concerned that use of a picture-based system, such as PECS, especially with very young children, could be detrimental to the potential acquisition of speech. "Research over the past 25 years (Carpenter & Charlop-Christy, 2000; Romski & Sevcik, 1996; Mirenda & Erickson, 2000) has shown not only that augmentative communication systems (aided or unaided) *do not* inhibit speech development but that use of these systems enhances the likelihood of the development or improvement of speech (Bondy & Frost, 2001)."

PECS will not inhibit speech development.

Transitioning from PECS to Other Modalities

When children develop speech while using PECS, the logical question teachers ask is, "Can we quit using PECS?" Implementing any alternative or augmentative communication system can be a labor-intensive endeavor for families and teachers. Initially we must gather pictures by taking and developing photographs, copying existing photographs or drawings, printing pictures from various computer software, or cutting pictures from boxes, magazines, or catalogs. Then we sometimes have to glue, cut some more, laminate or cover with contact paper, cut Velcro®, cut some more Velcro®, and then peel that stubborn strip off the back of the sticky-back Velcro®. Who wouldn't look forward to ending all of this?

As a result of tracking the progress of hundreds of children using PECS, we have found that ending PECS use as soon as the student is able to speak a few words can be detrimental to the further development of language skills. We have found that children who have developed speech while using PECS must progress through a "transitional" period during which time his speech skills must "catch up" with his PECS skills. For the majority of these children, this transition period has lasted a minimum of four months, but averages around eleven months. For speech to "catch up" with PECS, several events must occur:

1. **The student's "rate of initiation" must be as high with speech as it is with PECS.** During the transition period, we see many students who learn to say a few words initially, but then don't develop more for several weeks. What we also observe is that these students first develop speech WHILE using PECS. That is, most of these children "talk over" their sentence strips rather than instead of using their sentence strips. Essentially, PECS is supporting the speech. When the students hand the sentence strip to their communicative partner and the communicative partner "reads" it back using the delayed prompting procedure, the children typically imitate or repeat the communicative partner or they "fill in the blank" when the communicative partner pauses. These students initiated these interactions with PECS, though, not with speech. Over time, as the students develop more vocabulary and begin "saying" more and more of the words in the sentences they exchange, we observe them beginning to initiate interactions by speaking.

2. **The student's spoken vocabulary must be as large as his PECS vocabulary.** If the student has 70 pictures in his PECS vocabulary, he must have those 70 words in his spoken vocabulary. Of course, some of those pictures could be ones that have not been used frequently; therefore, we might not expect the student to develop that spoken word. Our goal is for the student not to "lose vocabulary" when he switches from PECS to spoken communication.

3. **The student's "length of utterance" must be as long with speech as it is with PECS.** Many children who first develop speech while using PECS do so a word or two at a time. It is quite common for these children to be able to construct 5-, 6-, or 7-picture sentences with PECS, but for many months not be able to speak in sentences of more than one or two words. Taking PECS away from a child who can not speak in sentences that are as comprehensive as his PECS sentences would be denying that student valuable communication skills.

4. **The student's speech must be intelligible to an unfamiliar communicative partner.** Many of our very young children who begin speaking while using PECS do so with "articulation" or "phonological" errors. We recommend discussing with the speech/language pathologist on the team whether the student would benefit from speech therapy. This therapy often occurs during the several months that the student's speech is catching up. Not until the student is understood at least 70% of the time by someone not familiar with his speech do we consider ending his PECS use.

How do we determine if all criteria have been met?

In order to determine if all criteria have been met, we design activities during which we formally assess each. These assessment activities must be ones the student is familiar with and ones in which he is accustomed to communicating. Ideally, the activities should occur regularly so that we can gather information across several days.

Each assessment activity will include two conditions: A "with PECS" condition and a "without PECS" condition. Each condition should last at least 10 minutes. When you repeat the assessment activity, vary which condition you start with. In the "with PECS" condition, the activity progresses in typical fashion. The teacher creates opportunities for and expects communication and the student uses PECS to communicate. The teacher must gather specific information on how many times the student initiates a communicative interaction, how many different pictures he uses, and the length and structure of each sentence. In the "without PECS" condition, the only change made is that the student does not have access to his PECS book. Again, the same information must be gathered. In addition, two people must transcribe everything the student says. The familiar listener (who understands what the student says) and the unfamiliar listener then compare their transcriptions in order to determine degree of intelligibility.

> To compare speech use to PECS use, assess both during familiar activities.

Once all criteria have been met, how do we discontinue PECS? Ending PECS typically is not something that happens all at once. It typically is a gradual process. What we observe is the student frequently approaching us (our first criterion) and using a variety of words (second criterion) in a variety of sentence forms (third criterion) that everyone understands (fourth criterion). When a student approaches a communicative partner and says, "I want three big blue blocks," or "I hear a loud fire truck," we don't say to him, "But you have to tell me with PECS." We get him the three big blue blocks or we go looking for the fire truck!! This type of spoken interaction occurs more and more frequently over time until one day we notice that the student has not used PECS all day, and that his communication has been just as sophisticated as it was when he did use PECS!

Transitioning to another modality

Sometimes students become very skilled at using PECS, but do not develop speech. For these children the question becomes, "Should we switch to a 'higher-tech' system." Many professionals and families want their student to have a "voice," so we might consider transitioning to some type of Voice Output Communication Aid (VOCA). The range of VOCAs available is extensive—from the very simple and relatively inexpensive ($100-$500) to the very complex and very costly (over $8000!!). If you decide that your student would benefit from using a VOCA, then your team should research the available devices, consult an augmentative/alternative communication specialist or an assistive technology specialist. When choosing a VOCA, we insist that essentially the same criteria must be met as was the case when transitioning to speech.

1. **Rate of initiating.** Initiation or approaching a listener is inherent in PECS. This is not the case with a VOCA wherein the student presses a button in order to activate the voice. We have observed some students who have switched from PECS to a VOCA who quit approaching a listener—rather, they sit with their device, activate the voice, and wait! This can result in a failed communicative attempt if no one hears the voice. When our student begins using a VOCA, because this is a new skill he is developing, we are careful to reinforce his use by listening carefully and responding to his communication. Eventually, though, to minimize the potential for the student to become a "sloppy" initiator, we develop lessons when introducing the VOCA in which the communicative partner purposefully does not respond to the student. Then we teach the student to

"repair" this communicative breakdown using a variety of strategies. We teach him to repeat the message, to turn up the volume (if possible), or to pick up the device, walk to the communicative partner, physically get her attention, and then repeat the message. Because this is initiation, we teach this using the 2-Person prompting procedure.

2. **Vocabulary size.** The student should be able to access as many words with his VOCA as he can with PECS. This can be a challenge when choosing a VOCA if the student has a vocabulary of more that 30-40 pictures. Many devices provide access to a limited number of words total or to a limited number of words that the student can access at any one time. Such devices often store vocabulary in different "levels" or "pages," which requires changing levels or pages (and sometimes physically changing the pictures on the device) in order for the student to access additional vocabulary. This can be especially problematic if the student is using sophisticated sentences with attributes, verbs, etc. For example, if a student can construct the picture sentence, "I want three big brown round cookies," and can do so quite easily by pulling pictures from pages within his book, he should be able to construct such a sentence just as easily using his VOCA. With devices that store a limited number of pictures on each page, constructing such a sentence would require that the page (and its corresponding physical overlay of pictures) be changed sometimes two or more times. When communicating becomes this laborious, many students begin simplifying their sentences. Many newer devices use a "dynamic" touch screen that eliminates the need for physically changing pictures as the "page" or "level" is changed. Many of our students who have used PECS have transitioned successfully to such devices and have been able to continue building their vocabulary

3. **Sentence length.** Many of the devices with the dynamic screens can be programmed to use a "sentence strip equivalent." This allows the student to see his sentence as he builds it picture-by-picture. In this case, through some creative programming, the students switching from PECS to a VOCA typically continue to build sentences as they did with PECS and to learn to build more and more sentence types.

4. **Voice intelligibility** is typically quite good with today's

VOCAs, so ensuring that the student is intelligible with the device is fairly straightforward. The devices either use recorded speech, which requires that someone record their own voice saying each word or synthesized speech, which is generated by the computer in the device combining individual speech sounds.

Once you have decided to switch to a VOCA and you have selected a specific device, consider the picture or symbol set that will be used with the device. Many VOCAs are pre-programmed with pictures that are specific to the device or the device manufacturer. Some of these allow you to "import" a symbol set of your choice via a computer. Some devices require that you make an overlay, so you can use pictures/symbols of your choosing. If you choose to switch symbol sets, plan to teach that vocabulary, if possible, before you switch from PECS to the device. If you are able to do this, then when you get the actual device, your student won't have to learn to use it AND learn a new symbol set. Many manufacturers' picture sets are available in paper form or computer program, so you can use either form to make PECS pictures. Begin by switching just a few symbols—we typically switch those that are most frequently used by the student. If your student adapts quickly to them, you most likely won't have to switch all of his pictures before beginning to use the device.

When the device arrives and we have programmed it or built the overlay for it, we teach the student to use it using the 2-Person prompting procedure just as we did in Phase I. We assess the student's picture discrimination using correspondence checks as we did in Phase III. We teach the student to construct sentences using the backward chaining strategy we used in Phase IV.

Once you switch to a "high-tech" device, remember that technology periodically breaks down. Anticipate that someone will forget to charge the battery, that the student will leave it at school or at home, or that it will need to be sent out for repairs. To prepare for this eventuality, periodically get out the student's PECS book and have him use it so that he can do so proficiently when he is without his device.

In summation, switching a student's communication modality from PECS to speech or another form of AAC depends upon ensuring that he does not lose any communication skills. Taking away skills is simply unethical.

15

PECS and Verbal Behavior

by Andy Bondy

According to Skinner (1957), it is more useful to understand the functional control of verbal behavior than to focus attention upon its form. Skinner defined a number of fundamental verbal operants, such as mands, tacts, intraverbals, and autoclitics. Each was defined in terms of its consequences and relatively narrowly defined stimulus conditions. In addition, Skinner discussed "impure" verbal operants and those under mixed or multiple control, in terms of both mixed antecedents and mixed consequences.

The development of certain communication training programs for children with a variety of severe handicaps, including autism, has been associated with Skinner's overall analysis (see, for example, Guess, Sailor, & Baer, 1976; Kent, 1974; Kozloff, 1974; Lovaas, 1977; Romanczyk, Matey, & Lockshin, 1994; Sundberg & Partington, 1998). There are an increasing number of training programs that address teaching children verbal operants using modalities other than speech (see Reichle, York & Sigafoos, 1991). However, a more detailed analysis of the stimulus control associated with particular training procedures may elucidate problems associated with the development of "spontaneous" communication (see Carr, 1982; Schreibman, 1988).

The Picture Exchange Communication System (PECS) was developed as an alternative/augmentative system for young children with autism (Bondy & Frost, 1994a). The design of PECS and the sequence of initial training steps were influenced by Skinner's description of verbal operants (1957) and a behavior analytic perspective regarding autism (Bondy, 1988). A number of techniques have been designed within PECS that directly address how an understanding of mixed verbal operants can assist in the rapid acquisition of complex verbal behavior in children who display marked deficits in their verbal repertoires.

My purpose here is to expand upon Skinner's analysis of "impure" verbal operants, especially in so far as it impacts upon the design of communication training programs. After describing a set of impure verbal operants, we will look at the training sequence within the PECS protocol as an example of how this type of analysis can lead to more effective training sequences for children with autism and related verbal deficiencies.

Verbal operants

Skinner (1957) defined several key verbal operants by delineating each operant's antecedent and consequence factors (see Table I). For example, a *mand* is a verbal operant "in which the response is reinforced by a characteristic consequence and is therefore under the functional control of relevant conditions of deprivation or aversive stimulation (p. 35-36)." Michael (1988) has sought to clarify the motivational conditions with a description of "establishing operations." Skinner notes that the term *mand* has its roots in the words 'com*mand*' and 'de*mand*.' Common examples of mands, especially for young children, include requesting specific items, requesting assistance, and rejecting offered items or activities.

	MAND
Antecedent conditions	*Deprivation or an aversive stimulus (EO))*
Behavior	Verbal Behavior
Consequence	Direct (tangible) / specified by the request

A *tact* is evoked by "a particular object or event or property of an object or event (p. 82)." Skinner created this word from 'con*tact*' because this verbal operant is controlled by contact with some aspect of the stimulating environment. Common examples of tacts include labeling or naming objects, events and activities, including the relationships between such items or events.

	TACT
Antecedent conditions	*Environmental object or event*
Behavior	Verbal Behavior
Consequence	Social/educational

The term *intraverbal* is used to define verbal behavior that is under the stimulus control of other verbal behavior, initially from other people but increasingly from oneself as one's verbal repertoire expands. Furthermore, the form of an intraverbal does not bear a direct relationship to the form of the preceding verbal stimulus. Common examples include answering questions such as "What's your name?" "How are you?" or responding to phrases such as "one, two, three..." and "roses are red, violets are ..." The *echoic* is a verbal operant that is also under the control of other verbal behavior, but its form matches (in part or whole) the form of the verbal stimulus. Common examples include verbal

	INTRAVERBAL
Antecedent conditions	*Other Verbal Behavior*
Behavior	Verbal Behavior
Consequence	Social/educational

imitation of sounds ("moo," "ahhhh", etc.), words ("cookie," "doggie,"etc.) or entire phrases ("I love you," "Thank you," etc.).

Perhaps the most difficult and complex to understand of the verbal operants defined by Skinner is the *autoclitic*. These verbal operants are under the control of the speaker's own verbal behavior (as 'auto-clitic' means 'self-leaning'). Autoclitics derive from the speaker's subtle impact upon the listener, and essentially bring the listener in contact with aspects of what is controlling the speaker's verbal behavior. For example, I could say "I want a cookie." However, if I said, "I *really* want a cookie" I am not informing you about some aspect of the cookie; rather, I am telling you more about myself as speaker or the conditions under which I am speaking. Skinner defined several different types of autoclitics including descriptive, quantifying, and qualifying, each in accordance to the type of environmental control.

	AUTOCLITIC
Antecedent conditions	*Verbal Behavior of the speaker*
Behavior	Verbal Behavior
Consequence	Social/educational/ impact on listener

In addition to differences in stimulus control, an important distinction between mands as opposed to the other verbal operants (i.e., tacts, intraverbals, echoics, or autoclitics) involves the type of reinforcement associated with each operant. Whereas the mand specifies its own reinforcer, the other verbal operants are established and maintained by the verbal community via what Skinner repeatedly calls "educational" reinforcement (see, for example, pp. 56, 74, and 84). Examples of these "educational" reinforcers most often used by Skinner are what can be identified as social reinforcers, i.e., "Right!" "Thanks!" etc.

	MAND	TACT	INTRAVERBAL	AUTOCLITIC
Antecedent conditions	Deprivation or an aversive stimulus (EO))	Environmental object or event	Other Verbal Behavior	Speaker's own Verbal Behavior
Behavior	Verbal Behavior	Verbal Behavior	Verbal Behavior	Verbal Behavior
Consequence	*Direct (tangible) / specified by the request*	*Social/ educational*	*Social/ educational*	*Social/ educational/ Impact on listener*

Early behaviorally-oriented communication training programs often did not distinguish between classes of verbal operants. This lack of distinction may be related to the observation that there were few attempts to define the target behaviors in terms of verbal operants (see Tarleton & Bondy, 1991). Most early programs began by attempting to establish echoic behavior (i.e., "Say 'ball'") and then intraverbal behavior, as in "What is this?" A common complaint stemming from these programs, in addition to the very long periods of acquisition (Carr, 1982), was the lack of "spontaneous" speech generated by even successful children (Schreibman, 1988). However, by noting the stimulus control inherent in echoics and intraverbals, it is clear that such responses occur following the verbal behavior of other people and that we should not expect a great deal of generalization across operant classes in such tentative repertoires. On the other hand, mands and tacts are operants for which "spontaneous" has a clearer fit— requesting or commenting "out of the blue." Neither of these operants is under the stimulus control of immediately preceding verbal stimuli.

Impure and mixed verbal operants

Skinner uses the term "pure" when describing a tact controlled by "a completely generalized reinforcer (p.83)." Skinner points out that the form of a pure tact
"is determined solely by a specific feature of the stimulating environment (p. 83)."
Thus, a
"...child who is taught to name objects, colors and so on when some generalized reinforcement (for example, the approval carried by the verbal stimulus Right!) is made contingent upon a response which bears an appropriate relation to a current stimulus (p. 84)"
has engaged in a pure tact. An "impure" tact is described as:
"A common result [of] a mixture of controlling relations characteristic of both tact and mand (p.151)."
For example, Skinner notes that
" When a housewife says Dinner is ready, not because of the generalized reinforcement characteristic of the tact, but mainly because her listeners will then come to the table, the response is functionally very close to the mand Come to dinner! (p. 151)."

It may be helpful to specify that an aspect of the "pure" tact is the complete absence of verbal stimuli as a part of the stimulating environment. That is, the specific feature of the stimulating environment does *not* involve verbal stimuli. When verbal stimuli are part of the effective environment complex, then the ensuing verbal operant would be under mixed control, and thus could be, in part, similar to an intraverbal (or more narrowly an echoic or textual, etc.). By carefully noting all aspects of the effective stimulus complex for particular verbal operants, teaching arrangements can be designed more effectively.

For example, if a teacher were to hold up an apple and say, "What's this?" the operant identified by the behavior of a child saying "apple" is a different one than if the child walked into the room and, upon seeing an apple on a table, said "apple." The latter would be a "pure" tact. Similarly, if the teacher said, "What is round and red and a fruit?" (without an apple present), and a child answered "apple," the child's answer would be characterized as a "pure" intraverbal. Verbal responses controlled both by prior verbal stimuli *and* specific features or aspects of the environment would better be characterized as mixed operants, in this case, a combination that we will identify as an *intraverbal-tact*. Within Table II a variety of mixed verbal operants is listed that are sensitive to combinations of stimuli as well as mixtures of controlling consequences.

	Intraverbal-Tact	Tact	Intraverbal
Antecedent conditions	• Apple in view • Hear, "What's this?"	• Apple in view •	• • "What is round and red and a fruit?"
Behavior	"Apple"	"Apple"	"Apple"

Several examples may help clarify each of the suggested mixed operants (See Table II). For instance, asking a child, "What do you want?" when there is nothing of high value in sight could result in an *intraverbal-mand,* if the child were to answer with a specific request. In this case, the *mand* portion of the operant is identified because it is the receipt of the item specified by the answer that serves as the reinforcer, as opposed to the educationally arranged (and often social) consequence provided by the listener. The teacher's question is regarded as the intraverbal aspect of the stimulus complex. The presence of the teacher's question alters the child's response from a "pure" mand to an "impure" mand. As Reichle & Sigafoos (1991) have noted, in training sequences in which children are taught to request in response to instructor questions, "...the learner may learn to make requests only when instructed or otherwise prompted to do so (p.103)." The lack of spontaneity frequently cited about children with autism (see Reichle & Sigafoos, 1991), includes the paucity of "pure" mands.

In similar fashion, if the specific item or event that a child mands is a part of the stimulating environment, such as the presence of a cookie or toy, then that verbal operant may be further specified by identifying it as a *mand-tact*, to distinguish it from both the pure mand and the pure tact. It also should be noted that the reinforcer for a mand-tact is most likely that which is specified by the statement, rather than the possibly accompanying social praise, especially for children with autism. If this form of mand were the only type of mand in which the child engaged, then the teacher must plan to remove (at least temporarily) the sight (or other controlling form of stimulation associated with the object or event) of the controlling stimulus before a pure mand could be acquired. Thus, it is unlikely that any child emits pure mands prior to mand-tacts.

In a more complex case, if a child were asked, "What do you want?" while an apple is held before him, the answer "apple" would be characterized as an *intraverbal-mand-tact*. The tact-portion of the operant is identified by the controlling relationship between the apple itself (as a specific feature of the environment) and the form of the answer. Here too, early in the development of functional communicative skills, it is unlikely that a child will generalize, without explicit training, to emit "pure" mands if such combined stimuli were used within the teaching procedure to establish the response.

	(pure) MAND	Intraverbal-Mand	Mand-Tact	Intraverbal-Mand-Tact
Antecedent conditions	• Apple deprivation • •	• Apple deprivation • • Hear, "What's do you want?"	• Apple deprivation • Apple in view •	• Apple deprivation • Apple in view • Hear, "What's do you want?"
Behavior	"Apple"	"Apple"	"Apple"	"Apple"

A similar examination may help in the analysis of imitation situations. In the "pure" echoic, the only prior verbal stimulus is exactly what is to be imitated. A teacher says, "Ball" and a child responds, "Ball." If the teacher adds another non-imitative stimulus to the complex, such as, "*Say* 'ball,'" and the child responds "ball," then that response is more accurately identified as an *intraverbal-echoic*. A "pure" echoic response would be identified if the child responded, "Say ball" (as do many children with autism who display "echolalic" responding). In addition, if a teacher held up a ball while saying "ball," the child's response of saying "ball" would best be characterized as an *echoic-tact*. Only if the child responded with saying "ball" solely in the presence of the ball, and thus without any prior verbal stimuli, would we designate a "pure" tact. In a similar manner, if the teacher said, "Say 'ball'" while holding up a ball, the child's response "ball" would be identified as an *intraverbal-echoic-tact* until such time as the individual stimulus elements controlling the response could be established.

	(pure) **Echoic**	**Intraverbal-Echoic**	**Echoic-Tact**	**Intraverbal-Echoic-Tact**
Antecedent conditions	• • Hear "ball"	• • Hear, "Say 'ball.'"	• Ball in view • Hear, "ball."	• Ball in view • Hear, "Say 'ball.'"
Behavior	"Ball"	"Ball"	"Ball"	"Ball"

O'Neill (1990) suggests that
> "*...the differences between the mand, tact, and the intraverbal should be more clearly recognized in language training programs*" (p.59).

It may be additionally helpful to identify examples of mixed verbal control when attempting to teach verbal behavior to children with communication impairments. Such an analysis may seem cumbersome at first. However, it also may be beneficial to identify such mixed verbal control when analyzing the failures of teaching methods and procedures. For example, if a child were taught to "label" a group of objects only when requested to do so, as in teaching the child to answer, "What's this?" with a variety of objects, then we should not expect the child to "spontaneously" label the same set of objects without explicit training. "Spontaneous" labels are functionally equivalent to pure tacts, and answers to questions regarding object "names" are a form of the mixed operant, the intraverbal-tact.

Communication training programs and children with autism

Children with autism often are described (especially when under 5 years of age) as displaying few social approaches to adults and as having impoverished repertoires designed to extend interactions initiated by others (Bondy & Frost, 1994b). For example, children with autism are noted to display limited eye-contact or even gaze-aversion, often preferring inanimate objects to interpersonal exchanges (Schreibman, 1988). One way of describing a host of social orientation deficits is by noting that these children seem relatively insensitive to social reinforcers (Bondy, 1988). When these children first attend school (or preschool) programs, they often do not display functional verbal repertoires. For example, Bondy & Frost (1994b) reported that 80% of preschool children with autism entering one statewide public school program over a three-year period did not display functional communication skills.

Attempts to teach these children functional communication skills must address their current repertoires and deficits as well as the types of consequences that may be effective in educational arrangements. Essentially, these children tend not be motivated by teachers' approval and praise (via displays of pleasure when the child accomplishes something). Thus, initial attempts to develop verbal operants such as tacts, intraverbals or echoics by necessity must involve "educational" reinforcers that are not social in nature. The arrangement of such "educational" reinforcers has at times been quite contrived, as when using M&Ms or other concrete rewards.

The sequence of training from a number of behaviorally oriented language training programs (see, for example, Guess, Sailor, & Baer, 1976; Kent, 1974; Kozloff, 1974; Lovaas, 1977) often begins with non-verbal responses such as eye-contact or compliance training. Some of these steps have been identified as "pre-speech attentive skills" (Romanczyk, Matey, & Lockshin, 1994). The next steps usually involve developing echoic repertoires, frequently for vocal sounds as opposed to whole words. (This step may be preceded by attempts to increase the operant level of vocal sounds.) The training protocols often do not distinguish between labels (i.e., tacts) and requests (i.e., mands). Teaching echoics typically leads to teaching echoic/tact verbal operants (the instructor holds up a ball and says, "Ball"). Sometimes this training also has an intraverbal component (intraverbal/echoic/tact) if the trainer

Some Traditional Communication Training Programs
Prerequisites
↓
Echoics
↓
Intraverbal/ echoics Tact
↓
Intraverbal/ Tact
↓
Tact
↓
Intraverbal/ Echoic/ Mand/ Tact
↓
Intraverbal/ Mand/ Tact
↓
Mand/ Tact
↓
Mand

uses the word, "Say," in her prompt and expects the student to NOT repeat it. If a "spontaneous" tact is the training target, the instructor must fade both the echoic and intraverbal components. In the end, though, the student can tact an item in the environment, but he has not learned to mand that item. If the training attempts to move on to mands, then often the sequence is to build upon the echoic repertoire already established, but with an intraverbal and tact component (as when the instructor holds up a ball and says, "What do you want? Say 'ball'").

It is often suggested that labeling should be established prior to requesting. In general, this sequential approach to language training has been justified, in part, due to its apparent similarity to the language development sequence of typically developing children, i.e., babbling before vocal imitation before one word utterances, etc.

There are a number of reasons why this pseudo-developmental/behavioral approach is inappropriate with children with autism. In *Verbal Behavior*, although Skinner (1957) writes about mands prior to echoics, intraverbals or tacts, he does not claim that mands are acquired before the other operants. Furthermore, Skinner suggests that these operants are acquired independently, and growing experimental evidence supports this view (see Oah & Dickenson, 1989, for a review).

Moreover, for typically developing children, where socially-based reinforcers are likely to be equally as motivating as various concrete rewards (in the absence of significant states of deprivation), there is no theoretical reason to suspect that one type of verbal operant should develop before another. Although the early attempts to systematically describe the initial language output of typical children were not behaviorally based (Brown, 1973; Nelson, 1973), and thus not functionally defined, a review of such records suggests that children are as likely to acquire "doggie" as a comment (non-imitative and consequated by social reactions) as they are to acquire the word as a request (non-imitative and consequated by the receipt of an item or action). Furthermore, it is readily apparent that typically developing children acquire echoic repertoires because of playful (i.e., social) interactions with people, rather than because someone has arranged to give them a piece of candy upon the imitation of the word "candy." As noted earlier, one critical difference between preschool children with autism and typically-developing children involves the types of reinforcers to which each is responsive.

Although children with autism may not be highly

motivated to obtain various socially-based rewards, often they are interested in a variety of objects and events in their surroundings (Bondy & Frost, 1995). They may have favorite foods or toys, etc., sometimes to the extent that they are called ritualistic or obsessive. It usually is relatively easy to identify a number of concrete items that an preschool child with autism is motivated to obtain. The question that we have attempted to answer within the framework of PECS is: given the power of particular concrete reinforcers and the relative paucity of socially based reinforcers for a preschool child with autism who has just entered a school program, what type of verbal operant should be taught first? To teach eye-contact or echoic responses (or even to follow an arbitrary type of matching-to-sample repertoire with objects, pictures or other symbols) necessitates the use of concrete rewards for repertoires that should be associated with the types of "educational" reinforcement that Skinner noted. Therefore, in PECS training, the first response involves reinforcers that are currently effective and does not involve the prior verbal behavior of someone else. Thus, the mand is the first verbal operant taught within PECS (see Table III).

```
┌──────────────┐
│    PECS      │
│              │
│   Mand/      │
│   Tact       │
│    ↓         │
│   Mand       │
└──────────────┘
```

PECS training and verbal operants

Training on PECS begins with a reinforcer assessment (Bondy & Frost, 1994b). Once the teacher has

Reinforcer Assessment

identified potential rewards (i.e., those items that the child persistently reaches for), one is selected with which to begin training. The communicative partner (the

Mand/Tact

listener) entices with the item, the child reaches for it, and the physical prompter (from behind the student) physically assists the child to give a picture of that item to the communicative partner. While the child is being assisted, the receiving teacher (the communicative partner) has one hand open (palm up) to the child. Upon receipt of the picture, the teacher says, "Oh, cookie!" (or something similar) and immediately gives the child the reward. There is no verbal prompting prior to the exchange. Therefore, a complex intraverbal is not being established. Although the receiving teacher does have an open hand during this early stage of training, this action acts to enhance the audience-effect of the listener for all forms of verbal behavior (see Skinner, 1957, p. 173 and 176) rather than specifically for a mand. An echoic repertoire is not being established because the exchange is physically prompted, and no modeling is used. However, during this initial phase of training, the object sought by the child is part of the stimulating environment and thus the function of the response may best be described as the compound *mand-tact*. In order to produce a pure mand, the objects manded must be removed from the stimulating environment.

It should be noted that the initial reach for the reinforcer by the child is not viewed as a communicative act- that is, it is not verbal behavior. The reach is controlled by the reinforcer and not by the social context. The child is as likely to pick up candy from an open hand as she is from the table-top. The aim of Phase I is to shape the non-verbal reach into verbal behavior directed to the listener rather than the reinforcer.

The physical prompts to pick up, extend, and exchange the picture are faded within a backward-chaining format. Thus, the last response usually taught (i.e., the physical prompt that is faded last) involves picking up the picture. Within a few trials of independently exchanging pictures for objects while the "listener" is within arms reach, the listener begins to move farther from the child in order to teach the child to seek out the listener wherever he or she may be in the environment. In addition, very early in training, other teachers take on the role of listener so that the child does not learn to associate the exchange solely with one person. A final aspect of this early phase of training is teaching the child to move to the picture and then find the listener. This contingency enhances searching for the picture even if the picture is not near the desired object nor near the listener. At the successful completion of this aspect of training, the child can find a single picture, pick it up, take it to someone who controls access to a desired object, and hand the picture to that person, thus eliminating the presence of the picture itself as part of the stimulus complex for manding. The child initiates the interaction, very often the first formal social interaction initiated by the autistic preschooler.

Persistence and Distance (Broadening stimulus control and setting events)

O'Neill (1990) has suggested that "Learners may need to be trained to mand for a listener's attention prior to manding for particular items or other outcomes (p. 120)." The PECS system does not require such prerequisite training because giving the picture to the teacher functions in a similar manner to the mand for attention noted by O'Neill. However, during the initial exchanges between child and adult, most children are looking at the hand of the teacher when they approach with their picture rather than at the teacher's eyes. In order to establish the importance of eye-contact as a critical feature of the *listener*, teachers are advised to sit with their head (and thus eyes) cast downward as the child approaches with a picture. A second teacher physically guides the child to touch the teacher's shoulders or gently lift the teacher's face prior to extending the picture. This step can be added only after the exchange is established. This training sequence essentially teaches the child that the eye-contact of the listener is important to set the occasion for the exchange. Thus, rather than the traditional approach of teaching the child to look at the teacher's eyes, within the PECS framework, a child is taught that it is important to make the teacher look at him.

During these early trials, the teacher presents only single pictures in each situation during which particular reinforcers are most likely to be effective. The next phase introduces discriminating between pictures. A variety of techniques may be used to develop such discrimination, but one strategy is to use pairs of pictures in which one picture is strongly associated with contextual cues for a particular reward while the other picture is associated with something that does not fit the immediate context. For example, assume that a child has learned to mand a spoon when a bowl of cereal is visible on the kitchen table. Furthermore, the child has learned to mand turning on the TV while in the living room. In a situation where

> Discrimination of symbols
> (Narrowing stimulus control)

the strength of manding for the TV is very high, if the child selects the spoon picture when paired with the TV picture, he is given the spoon (rather than being told he is wrong or has made a mistake). If the boy does not seem to care about the outcome (i.e., he seems as content with the spoon as with having the TV turned on) then he is unlikely to attend to the visual stimuli associated with making an appropriate discrimination between the pictures. However, a child who react with "surprise" or "annoyance" to receipt of the spoon, often follows with correct discriminations of the pictures. The same analysis extends to presenting a highly-preferred item and a non-preferred item.

After a child has learned to accurately mand when given a choice between pairs or even an array of pictures, an important step is to teach the child to engage in a new or different verbal operant. However, at the phase wherein the child can use only a singly presented picture, it may be difficult for the communicative partner to understand how the child is using the picture. Is it a mand or a tact? At a comparable point in language development, when typically developing children are using single word utterances, they can both mand and tact. We can discriminate which verbal operant he speaks by hearing differences in the child's inflections (or intonation patterns) that accompany these single words. Intonation functions as an autoclitic (Skinner, 1957, p. 315 and p. 355), and it is important to develop an equivalent autoclitic to intonation at this phase of PECS training in order for children to be able to clarify the function of the pictures they use.

One autoclitic developed within PECS is designed to function as an "autoclitic frame" (Skinner, 1957, p.336). The

| Mand w/ autoclitic frame |

frame is added to the single picture previously established without changing the nature of the overall function. For example, when a child gives a teacher the single picture of a cookie, the child is manding the cookie. Next, the child is taught to construct the sentence "I want" "cookie" with two distinct pictures. The "I want" frame is a single picture. The sentence "'I want' 'cookie'" also is a mand but adds the autoclitic frame. The use of the frame is taught in a backward chaining format, with the "I want" icon initially being placed upon a removable card, called the "sentence strip," by the teacher. The child is physically guided to add the picture of what is wanted to the sentence strip and then is guided to give the entire strip to the teacher. Upon its receipt, the teacher "reads" the sentence to the child and acts in accordance with the mand. The child is then taught to take the "I want" card and place it on the sentence strip prior to adding the picture that corresponds to the desired object. It is useful to note that the child is still engaging in a mand, and if the desired object has been removed from part of the stimulating environment, then the response is a pure mand elaborated with an autoclitic frame.

The next phase of training brings the child's request

| Intraverbal/Mand |

under the influence of words spoken by someone else- that is, we introduce an *intraverbal-mand*. This step is accomplished by asking, "What do you want?" while simultaneously pointing to the "I want" card. The form of the response- using the sentence strip to create "I want" "cookie" already is available within the child's repertoire; however, the use of the question by the teacher brings the response partially under the control of the verbal stimulus introduced by the teacher. At this point in training, the child can mand or respond to a question with an intraverbal-mand. This compound function leads into the next phase.

During the next phase of training, the teacher introduces

| Intraverbal/Tact |

new autoclitic frames to the communication board. These frames include "I see," "I have," "I hear," etc.

With a minimally desired object in sight, the teacher asks, "What do you see?" while simultaneously touching the "I see" card. This gestural prompt, established in the previous phase of training, is likely to be sufficiently effective so that the child picks up the card and places it on the sentence strip. The child then is likely to place the corresponding picture upon the sentence strip and give it to the teacher. Upon its receipt, the teacher reads back, "Oh. I see the ball!" or something similar but does *not* give the ball to the child. The response being established is an *intraverbal-tact* controlled by both the preceding verbal stimulus and a particular aspect of the environment resulting in educational consequences but not that are specified by the response itself. Were the teacher to provide the ball, the child may simply be learning another form of a mand.

> Tact

In order to develop pure tacts the verbal aspect of the stimulus complex preceding an intraverbal-tact must be faded. A variety of procedures may be used. Some involve introducing a general mand or tact prior to the specific mand "What do you see?" or a general mand, such as "Look!" or "Wow!" Subsequent trials would then fade the specific or general mand and retain the tact. Over time these vocal prompts are faded and replaced by non-vocal prompts such as an arched eyebrow or an expectant look by the teacher. To the extent that tacts are emitted solely in association with even general mands, then we must recognize that a pure tact has not been established.

Summary

The development of effective communication training programs has, in part, been associated with Skinner's functional analysis of verbal behavior. Strategies that address issues related to stimulus control and sources of reinforcement have yielded effective training protocols. It is suggested here that the difficulties in establishing some types of verbal behavior, especially with populations that display weak responding to socially-based reinforcers, may be reduced by a more detailed analysis of complex verbal operants wherein sources of stimulus control may be described as "mixed." A variety of mixed verbal operants has been described with the intention of stimulating discussions regarding procedures to improve how stimulus control is manipulated across communication training procedures.

The analysis suggested was applied to PECS. A similar analysis may be beneficial when reviewing other communication training programs, whatever their stated theoretical underpinnings. That is, regardless of why a particular training sequence is arranged, a behavior analysis may proceed to describe how stimulus control and control by consequences is arranged over time within the recommended training steps. For example, someone may claim to teach "expressive labeling." Regardless of the term used, the actual teaching protocol can be analyzed in order to determine which stimuli, i.e., from environmental, verbal and social sources, and which types of consequences, i.e., direct or social, actually are associated with specific behaviors. The description of the three-term contingency defines the operant, rather than the intentions or philosophy, of the trainer. This emphasis upon observing actual teacher-learner interactions equally applies to trainers claiming to teach specific verbal operants. That is, a protocol to teach manding may be described without adequate elaboration that the mands are not "pure" but are partially controlled by teacher questions or comments.

It may well be that specialists with non-behavioral backgrounds have developed effective communication training strategies. Their use of terms unfamiliar to us should not deter us from an analysis of what operants are actually taught by the described protocols. Such an analysis may broaden our own teaching strategies and lend a common language base to the comparison of otherwise disparate orientations.

Table I. Pure Verbal Operants

		PURE MAND	PURE TACT	INTRA-VERBAL (IV)	ECHOIC	AUTOCLITIC
Antecedent conditions		Establishing Operation (EO)	Aspect of the environment	VB of another person	VB of another person	VB of the Speaker
Behavior		Verbal Behavior	Verbal Behavior	Verbal Behavior	Verbal Behavior that is identical to the speaker's VB	Verbal Behavior
Consequence		Specified by EO	Educational (including social)	Educational	Educational	Impacts the behavior of the listener relative to the speaker (educational)
Example	**A**	•EO • •	• •M&M in view, •	• • •Hear :1,2,3,..."	• • •Hear "Ball"	•EO • •
	B	↓ *"I want M&M"*	↓ *"M&M!"*	↓ *"four five"*	↓ *"ball"*	↓ *"I really want a cookie"*
	C	↓ receive M&M	↓ "That's right!"	↓ "That's right!"	↓ "That's right!"	↓ receive cookie (tells you more about the speaker than the cookie)

Table II. Mixed Verbal Operants

	MAND-TACT	IV-MAND	IV-TACT	IV-MAND-TACT	ECHOIC-TACT	IV-ECHOIC	IV-ECHOIC-TACT
Antecedent conditions	EO plus a specific aspect of the environment	EO plus VB of another person	VB of another person and an aspect of the environment	EO plus VB of another person and an aspect of the environment	Pure model stimulus plus specific object or aspect of environment	VB (a mand for action) plus VB (as a model)	VB of another person and an aspect of the environment
Behavior	VB	VB	VB	VB	**VB** that matches verbal stimulus	**VB** that matches the modeled portion only	**VB** that matches speaker's **VB**
Consequence	Specified by the EO and the specific aspect of the environment	Receipt of specified R+ plus educational	Educational	Receipt of specified R+ plus educational	Educational	Educational	Educational
Example A	•EO •M&M present	•EO • •hear "What do you want?"	• •pencil in view •hear "What's this?"	•EO •ball present •hear "I want..."	• •ball present •hear "ball"	• • •hear, "Say "ball'	• •pencil in view •hear, "Say "pencil"
B	↓ *"I want M&M"*	↓ *"cookie"*	↓ *"pencil"*	↓ *"ball"*	↓ *"ball"*	↓ *"ball"*	↓ *"pencil"*
C	↓ receive M&M	↓ get cookie and smile	↓ hear "that's right"	↓ get ball and "that's right!"	↓ "that's right!"	↓ "Good!"	↓ "that's right!"

Table II

Table III. PECS and Verbal Operants

PECS Phases	Verbal Operants		
	Antecedent	Behavior	Consequence
	SD →	R	← SR+
Phase I---<u>Physical Exchange:</u> Icon of preferred is given to the listener. *Learner requests desired item via exchange with item in sight.*	E.O Reinforcer in sight	Mand-Tact (Impure Mand)	Receipt of item requested Same same
Phase II – <u>Distance and Persistence</u> Speaker seeks audience in different settings/ locations and gets own PECS book. Learner initiates request within a social framework.	E.O. Reinforcer not in sight	Pure Mand	Receipt of item requested
Phase IIIA – **Discrimination of symbols** Discrimination is under the control of the reinforcing value of the desired item. **(Not conditional discrimination)**	E.O. Reinforcer in sight or not in sight	Pure Mand or Mand-Tact	Receipt of item requested
Phase IIIB – **Discrimination of requests** Learner chooses an icon from several and then takes Item requested **(conditional discrimination)**	E.O. Reinforcer in sight or not in sight	Pure Mand or Mand-Tact	Receipt of item requested
Phase IV – **Sentence structure-** Speaker learns to request with phrase "I want _____."	E.O.	Pure mand w/ autoclitic frame	Receipt of item requested
Attributes – development of complex mands using attributes – correspondence checks ensure conditional correspondence	E.O. Some aspect of reinforcer (aspect of environment)	Mand/Tact with autoclitic frame	Receipt of specific item requested
Request of multiple reinforcers – with correspondence checks	"	Mand/Tact with autoclitic frame	Receipt of multiple reinforcers
Phase V – **Answering "What do you want?"** – bringing requests under control of another's verbal behavior. All previous skills maintained	E.O. Verbal Stimulus	Intraverbal/ Mand	Receipt of requested item
Phase VI – **Commenting in response to a question** – describing aspect of environment	Verbal stimulus Aspect of environment	Intraverbal-Tact	Generalized social reinforcement
Spontaneous commenting - Learner comments about aspect of environment	Aspect of environment	Pure Tact	Generalized social reinforcement

Table III created by Brenda Terzich. M.ED. of Applied Behavior Consultants, Sacramento, California

References

Apel, K. and Masterson, J. (2001). *Beyond Baby Talk.* Kima Publishing.

Bondy, A. (May, 1988). Autism and initial communication training: How long have we been wrong? Paper presented at the Association for Behavior Analysis convention, Philadelphia.

Bondy, A. & Frost, L. (May, 1992) Autism as an autoclitic disorder. Paper presented at the annual Association for Behavior Analysis convention, San. Francisco, CA.

Bondy, A. & Frost, L. (1994a). The Picture Exchange Communication System. *Focus on Autistic Behavior*, **11**, 1-19.

Bondy, A. & Frost, L. (1994b). The Delaware Autistic Program. In S. Harris & J. Handleman (Eds.), *Preschool Education Programs for Children with Autism* (pp. 37-54). Austin, TX: Pro-Ed.

Bondy, A. & Frost, L. (1995). Educational approaches in preschool: Behavioral techniques in a public school setting. In E. Schopler & E. Mesibov (Eds.), *Learning and Cognition in Autism* (pp. 311-333). New York: Plenum Publishing Corporation.

Bondy, A. (1996). *The Pyramid Approach to Education.* Newark, DE: Pyramid Educational Consultants, Inc.

Bondy, A. & Frost, L. (1998). The Picture Exchange Communication System. *Seminars in Speech and Language.* 19, 373-389.

Bondy, A., Ryan, L., and Hayes, M. (1991) Tact training following mand training using the Picture-Exchange Communication System. Paper presented at the Association for Behavior Analysis Conference, Atlanta, GA.

Bondy, A. & Frost, L. (2001). The Picture Exchange Communication System. *Behavior Modification*, 25, 725-744.

Brown, R. (1973). *A first language: The early stages.* Cambridge, MA: Harvard University Press.

Carpenter, M., Charlop-Christy, M., LeBlanc, L. & Le, L. (May, 1998).An evaluation of spontaneous speech and verbal imitation in children with autism after learning the picture exchange communication system (PECS). Paper presented at the meeting of the Association for Behavior Analysis, Orlando, FL.

Carpenter M. & Charlop-Christy, M.H. (May, 2000). Verbal and nonverbal communication in children with autism after learning the Picture Exchange Communication System (PECS). Paper presented at the meeting of the Association for Behavior Analysis Conference, Washington, D.C.

Carr, E. (1982). Sign language. In R. Koegel, A. Rincover, & A. Egel (Eds.) *Educating and Understanding Children with autism* (pp. 142-157). San Diego: College-Hill Press.

Charlop-Christy, M.H. (March, 2001). Using PECS as functional communication training: Like water for chocolate. Paper presented at the 2nd annual PECS Expo, Philadelphia, PA.

Frost, L. & Scholefield, D. (May, 1996). Improving picture symbol discrimination skills within PECS through the use of three-dimensional objects and fading: A case study. Paper presented at the Association for Behavior Analysis. San Francisco, CA.

Frost, L., Daly, M. & Bondy, A. (April, 1997). Speech features with and without access to PECS for children with autism. Paper presented at meeting of the New Jersey Center for Outreach and Services for the Autism Community, Inc. (COSAC). Long Beach, NJ.

Glennen, S.L. (1997). Introduction to augmentative and alternative communication. In, S.L Glennen and D.C. DeCoste, Handbook of augmentative and alternative communication (pp. 3-20). San Diego: Singular Publishing Group, Inc.

Guess, D., Sailor, W., & Baer, D. (1976). *Functional Speech and Language Training for the Severely Handicapped.* Lawrence, KS.: H & H Enterprises.

Halle, J.W., (1984). Arranging the natural environment to occasion language. *Seminars in Speech and Language*, 5, 185-196.

Hart, B. and Risley, T. (1999). *The social world of children learning to talk.* Baltimore: Paul H. Brookes.

Hart, B., & Risley, T. R. (1982). How to use incidental teaching for elaborating language. H & H Enterprises, Inc., Lawrence, KS.

J. Handleman (Eds.), *Preschool Education Programs for Children with Autism* (pp. 37-54). Austin, TX: Pro-Ed.

Kent, L. (1974) *Language Acquisition Program for the Severely Retarded.* Champaign, IL.: Research Press.

Kozloff, M. (1974). *Educating Children with Learning and Behavior Problems.* New York: John Wiley and Sons.

Le, L. & Charlop-Christy, M.H. (February, 1999). PECS and social behavior. Paper presented at the meeting of the California Association for Behavior Analysis, San Francisco, CA.

Le, L., Charlop-Christy, M.H., Carpenter, M. & Kellet, K. (May, 1999). Assessment of social behaviors following acquisition of PECS for children with autism. Paper presented at the meeting of the Association for Behavior Analysis Conference, Chicago, IL.

Lovaas, O. I. (1977). *The Autistic Child: Language Development through Behavior Modification.* New York: Irvington.

Michael, J. (1988). Establishing operations and the mand. *The Analysis of Verbal Behavior, 6,* 3-10.

Michael, Jack (1983). Evocative and Repertoire-Altering Effects of an Environmental Event. *Journal of the Analysis of Verbal Behavior, 2,* 19-21.

Mirenda, P. & Erickson, K. (2000). Augmentative communication and literacy. In A. Wetherby & B. Prizant (Eds.), Autism Spectrum Disorders (pp. 333-367). Baltimore: Paul Brookes Pub. Co.

Nelson, K. (1973). Structure and strategy in learning to talk. *Society for Research in Child Development Monograph No. 141,* Chicago, IL: The University of Chicago Press.

Oah, S. & Dickenson, A. (1989). A review of empirical studies of Verbal Behavior. *The Analysis of Verbal Behavior, 7,* 53-68.

O'Neill, R. (1990). Establishing verbal repertoires: Toward the application of general case analysis and programming. *The Analysis of Verbal Behavior, 8,* 113-126.

Peterson, S., Bondy, A., Vincent, Y., & Finnegan, C. (1995). Effects of altering communicative input for students with autism and no speech: Two case studies. *Augmentative and Alternative Communication, 11,* 93-100.

Pryor, K. (1999). *Don't shoot the dog: the new art of teaching and training.* New York: Bantam Books.

Reichle, J. & Sigafoos, J. (1991) Establishing an initial repertoire of requesting. In J. Reichle, J. York, & J. Sigafoos (Eds.), *Implementing Augmentative and Alternative Communication Strategies for Learners with Severe Disabilities* (p. 89-114). Baltimore: Paul H. Brookes Publishing Co.

Reichle, J., York, J. & Sigafoos, J. (1991). *Implementing Augmentative and Alternative Communication Strategies for Learners with Severe Disabilities.* Baltimore: Paul H. Brookes Publishing Co.

Romanczyk, R. G., Matey, L., & Lockshin, S. B. (1994) The Children's Unit for Treatment and Evaluation. In S. Harris & J. Handleman (Eds.), *Preschool Education Programs for Children with Autism.* (181-223). Austin: Pro-Ed.

Romski, M.A., & Sevcik, R.A. (1996). *Breaking the speech barrier: Language development through augmented means.* Baltimore: Paul H. Brookes.

Schreibman, L. (1988). *Autism.* Newbury Park, Sage Publications.

Schwartz, I., Garfinkle, A. & Bauer, J. (1998). The Picture Exchange Communication System: Communicative Outcomes for Young Children with Disabilities. *Topics in Early Childhood Special Education,* 10-15.

Sigafoos, J., O'Reilly, M., Drasgow, E. & Reichle, J. (2002). Strategies to achieve socially acceptable escape and avoidance. In J. Reichle, D. Beukelman, &J. Light (Eds.), *Exemplary Practices for Beginning Communicators: Implications for AAC* (pp. 157-186). Baltimore: Paul H. Brookes Publishing Co, Inc.

Silverman, F. (1995). *Communication for the speechless* (3rd ed.). Boston, MA: Allyn & Bacon.

Skinner, B. F. (1957). *Verbal Behavior.* Englewood Cliffs, NJ.: Prentice-Hall, Inc.

Sulzer-Azaroff, B. and Mayer, G. R. (1991). *Behavior analysis for lasting change.* Fort Worth, TX: Holt, Rinehart and Winston, Inc.

Sundberg, M.L. & Partington, J.W. (1998). *Teaching Language to Children with Autism or Other Developmental Disabilities.* Behavior Analysts, Inc.: Danville, CA.

Tarleton, R. and Bondy, A. (May, 1991. Tumbling the tower of babel: An analysis of verbal operants in JABA. Presented at the Association for Behavior Analysis, Atlanta, GA.

Wetherby, A. M. and Prizant, B. M. (1989). The expression of communicative intent: assessment guidelines. *Seminars in Speech and Language,* 10, 77-91.

Appendix A

Sample IEP Objectives

Sample Picture Exchange Communication System Objectives©

Student: _____ **Site:** _____

Objective	Criterion	Current Level	Date begun	Date met
I. Upon seeing and wanting a particular item, and with a picture of that item in reach, S will pick up the picture, reach to person holding the item, and release the picture into that person's hand.	Independently complete request sequence on 10 of 10 opportunities when trainer is within 1 foot for 5 different reinforcers across 3 trainers and 3 activities.	Reaches for desired item.		
IIa. Upon seeing and wanting a particular item, and with a picture of that item alone on a communication book within reach, S will remove the picture from the book, go to the communicative partner, and give picture.	Independently complete request sequence on 9 of 10 opportunities when communicative partner is: a. 5 feet away b. 10 feet away c. across the room across 5 different reinforcers and across 5 trainers	Gives picture when trainer is within 1 foot.		
IIb. Upon seeing and wanting a particular item, and with a picture of that item alone on a communication book, S will go to the book, remove the picture, go to communicative partner, and give picture.	Independently complete request sequence on 9 of 10 opportunities when book is a. 5 feet away b. 10 feet away c. across the room across 5 different reinforcers and across 5 trainers	Gives picture when book is within 1 foot. Can travel 5 feet to trainer.		
IIIa. Upon seeing and wanting a particular item and with the communication book available with corresponding picture and picture of a distracter item on it, S will request that item by giving communicative partner the correct picture.	a. Give correct picture on 9 of 10 trials b. Give correct picture on 9 of 10 trials when book and communicative partner are more than 2 feet from S.	Gives pictures presented one at a time.		
IIIb. Upon seeing 2 reinforcing items and with the communication book available with those pictures on it, S will request that item by giving communicative partner one picture and then selecting corresponding item when then told "Go ahead, take it."	a. Give correct picture on 9 of 10 trials b. Give correct picture on 9 of 10 trials when book and communicative partner are more than 2 feet from S.	Gives correct picture when that picture distracter picture are on book.		
IIIc. Upon seeing a variety of reinforcing items, S will go to communication book, select picture from all available pictures (on cover or inside), take and give picture to communicative partner, and then when told "Go ahead and get it," will get corresponding item.	9 of 10 opportunities completed independently across a variety of objects.	Gives picture from field of two and gets corresponding item.		

Objective	Criterion	Current Level	Date begun	Date met
IIId. With reinforcing items not in sight, S will go to communication book, select picture from any page within it, take and give picture to communicative partner, and then when told "go ahead and get it," will get corresponding item.	9 of 10 opportunities completed independently across a variety of objects, activities, communicative partners, and environments.	Travels to book, get correct picture from field of 5, take picture to communicative partner and get corresponding item.		
IVa. Given communication book with a variety of pictures and a sentence strip with an "I want" picture attached to L end of it, S will request item by attaching R+ picture to R end of sentence strip and giving strip to trainer.	9 of 10 opportunities completed independently across a variety of objects, activities, communicative partners, and environments.	Makes single picture requests.		
IVb. Given communication book with a variety of R+ pictures , an "I want" picture, and a sentence strip, the S will request desired items by removing "I want" picture and affixing to left end of sentence strip, removing R+ picture and affixing to right end of sentence strip, and giving entire sentence strip to trainer.	9 of 10 opportunities completed independently across a variety of objects, activities, communicative partners, and environments.	Requests by putting R+ picture on sentence strip already containing "I want picture."		
IVc. Upon wanting a particular item, S will go to communication book, construct entire sentence strip, go to communicative partner and exchange strip.	9 0f 10 opportunities completed independently across a variety of objects, activities, communicative partners, and environments.	Requests using sentence strip when book and communicative partner are nearby		
Attributes a. When shown two examples of an item (one preferred and one non-preferred such as blue and green candies), and given a PECS book, "I want" icon, desired item icon, and attribute icon representing specifically desired item, S will request the item using a three-picture sentence.	9 of 10 opportunities completed independently.	Requests items using sentence strip and demonstrates preference for a specific example of desired item.		
Attributes b. When shown two examples of an item (one preferred and one non-preferred), and given a PECS book with "I want" icon, desired item icon and two attribute icons-one of the specifically desired item and one of the non-desired item, S will request the specifically desired item using the correct attribute icon in a three-picture sentence.	9 of 10 opportunities completed independently for at least two exemplars of the desired attribute (blue marker and blue M&M).	Requests specifically-desired item using three-picture sentence when no attribute icon discrimination is required.		
Attributes c. Given communication book, and when shown two preferred examples of a desired item varying by one attribute, S will construct and exchange a sentence strip using an attribute icon in correct sequence and then when told, "Take it," etc., will take the corresponding item.	9 of 10 opportunities completed independently for at least three different icons (3 colors of M&Ms) and across at least 2 exemplars (3 colors of M&Ms AND 3 colors of markers).	Requests desired item using three-plcture sentence and discriminates between 1 high-preference and 1 low-preference attribute icons.		

Objective	Criterion	Current Level	Date begun	Date met
Va. When asked, "What do you want?" S will answer by constructing sentence strip with "I want and R+ picture and giving sentence strip to trainer.	9 of 10 opportunities completed independently across a variety of objects, activities, communicative partners, and environments.	Spontaneously requests item using phrase "I want ___."		
Vc. When asked, "What do you want?" or when provided an opportunity to spontaneously request, S will go to book, construct sentence strip, go to communicative partner and exchange strip.	9 of 10 opportunities completed independently across a variety of objects, activities, communicative partners, and environments when opportunities to spontaneously or responsively request are randomized.	Asks and/or answers during structured activities with no mixing of stimuli.		
VIa. Given access to communication book and asked, "What do you see?" S will answer by constructing sentence strip with "I see" Sentence Starter and object picture and giving sentence strip to trainer.	9 of 10 opportunities completed independently across a variety of objects, activities, communicative partners, and environments.	Spontaneously requests and can answer "What do you want?"		
VIb. Given access to communication book and randomly asked "What do you see?" and "What do you want?" S will answer by constructing sentence strip with correct "I see" or "I want" Sentence Starter plus noun picture and give strip to trainer.	9 of 10 opportunities completed independently when questions are randomized and across a variety of materials about which either question can be asked	Answers "What do you want?" and "What do you see?" when presented singly .		
VIc. Given access to communication book and randomly asked "What do you see?" and "What do you want?" and provided with opportunities to spontaneously request, S will answer question appropriately using "I see" or "I want" Sentence Starter, or will spontaneously request desired item using "I want" Sentence Starter.	9 of 10 opportunities completed independently when questions and opportunities to request are randomized and across a variety of materials that are desired and about which either question can be asked.	Answers "What do you want?" and "What do you see?" and requests using appropriate Sentence Starters.		
VId. Given access to communication book and shown specific item and asked "What is it?" S will answer using "It is" Sentence Starter and correct noun picture.	9 of 10 opportunities completed independently across a variety of familiar objects.	Answers "What do you want?" and "What do you see?" and can request using appropriate phrases.		
VIe. Given access to communication book and randomly asked "What do you see?" "What is it? and "What do you want?" and provided with opportunities to spontaneously request, S will answer question appropriately using "I see," "It is," or "I want" Sentence Starter or will spontaneously request desired item using "I want" Sentence Starter.	9 of 10 opportunities completed independently when questions and opportunities to request are randomized, and across a variety of materials that are desired and about which either question can be asked.	Answers questions individually and can request spontaneously.		

Objective	Criterion	Current Level	Date begun	Date met
VIf. Upon seeing a familiar item within a novel context and provided access to communication book, S will spontaneously comment on the item using phrase "I see__" or "It is__"	9 of 10 opportunities completed independently.	Comments in response to a question.		
Help-a Upon encountering an obstacle, S will bring a "help" icon to a communicative partner	9 of 10 opportunities completed independently.	Approaches communicative partner to exchange a single picture (Phase I, early Phase II of PECS).		
Help-b Upon encountering an obstacle, S will construct and bring a sentence strip to a communicative partner containing "I want" Sentence Starter and "help" icon in correct sequence	9 of 10 opportunities completed independently.	Exchanges single "help" icon.		
Help-c Upon encountering an obstacle, S will construct and bring a sentence strip to a communicative partner containing "I want" and "help" and obstacle icon in correct sequence. ("I want" "open" "door." or "I want" "help" "door.").	9 0f 10 opportunities completed independently.	Constructs and exchanges sentence strip with "I want" and "help" icons on it in correct sequence.		
Break-a Given a stressful situation, S will exchange a "break" Icon with communicative partner	9 of 10 opportunities completed independently.	Requests desired items by exchanging an icon with a communicative partner.		
Wait-a When given a "wait card," S will sit/stand quietly.	9 of 10 opportunities completed independently in at least 3 environments for: a. 5-10 seconds b. 10-30 seconds c. 30 seconds-3 minutes d. >3 minutes	Requests a desired item by exchanging a single picture.		
Wait-b When given a "wait card," S will sit/stand quietly and occupy self with manipulative/interactive toy (not highly reinforcing item).	9 of 10 opportunities completed successfully in at least 3 environments for: ____minutes ____minutes ____minutes	Waits quietly for up to 3 minutes		
"No" When asked, "Do you want ____?" or "Do you want this?" regarding a non-preferred item, S will indicate "no" with a head shake.	9 of 10 opportunities completed independently when items are in sight. 9 of 10 opportunities completed independently when items are not in sight.	Requests a desired item by exchanging a single picture.		

Objective	Criterion	Current Level	Date begun	Date met
Yes" When asked, "Do you want ____?" or "Do you want this?" regarding a preferred item, S will indicate "yes" with a head nod.	9 of 10 opportunities completed independently when items are in sight. 9 of 10 opportunities completed independently when items are not in sight.	Requests a desired item by exchanging a single picture.		
Follow directions When told/shown a direction related to a functional outcome, S will comply correctly.	9 of 10 opportunities completed independently when told to go to: ____ areas of room or to retrieve: ____ items.	Engages in appropriate activity in area where direction terminates (plays once he/she reaches play area, pours juice into cup when given cup, etc.)		
Transition between activities When shown the next available reinforcer and told to transition to the next activity, S will comply correctly with no inappropriate behavior.	9 of 10 opportunities completed independently across an entire day.	Indicates preferences via PECS or other modality.		
Follow a visual schedule Upon arriving at school or awakening at home, S will: 1. go to schedule 2. remove top picture 3. Place picture on "current activity" slot 4. Complete activity 5. Return to schedule 6. Remove current activity picture 7. Place picture in "finished" envelope S will repeat steps 2-8 throughout day	All steps completed independently entire and sequence repeated across day.	Responds to single picture directions.		

Appendix B

Critical Communication Skills Checklist

CRITICAL COMMUNICATION SKILLS CHECKLIST©

Name:	Age:	Date:

Skill	Example	Appro-priate?
1. Request reinforcers		
edibles		
toys		
activities		
2. Request help/assistance		
3. Request break		
4. Reject		
5. Affirm/Accept		
6. Respond to "Wait"		
7. Respond to directions		
VISUAL DIRECTIONS		
Orient to name being signaled		
"Come here"		
"Stop"		
"Sit down"		
"Give it to me"		
"Go get…" (familiar item)		
"Go to…" (familiar location)		
"Put it back/down"		
"Let's go/ Come with me."		
ORAL DIRECTIONS		
Orient to name being called		
"Come here"		
"Stop"		
"Sit down"		
"Give it to me"		
"Go get…" (familiar item)		
"Go to…" (familiar location)		
"Put it back/down"		
"Let's go/ Come with me."		
8. Transition b/w activities		
9. Follow visual schedule		

Appendix C

Reinforcer Worksheet

Reinforcer Worksheet©

Name: Age: Date:

Item	Rejects	No reac-tion	Reaches for	Protests when taken away	Shows signs of pleasure	Takes again

Appendix D

Vocabulary Selection

Vocabulary Selection Worksheet©

Student/Child:	
Person completing form:	
Date:	

Instructions: List up to 5-10 items for each category. Include only those items that your student or child currently enjoys (or dislikes for final category).

Things your student/child likes to eat	
Things your student/child likes to drink	
Activities your student/child likes (watching television, spinning, sitting in a special chair, squeezes)	
Social games your student/child likes (Peek-a-boo, chase, tickles, etc.)	
Places your student/child likes to visit	
What your student/child chooses to do during free time	
People your student/child recognizes and enjoys being with	
Items, activities your student/child DOES NOT like	

Attribute Worksheet

Name
: _____   Date: _____

Concept	Current Reinforcers						
Size							
Color							
Shape							
Texture							
Speed							
Body Parts							
Action							
Position							

Appendix E

PECS Implementer Skills Assessment

PECS Implementer Skills Assessment©

Implementer:	
Reviewer:	
Review Date:	
Site:	

	Pass	Redo	Comments
General Issues:			
Plans for PECS training to occur across a range of activities			
Plans for a variety of trainers to participate			
Plans for student to request a variety of reinforcers			
Notes:			
Phase I Communicative Partner:			
• Arranges training environment effectively – pictures available one at a time, trainers positioned appropriately, control of reinforcers			
• No verbal prompting			
• Entices appropriately			
• Uses open hand prompt effectively- appropriate timing			
• Reinforces within ½ second and provides social praise			
• No insistence on speech			
• Returns picture (while student consumes/plays with R+)			
Notes:			

Phase I Physical Prompter:			
• Waits for student to initiate (reach for REINFORCER)			
• Physically guides to pick up, reach, release			
• Fades prompts effectively			
• Interrupts/prevents student's interfering behaviors			
• No social interaction with student			

Notes:

Phase II Communicative Partner:			
• Plans for each student to have own communication book			
• Arranges training environment appropriately –pictures available one at a time, trainers positioned appropriately, control of reinforcers			
• Entices appropriately			
• Gradually increases distance between student and communicative partner			
• Teaches student to cross room to reach communicative partner			
• Gradually increases distance between student and communication book			
• Teaches student to cross room to reach communication book			
• Turns away from student-eliminates "body language" cues			
• Reinforces appropriately—new behavior within ½ second			

• Eliminates subtle trainer prompts (body orientation, eye contact, expectant look, etc.)			
• Does not insist on speech			
• Teaches student to travel from room to room			

Notes:

Phase II Physical Prompter:

• Waits for initiation			
• Prompts removal of picture from book if necessary			
• Physically guides student to trainer if necessary			
• Physically guides student to communication book if necessary			
• Does not interact socially with the student			
• Uses backstepping if necessary			

Notes:

PHASE IIIA- high vs. distracter discrimination

• Arranges effective training environment			
• Entices with both items			
• Socially reinforces as soon as student touches correct picture			
• Appropriate reinforcement with requested item			
• Uses a variety of distracter items and a variety of target pictures			

• Conducts error correction procedures correctly- high vs. non-desired
    ▪ Gives non-desired item
    ▪ Elicits negative response
    ▪ **Model**
    ▪ **Prompt**
    ▪ **Switch**
    ▪ **Repeat**
 	
• Second error correction if necessary			

• Moves pictures around on book (diagonal, vertical, horizontal)			
• No insistence on speech			
Notes:			
Phase IIIB multiple preferred discrimination			
Arranges effective training environment			
Entices with all items			
Conducts correspondence check			

• Conducts error correction procedures correctly- high vs. high with correspondence check
    • Prevents student from taking non-corresponding item
    ▪ Model picture of item reached for
    ▪ Elicits negative response
    ▪ **Model**
    ▪ **Prompt**
    ▪ **Switch**
    ▪ **Repeat**
• Second error correction if necessary			

• Moves pictures around on book (diagonal, vertical, horizontal)			
• Teaches 3, 4, 5-way discrimination			
• Uses a variety of target pictures in the 2-, 3-, 4-, or 5-way mix			
• Teaches looking inside book			
• No insistence on speech			

Notes:

Phase IV

• Begins with "I want" already on sentence strip			
• Waits for initiation			
• Physically guides student to put R+ picture on strip and exchange strip			
• Fades physical guidance to put R+ picture on strip and exchange strip			
• Verbal praise + turns strip around and "reads" sentence			
• Teaches assembly of entire strip- backward chaining			
• Reinforces new behavior within ½ second			
• Appropriately reinforces with tangible item			
• Uses physical assistance to teach student to point while strip is being "read"			
• Uses delay (3-5 seconds) in "reading" strip			
• Differentially reinforces if student speaks			
• Avoids verbal prompting			
• Conducts error correction for incorrect picture sequence			

• Organizes communication book appropriately			
• Does not insist on or drill speech imitation/production			
Notes:			

Attributes:

• Assesses current reinforcers for potential attributes			
• Teaches three-picture construction			
• Reinforces new behavior within ½ second			
• Teaches discrimination between attribute icons			
• Conducts correspondence check with attributes			
• Conducts error correction for attribute icons			
• Conducts error correction for incorrect picture sequence			
• Teaches variety of attributes within same class (several colors, variety of sizes)			
• Teaches multiple exemplars of each attribute (several "red" items)			
Notes:			

Phase V:

• Uses delayed prompting to teach "What do you want?"			
• Uses differential reinforcement if student "beats" the second prompt			
• Reinforces new behavior within ½ second			

• Creates multiple opportunities for spontaneous requesting AND answering, "What do you want?" within same lesson			

Notes:

Phase VI:			
• Uses delayed prompting to teach commenting in response to comment			
• Continues to create opportunities for spontaneous requesting			
• Differentially reinforces commenting/requesting			
• Teaches "comment question" vs. "What do you want?" discrimination (sentence starter discrimination)			
• Uses error correction for incorrect discrimination between sentence starters			
• Teaches "comment question" vs. "What do you want? vs. spontaneous requesting			
• Creates lessons to elicit spontaneous commenting			
• Fades "comment question" to elicit spontaneous comment			
• Incorporates attributes into comment lessons			
• Teaches additional comments and/or "comment" questions			
Notes:			

Appendix F

Communication Training Timeline

Communication Training Timeline©

Phase I					
	Phase II				
		Phase III			
			Phase IV		
				Phase V	
					Phase VI
				Attributes	
		"Do you want?"			
			Request "help"	"I want help"	"I want help with…"
			Request "break"		
			Respond to "wait"		
		Picture Direction Following			
			Schedule Following		
	Let's Make a Deal				
		Visual Reinforcement Systems			

Acquisition	Maintenance

Appendix G

Data Collection

Picture Exchange Communication System- Long-term Progress©

Name: Data Period:

Phase VI	Spontaneously comments																													58
	Discriminates all Sentence starters																													56
	2nd comment question																													54
	Com ? + Request ? + Spont. request																													52
	Discrim. comment vs. request S.S																													50
	First comment question																													48
Phase V	Answers AND spontan. requests																													46
	Answers independently																													44
	3-5 second delay																													42
	0 second delay																													40
Attributes	Uses multiple attributes																													38
	Uses multiple exemplars																													36
	Discrim 2+ prefer. attribute icons																													34
	Discrim. High vs. low attribute icon																													32
	Constructs 3-icon sentence																													30
Phase IV	Points to pictures during read-back																													28
	Constructs entire strip																													26
	Adds R+ icon to sentence strip																													24
Phase III	Looks inside book																													22
	5 High Preference																													20
	4 High Preference																													18
	3 High Preference																													16
	2 High Preference																													14
	High preference vs Low/non preference																													12
Phase II	Travel to book																													10
	Travel to Comm Partner																													8
	Remove picture from book																													6
Phase I	Independent Exchange																													4
	Physically Assisted Exchange																													2
	DATE																													

W = Number of spoken words   P = Number of pictures   Shaded Area = PECS Acquisition

PECS Phase I Trail-by-Trial

Name:				Location:		

Date	Trial	Pick Up	Reach	Release	Picture	Activity
	1					
	2					
	3					
	4					
	5					
	6					
	7					
	8					
	9					
	10					
	11					
	12					
	13					
	14					
	15					
	16					
	17					
	18					
	19					
	20					

+ = Independent;   **FP** = Full Physical Prompt;   **PP** = Partial Physical Prompt

PECS Phase I Anecdotal©

Name:			Location:		

Date of Session/ Activity	Approximate # trials	Location and Length of session	List icon(s) used	Initials of Trainers	Status of Physical Assistance

This form created by Anne Hoffman, M.Ed. of Pyramid Educational Consultants, Inc.

PECS Phase II Shaping©

Name:			Location:	

Date/ Trainer initials	Item(s) requested	DISTANCE TO LISTENER start: 0 1 2 3 4 5 6 7 8 9 10 end: 0 1 2 3 4 5 6 7 8 9 10	# trials at target distance:	# independent trials at target distance:
		DISTANCE TO BOOK start: 0 1 2 3 4 5 6 7 8 9 10 end: 0 1 2 3 4 5 6 7 8 9 10	# trials at target distance:	# independent trials at target distance:

Notes:

Date/ Trainer initials	Item(s) requested	DISTANCE TO LISTENER start: 0 1 2 3 4 5 6 7 8 9 10 end: 0 1 2 3 4 5 6 7 8 9 10	# trials at target distance:	# independent trials at target distance:
		DISTANCE TO BOOK start: 0 1 2 3 4 5 6 7 8 9 10 end: 0 1 2 3 4 5 6 7 8 9 10	# trials at target distance:	# independent trials at target distance:

Notes:

Date/ Trainer initials	Item(s) requested	DISTANCE TO LISTENER start: 0 1 2 3 4 5 6 7 8 9 10 end: 0 1 2 3 4 5 6 7 8 9 10	# trials at target distance:	# independent trials at target distance:
		DISTANCE TO BOOK start: 0 1 2 3 4 5 6 7 8 9 10 end: 0 1 2 3 4 5 6 7 8 9 10	# trials at target distance:	# independent trials at target distance:

Notes:

This form created by Victoria Bluett-Murphy of Applied Behavior Consultants, Inc.

PECS Phase II Trial-by-Trial©

Name:						Location:	

Date	Trial	Travel To Trainer	Distance To Trainer	Travel To Board	Distance To Board	Picture	Activity
	1						
	2						
	3						
	4						
	5						
	6						
	7						
	8						
	9						
	10						
	11						
	12						
	13						
	14						
	15						
	16						
	17						
	18						
	19						
	20						

+ = Independent   **-** = Prompted   Note distance in inches, feet, room-to-room, etc.

PECS Phase II Trial-by-Trial©

Name:				Location:			

Date	Location/ Length/ Activity	Icons used	Comm. Partner (s)	Status of Physical Assistance	Distance to Comm. Partner	Position of Comm. Partner	Distance from Comm. book

This form created by Anne Hoffman, M.Ed. of Pyramid Educational Consultants, Inc.

PECS Phase IIIA ©

Name:				Location:	

Date	Trial	Discrimination Level (circle picture student gives)	negative reaction? Y or N	Pictures
	1			
	2			
	3			
	4			
	5			
	6			
	7			
	8			
	9			
	10			
	11			
	12			
	13			
	14			
	15			
	16			
	17			
	18			
	19			
	20			

H = Highly Preferred   **D** = Distracter

PECS Phase IIIB ©

Name:				Location:		

Date	Trial	Discrim. Level	Correspon- dence check	Item Selected	Distance to book	Distance to trainer
	1					
	2					
	3					
	4					
	5					
	6					
	7					
	8					
	9					
	10					
	11					
	12					
	13					
	14					
	15					
	16					
	17					
	18					
	19					
	20					

P= Preferred item   **D**= Distractor (non preferred/blank/negative/neutral)

For correspondence check: **+** = took same item as requested   **-** = took incorrect item

PECS Phase IV ©

Name:			Location:			

Date	Trial	Put "I want" on strip	Put picture on strip	Exchange strip	Point to pictures	Correspondence Checks
	1					
	2					
	3					
	4					
	5					
	6					
	7					
	8					
	9					
	10					
	11					
	12					
	13					
	14					
	15					
	16					
	17					
	18					
	19					
	20					

+ = Independent;   **FP =** Full Physical Prompt;   **PP =** Partial Physical Prompt

PECS Attributes ©

Name:					Location:		

Date	Trial	Constructs 3-picture sentence strip	Target Attribute	Number of Available: Icons Items		Uses correct attribute	Correspon. Check
	1						
	2						
	3						
	4						
	5						
	6						
	7						
	8						
	9						
	10						
	11						
	12						
	13						
	14						
	15						
	16						
	17						
	18						
	19						
	20						

+ = Independent;   **FP =** Full Physical Prompt;   **PP =** Partial Physical Prompt

PECS Phase V©

Name:				Location:		

Date	Trial	Delay Interval	Answer question	Beat prompt?	Spontaneous Request	Correspon-dence Check
	1					
	2					
	3					
	4					
	5					
	6					
	7					
	8					
	9					
	10					
	11					
	12					
	13					
	14					
	15					
	16					
	17					
	18					
	19					
	20					

+ = Independent;   **y** = yes;   **n** = no

PECS Phase VI without spontaneous commenting©

Name:						Location:			

Date	Trial	What see?		What want?		Spont request		_____	
		SS	pic	SS	pic	SS	pic	SS	pic
	1								
	2								
	3								
	4								
	5								
	6								
	7								
	8								
	9								
	10								
	11								
	12								
	13								
	14								
	15								
	16								
	17								
	18								
	19								
	20								

Key: **+** independent response **P** prompted response **-** Incorrect response

PECS Phase VI **with** spontaneous commenting©

| Name: | | | | | | Location: | | | |

Date	Trial	_____?		_____?		Spont request SS pic		Spont comment SS pic	
	1								
	2								
	3								
	4								
	5								
	6								
	7								
	8								
	9								
	10								

Key: **+** independent response   **P** prompted response   **-** Incorrect response

Appendix H

4-Step Error Correction Procedure

4-Step Error Correction Procedure
High Preference vs. Distracter

Step	Teacher	Student
	Entice with both items	
		Gives incorrect picture
	Give corresponding item	
		Reacts negatively
MODEL or SHOW	Show or tap target picture (get S to look at the target picture)	
PROMPT	Hold open hand near target picture or physically prompt	
		Gives target picture
	Praise (do not give item)	
SWITCH	"Do this," pause, etc.	
		Performs switch
REPEAT	Entice with both items	
		Gives correct picture
	Praise and give item	

4-Step Error Correction Procedure
Correspondence Checks

STEP	TEACHER	STUDENT
	Entice with both items	
		Gives a picture
	Say, "Take it," "Go ahead," etc.	
		Reaches for wrong item
	Block access	
MODEL or **SHOW**	Point to, tap correct picture (of item student reached for)	
PROMPT	Hold open hand near target picture or physically/gesturally prompt to give picture	
		Gives target picture
	Praise (do not give item)	
SWITCH	Say, "Do this," or other known task	
		Performs switch
REPEAT	Entice with both items	
		Gives picture
	"Go ahead," etc.	
		Takes corresponding item
	Allow access and praise	

4-Step Error Correction Procedure
Attribute Icon Discrimination

Step	Teacher	Student
	Entice with preferred and non-preferred	
		Exchanges strip with incorrect attribute icon
	Give corresponding item	
		Reacts negatively
	Put attribute icon back on book	
MODEL or SHOW	Show/tap/ target picture (get S to look at it)	
		Looks at target picture on book
PROMPT	Hold open hand near target picture, gesture or physically prompt to put pic on S.Strip	
		Adds target picture to sentence strip
	Praise (do not give item)	
SWITCH	"Do this," or pause, etc.	
		Performs switch
REPEAT	Entice with both items	
		Adds correct picture to sentence strip
	Read strip, praise and give item	

4-Step Error Correction Procedure
Attributes and Correspondence Checks

Step	Teacher	Student
	Entice with 2 or more preferred examples of the attribute	
		Exchanges 3-icon strip with attribute icon
	" I want hmmm candy," "Take it."	
		Reaches for incorrect item
	Block access to item	
	Put attribute icon back on book	
MODEL or SHOW	Show/tap target picture (get S to look at it)	
		Looks at target picture on book
PROMPT	Hold open hand near target picture or physically prompt OR gesture to empty spot on sentence strip	
		Adds target picture to sentence strip
	Praise (do not give item)	
SWITCH	"Do this," or pause, etc.	
		Performs switch
REPEAT	Entice with both items	
		Adds picture to sentence strip
	"I want that candy." "Here," while holding out both.	
		Takes corresponding item
	Read strip and praise.	

Appendix I

Communication Planning Worksheets

Classroom PECS Spot-Check©

Date:					
Observer:					
1. PECS books available to all.					
2. Students involved in functional activities.					
3. Environment "engineered" to elicit communication.					
5. Staff expect communication.					
6. Spontaneous requesting occurring.					
7. Functional direction following training occurring.					
8. Appropriate prompting strategies used.					
9. Appropriate error correction used.					

Communication Planning Across the Day©

Class: _____   Date: _____

Time	Activity	Functional Objectives	Communication Goals	Who	Direction Following	Who

Communication Planning Across the Day©

Class: _____ **Date:** _____

	Activity Objectives	Productive Goals	Receptive Goals
Time Activity Where Who			
Time Activity Where Who			
Time Activity Where Who			
Time Activity Where Who			
Time Activity Where Who			

Routines and Communication in the Home and Classroom Worksheet©
summary of routines

Location: _____		Time: _____	
Routine	**Reinforcement (routine itself or**	**Area of House/**	**Materials**

Routines and Communication in the Home and Classroom Worksheet©
summary of routines

Name: _____

Location: _____ **Time:** _____

Routine	Reinforcement (routine itself or finishing routine)	Area of House/ class	Materials

Routines and Communication in the Home and Classroom Worksheet©
steps within routines

Name: _____

Routine	Steps	Vocabulary for Requesting
	1.	1.
	2.	2.
	3.	3.
	4.	4.
	5.	5.
	6.	6.
	7.	7.
Sabotage strategy once routine is mastered:	8.	8.
	9.	9.
	10.	10.
	11.	11.
	12.	12.
	Reinforcement:	

Date										
Item										
Response										
Staff										